Mark Rice-Oxley is an editor at the *Guardian* specialising in foreign news. He was born in Hampshire in 1969, educated at Portsmouth Grammar School, Exeter University and Voronezh University in the USSR. He joined the *Guardian* after ten years reporting and writing from Moscow, Paris and Eastern Europe. He lives in Kingston with his wife and three children.

UNDERNEATH
THE LEMON TREE

A Memoir of Depression and Recovery

Mark Rice-Oxley

ABACUS

First published in Great Britain in 2012 by Little, Brown
This paperback edition published in 2015 by Abacus

13 5 7 9 10 8 6 4 2

A CIP catalogue record for this book
is available from the British Library.

ISBN 978-0-349-14030-8

Typeset in Bembo by M Rules
Printed and bound in Great Britain by
Clays Ltd, St Ives plc

Papers used by Abacus are from well-managed forests
and other responsible sources.

MIX
Paper from
responsible sources
FSC
www.fsc.org   FSC® C104740

Abacus
An imprint of
Little, Brown Book Group
Carmelite House
50 Victoria Embankment
London EC4Y 0DZ

An Hachette UK Company
www.hachette.co.uk

www.littlebrown.co.uk

For my wonderful children,
and for Sharon

Contents

RECOVERY

Acknowledgements

There are people who helped me get well and people who helped me write the book. And a few who did both. In the first instance I was very lucky to get sympathetic, comforting and effective medical treatment from Dr John Wilkins, Sacha Khan and Dr Nerida Burnie. Thanks also to Heather Campbell and Alex Baden for shepherding me back to work so well. At work, my colleagues kept in touch during the vacant months and welcomed me back warmly. So thanks to Harriet Sherwood and David Munk for being patient bosses, to Judith Soal for caring, to Jamie Wilson, Paul Hamilos, Max Benato and Martin Hodgson for making it easy to slip back into the groove, and to Charlie English and Ian Katz for finding interesting things for a man on the mend to do.

I want to mention friends and family for their love, particularly Ju, Caro, Kerry, Dad, Sid and Pauline and everyone else who brought over lunch or put something in the post (depression victims don't generally receive 'Get Well' cards). Then there are my fellow sufferers, all of you wherever you are, but particularly those who have shared your stories with me. I mention no names as sadly most of us don't want the world to know about our thing. One day . . . Thanks to all the clinicians and academics who give this book a veneer of expertise. The sources are too many to mention, but particular thanks to Dr Tim Cantopher, Professor Mark Williams, Professor Colin Espie, Professor David Healy and Dr John Sharp for their thoughts which I have tried not to present as my own. And also to my *Guardian* colleagues Tom Parfitt, Tania Branigan, Giles Tremlett and Helen Pidd for helping me understand how other languages render the word 'depression', and to Clemence Cleave-Doyard for the same.

This book would not have come about without the publishing pros who 'spotted' the idea and gently encouraged me to write. I'm deeply grateful to Annabel Merullo and Tim Binding at PFD for believing in me, to Tim Whiting and Zoe Gullen at Little, Brown for making this book better, and to Susan de Soissons and Zoe Hood for their support.

Finally, to the people who really saved me. This is probably the hardest bit of the book to write. How to say thank you when you've said it a thousand times and it still doesn't express the magnitude of the great debt you owe? Mum, you showed me that a parent's job is never quite done with, however old the offspring. The only way I can think to repay you for helping me through this is to look after your grandchildren the same way you looked after me.

Sharon, simply thank you and I love you and let's get on with the second half.

Prologue

The *London Rose*

I am on a boat on the Thames. The *London Rose*, it is called, and it's a bit shabby, like something that might sink in the Philippines, though it's scrubbed up OK for my birthday party. There's a dance floor and a bar, which sells water for £2.50, and some mighty speakers that are so loud that they leave a noise like *xoxox* in your ears. My brother-in-law is dressed as James Brown, which doesn't happen every day. The outlaws are John and Yoko, while my mum and dad are Sonny and Cher. The vibe is sort of Woodstock-meets-the-Gosport-Ferry. Friends are congratulating me on a thoroughly good idea.

I, however, am having the most frightening time of my life. I don't know it, but I am having what they used to call a nervous breakdown. In the weeks that follow I will travel to the edge of madness, scaring the hell out of everyone around me.

I will spend a good part of the next year on the sidelines of my own life. I will think myself stupid, staying awake night after night, doing battle with the hours I used to love so much. I will pace nervously, stare at walls, tremble and thrum like I'm full of some undiscovered radioactive isotope. In the blackest moments, I will contemplate suicide.

I will be washed ashore on the forbidden reaches of depression, but I will also learn more about myself than I have done in all of the first forty years put together. I will be reborn and start to get a sense of how to live better, slower, less frantically.

But that's in the future. For now I am on a boat on the Thames, having a nervous breakdown. Hammersmith, Chelsea, Westminster scroll past, a two-dimensional backdrop to a cheap horror film. The music washes in and out like it's in a nearby room and the door keeps opening and closing. The pitching of the boat isn't helping at all. And it's uncommonly mild. Early October often is. From under my unconvincing Jimi Hendrix wig I whisper to my mother, 'Stay close,' and grip her hand like it's the first day at school.

I can't look at anyone for more than three seconds without a pulsating acceleration of sound and vision. There's a fluttering in my breastbone like a bird with a broken wing is in there, learning how to fly again. I try circulating but need to sit. When I sit I instantly need to get up and move about. I try telling people that I've been unwell and am not sure what it is. But it's not the most promising conversational gambit on a party boat. I try eating; the food is good, but not good for me. I toast myself with water in a champagne glass.

The people, my people, are all here. There are several layers of friendships. People I've known for just a few months, school-gate dads and mums who think of me chiefly as an affable, unremarkable dad of three. There are colleagues present and past who know me in a different way, as a semi-serious journalist. There are people who knew me as a student. Others go back further still and can remember me with braces on my teeth and mischief on my mind. Some, like my sisters, have known me before I could walk. Everyone is here who needs to be. Except me.

My trio get up to play a set. Music truly was my first love, and yet here I can't stand it. The sound, channelled through two ageing amplifiers, is rotten. I take great chunks out of simple chords, massacre a bossa nova and then bang out a blues number I wrote for the occasion, 'The "How-did-I-end-up-forty?" Blues'. People laugh. They think I'm joking. I sing the chorus: 'I'm turning forty. Seems to me like front-page news. And all I wanna do is sing the "How-did-I-end-up-forty?" Blues . . .'

It is a big moment. Forty. When we're young, we have no inkling of what it will be like, the gradual loss of potential that comes with getting older. We can still think of ourselves as promising. Most people in the papers are older than us. The birthdays of the famous still predate our own by several years, though they are starting to creep closer. There's still time. We appear rather fresh and precocious when we tell people we were born in 1969. Any achievement at this age is worth double. We don't have to fret too much about making something of ourselves. Time will take care of that. But what happens when time starts to run out? When you have been overtaken by people born in the eighties? It's a nasty realisation: actually, we might not fulfil any of that potential at all. I have a strong sense that if something's going to happen to you, something big, then it's probably going to have happened by the time you're forty. I try the second verse:

> Well, some people tell me
> That forty's the new thirty,
> But ten years ago there was more totty at my party . . .

I have to work hard at the vowels to rhyme thirty with party, but it's worth it because there is more laughter. But it's not really true: ten years ago, I was newly married to the woman I still love. Totty didn't really come into it. In fact, I'm not sure it ever did. By now I'm convinced I've been behaving strangely for the last few minutes. Photos of the event bear this out: my eyes are bulging and I am green. I plough on to verse three.

I'm not a glass-half-empty person. I'm a lucky man. There has always been plenty to look forward to, but something had changed, perhaps in the past two or three years. It was as if I had joined the first forty dots of my life and then smarted at the surprise of seeing the features not of a happy man, but of a sour old thing leering back at me. There was much to be grateful for, but I always came back to negatives: the burden of childcare, the exigencies of work, the sense that every bit of my time and effort was taken up in dutiful subservience to someone else.

We crash out of the set and then dance like it is the last night of the sixties. I try for the umpteenth time to push it to the back of my mind, but I can no longer pretend there isn't something urgently wrong. The music is so loud that our teeth rattle in our heads. 'I think something's seriously wrong,' I yell at a number of ears. But all I get is grinning faces and groovy dancing; no one can hear a thing. There are colleagues aboard who think I pulled a sickie when I fled the office on Thursday. I try to explain: I'm ill, there's something wrong. I don't think I'll ever be able to set foot in that office again, I tell them. They think I am drunk. But I'm drinking water.

Somehow midnight arrives at the same time as Putney pier. The *London Rose* bobs giddily into dock. We step off into the London night; partygoers disperse to the promise of tomorrow and the rest of their lives. I load up the guitar and amplifiers and generally grimace a lot. 'Let's get you home and get you better,' Sharon says. At last, I think, she's taking me seriously. I dread the moment of arriving home, the point at which the party is officially over and there is nothing left between me and what's happening to me. The coach pulls into the close and we disembark, wigs awry. Babysitters wave goodbye and saunter off back to their effortless weekends. We lug various sleepover children around, disperse them evenly among the houses. Then people settle. It's night-time. The house falls quiet.

Lying in bed, my heart races like a hamster in an experiment; my eyes stare into the future and see a bedridden misery, a tossing and turning wretch who cannot get comfortable in his skin. The hot water system is thrumming in sympathy so I get up to reset the boiler. It is the first of about half a dozen trips to the kitchen, bathroom and elsewhere that night as I seek somewhere peaceful, away from myself. But that place doesn't exist. It is 2:30, 3:17, 4:09 and still I am alert, a dry hissing in my ears like after you've been to see ageing guitarmen do their thing and stood a bit too close to one of the speakers. I think I drift off somewhere around five, but awaken forty minutes later. At 6:45 I get up and go downstairs.

The next hours are shattering. I blurt out stuff to my father-in-law and hear myself say, 'I think I've got ME.' By the look on his baffled, hungover face I can tell he is alarmed and uncomfortable all at the same time. I crave things – an apple, a cup of tea – then don't want them. As they hit my stomach they make me wired, jittery. I start pacing but make myself disoriented; I try to rest on a chair but have to pace again. I am hungry but don't fancy anything. I want Mum and Dad to come over for breakfast, but once they are there I want breakfast over and the house cleared. They leave. My wife turns to me and weeps. It is just the beginning.

BREAKDOWN

BREAKDOWN

1

Beginnings

I can't say for sure when it all started. Maybe it was the day in July 2009 when a headache in the shape of a question mark curled itself around my right eye and hung there for a few days. I thought it was swine flu, though I didn't really feel very bad. Just slightly detached and feeble. Occasionally I'd do something like flush the toilet and the sound would distort and stretch out, as if it had been processed through a machine invented by Brian Eno. Or else someone would be talking to me and their face would become misshapen, as though seen through the bottom of a highball glass. I'd zone out and think things like, 'He's got a funny face: three moles on his cheek – what if I joined them all together to make a triangle? Would it be scalene, isosceles or equilateral?'

The headache went, and then came back and made itself at home. It was joined in early September by a fatigue that poured itself into my legs like molasses. My digestive system seemed a little awry. I had a cold ringing in my ears, a kind of tinnitus that, as well as being supremely irritating, remains a symptom that I'm still not sure how to pronounce. I stumbled around like a drunk, finding it curiously difficult to judge the length of my legs. Meeting rooms and station platforms appeared frozen in time, hissing with feedback as though recorded on an old Betamax cassette. As weeks went by a heavy chainmail duvet of exhaustion wrapped tight around me. The autumn was beckoning but its colours and mutability just seemed to be the harbinger of death for another year.

As September progressed, I began to be alarmed by brief episodes. A kind of surreal impression of the world around me, horizontals and verticals askew like a bad Picasso forgery, and an internal quickening that felt like I'd had a dozen espressos without stopping to draw breath. The episodes lasted just a couple of minutes, and came and went infrequently; between times I was well enough to wonder if I wasn't imagining it all.

By early October I was congratulating myself. It was all over! I'd felt great for two or three days. An MRI scan, commissioned because of the persistent headaches, came up empty and so I decided: that's it, enough of being a stupid hypochondriac – just get on with life. The next day one of those disquieting episodes shuddered through me like dysentery, far worse than before. I was suddenly unable to read my computer screen or take in information from the dozen or so windows

I had open. I dashed off an edit of a story on Silvio Berlusconi and sent it through to the subs without caring whether it made sense or not. A colleague arrived and began gabbling at me. It made me shake and quiver to try to concentrate on the words coming out of his mouth. I had to look past his face and focus on the middle distance or I felt I would lose my balance. I spent half the morning in the toilet trying to calm myself, doing some forward bends as if that would straighten everything out. Eventually I went home to bed, trying to fool myself into believing I had the flu. The next day, I was forty. Sharon and I went into London for a treat – meal, theatre, hotel. I couldn't be still. It wasn't right. Panic bounced off the four walls of our narrow hotel room. The noise and movement of the television were insupportable. We saw *War Horse* and all I can remember thinking was, 'It could be worse, Marko. You could be stuck in the trenches.' The next morning, walking to the station along the Embankment with the night on the Thames looming in front of me, I began to look enviously at other people: he's not me, she's not me, they're not me. What is wrong with me?

These were all milestones on the descent that had started much earlier that year. I had been grumpy, irritable, for a while and became ambivalent about things I used to love, like playing football or hosting friends. I became aware that I was avoiding social situations: the prospect of a quiet beer in a bar with a mate appalled me. Alcohol didn't appeal, while television made me inexplicably nervous and unable to concentrate. When we watched films I noticed that, instead of looking at the screen, I was watching the numerical counter on the DVD player to see how much more of the thing we still had to get through. It was all about getting through.

Or perhaps the rot started a few months earlier, when I began waking at four or five and staring into the midsummer half-light. Or maybe earlier still, when I got a promotion at work and started working long hours while still trying to be a present and active father to my three small children. Maybe the seeds were sown during the long years of babies and night work, when I went to bed so late and got up so early that sometimes the two almost met in the middle.

So I can't really say for sure where it all started. Who knows how far back you have to go. All of us come from childhoods that, however happy and unremarkable, will shape our adult psyches. Like when you roll up a tent: if you get an air kink stuck in the lining early on it will magnify several-fold and then you won't be able to get the tent back in its bag. (If you still have the tent bag, that is. I'm not sure I do.)

I was born at the tail end of 1969 in a cold, aloof house in Hampshire. The time and place are crucial. They always are. Thin lines of essence from the period poured into me and got trapped. A spare folk song – Nick Drake or Joni Mitchell – can still hollow me out like news of a death. Ancient leaves and low-ering skies, dusk at teatime and headlights in the lane remind me of where I come from and why I'll never end up too far away from it all. The moon, the guitars, Vietnam, the counter-culture. I'm endlessly fascinated by it all. A sixties baby, gentle, autumnal, just too late for the main event and wistful at times gone past. That's me.

My parents still live at Glendene, but it was a different house then. It was tall and thin, three bedrooms and an outside loo with a newspaper front page from 3 September 1939. I still remember the headline: 'Stand Calm United, We Shall Prevail: The King.' There was a pre-war piano that seemed to produce tones from the same era, sad looping melodies that my sister or mother would play. I taught myself to write music on that piano, but because of its tone they are only ever sad songs. There was a master bedroom, another for the baby and one that I shared with my two elder sisters. There was a car whose rear door swung open when you went round corners and a TV that would always overheat; you could change the channel by jingling coins in your pocket.

In the seventies Glendene felt remote. It was a mile away from school and a mile away from church, and both felt like long, long walks. It was a dot in acres of green. In winter the place was draughty and frigid, but I don't remember ever feeling too cold. The house really came into its own in the summer. Long childhood hours were passed outdoors, me whining at my sisters to build dens and play cops and robbers, or go in goal while I took penalties with the toe of my wellington boot. In the days before skin cancer and paedophiles we lay in the sun and trotted to and from school on our own. The sun shone, and when it didn't we went indoors and hid behind sofas and in the cupboard under the stairs. When we fell out I would go and stare at my dad's clock. It was one of the early attempts at digital, but better because the numbers would flick into place with the metronomic rhythm that time does so well. I found it absorbing that a 2 became a 3 with just one deft click, that an 8 turned into a 9 with a simple stroke. I loved the change of the hour, which seemed to amount to a glorious resolution, albeit an impermanent one.

There were power cuts and board games, and TV shows that started at 7:55 or 3:24. We fell out and made up, squabbled and hit. When Mum got fed up with us she would send us out into the garden with a picnic, which consisted of a few raisins, an apple and a lump of cheese in a Tupperware container. We tried to learn the names and dates of all the kings and queens of England in order: my dad promised twenty-five pence to anyone who could crack it by Silver Jubilee day. Occasionally I get a strong backdraft from the seventies and marvel at what a fine decade it was for me. If I wasn't writing this book, I'd be writing Andrew Collins's brilliantly titled book, *Where Did It All Go Right?*

My siblings and I all shared baths and books and bedrooms until I was about six. Then Dad built a panel wall down the centre of a bedroom to split it in two. At last, some privacy. It wasn't the last cosmetic change to Glendene. Age has added bulk to the place: new rooms to house my grandmother, an extension at the back. The garden is not the wilderness it was in 1973; pictures of a bonfire from that era make us look like we are on a survival weekend in Kazakhstan. Since then, several sheds and a greenhouse have sprung up, as well as a modest stand-up pool that is still going strong after thirty-five years;

there are vegetable patches and something that my mum rather grandly calls an arboretum.

Some things never change, though. An oak tree that dominates the back garden, a path made of paving slabs that follow each other like a hopscotch grid down past the greenhouse. An open fire for warming old bones and drying wet dogs. A wood-pigeon that must be about 108 in bird years by now. The people too: my dad, restless and hearty, tall and impatient, always about to build another shed or mix some concrete; my mum, loving a good hug, still answering the phone by repeating the phone number back down the line. I've never been too sure why she does that. And me too. I haven't really changed that much. I still write notes to myself on my hand, still glance at my reflection in parked cars. I'm still addicted to HP Sauce and dry-roasted peanuts. In a meeting room full of grown-ups, I still feel like a small boy at times. My favourite colour is green, my funniest animal is a horse. My worst feature is my toes, quickly followed by my hair, which is dry and frazzled like it has been trying to grow in the desert. I still love games and songs and a good cup of tea.

But I'm not just a sixties baby and a country boy. I'm a Generation Xer and a brother three times over, and that's important. They were good girls, my sisters, equal in my affections. Julianne was the closest I would have to a brother. We invented clubs and languages, and made disgusting sandwiches that we would dare each other to eat. We quoted long segments of *Monty Python* and *Not the Nine O'Clock News*, and recorded aimless banter on an ancient reel-to-reel machine then listened to it so often the tape wore out. She did a famous impression of a mail bag being picked up by an aircraft. I would wake her at seven on summer mornings for the fun to start again. She was never too academic. In France one year, she was trying to explain my hay fever to our host. 'Er, *le soleil fait-il brrthrrsppp,*' she said, miming in quite spectacular fashion the act of someone sneezing. It became one of many family catchphrases. Ju left home for dancing college in 1982 and I remember feeling a bit lost for a while. About 90 per cent of the *Boy's Own* stuff I got up to at home was under the loving tutelage of a future ballerina.

Carolyn was the bookish one, always reading or practising her piano scales when we wanted to involve her in a game. When she repeatedly refused to join us we would sing 'Read a book, no, no, no, no, no' at her bedroom door until she came out and pulled our hair. But she truly cared as well: she taught me how to read and do sums when I was three or four, and how to play card games and read music. We became closer as we got older and had more and more in common: languages, university careers, stints in Europe and boy-boy-girl families of our own.

Kerry was the baby. She called me 'Wowa' – brother in baby-speak – and still does sometimes. We shared the room that Dad split with a stud wall, so were always annoying each other. She wanted the door open at night, I wanted it closed, so it had to be at forty-five degrees, which suited neither of us. I teased her mercilessly, stole a library book from her room and gave it back to her six months later when it was expensively overdue. We developed a system of grunts to inform one another of how awake we were at night. Later we perfected the art of 'sloping': disappearing just when there were chores to be done or a major confrontation to be had. We watched loads of telly. There was none of the rationing we subject our own children to. Moderation was imposed by the schedules of the day.

In our halcyon reflections, we fondly imagine there were long years of games involving all four of us in a garden big enough to get lost in. But there are seven years between Julianne and Kerry. By the time K was big enough to join in properly, Ju was already doing pas de deux on the stage in London. There were probably only three or four years when we could all play the same thing together, and then we only really did so when there were visitors: cousins or French family friends spending the summer with us to improve their English. There was 195, a great hide-and-chase game that I think came from the French; a more obscure thing called Pencil and Paper, which had nothing to do with either pencil or paper. My favourite was always sardines. I loved the subterfuge, the drama when the hunting pack suddenly thinned down to just two or three. I quite liked squeezing into small spaces with strange girls who sometimes kissed me.

There were dogs too: Teleta, a collie who had to be put down after eating things she wasn't supposed to, like the flesh of small children. Sandy, a crafty old thing who played a long game, unless there was mud involved in which case she would plunge in with no thought for us and the long car journey home. Gemma, her daft daughter, was the runt of the litter, and

11

struggled for life until my grandmother drip-fed her from a bottle of Armagnac. There was a cat called Cleo who stalked around, unamused and impervious to everything. There were chickens who led short, nasty lives in a pen, laying eggs and pecking each other and shitting everywhere.

There was my gran, who lived with us from about 1972, an unreconstructed grande dame with a tendency to outrageous outbursts while watching the news. She peppered our childhoods with her pithy catchphrases ('Four'nce for that!' 'Pot on you!') and called hiccups 'hiccoughs'. She had friends with names like Maud and Bea, which we thought quite hilarious as how could someone have just a letter for a name? Gran outlived three husbands, several dogs and cats and a Triumph 1300, and bought herself a new graphite tennis racket for her eightieth birthday. She walked the South Downs Way at ninety and, as I write, is still with us.

My parents both endured quite singular upbringings in houses dominated by patriarchy and the *Daily Telegraph*. My dad was an only child, my mother an afterthought to a great tribe of free-spirited siblings. Their first encounter is the stuff of legend. My dad was on leave from the Navy and between girlfriends. His father, Ted, told him there was this girl he should meet, the daughter of an occasional drinking chum who shared some of his passions for gin, ciggies and the occasional flutter. Dad was ambivalent, but Ted insisted and suggested he pop into the Rose and Crown in Tonbridge at lunchtime to meet her.

'I'm not sure I've got time,' said Dad. 'I've got things to do in town.'

'Come on, boy, you can spare half an hour.'

'How will I know she'll be there?' Dad asked. He wasn't going to go on an empty promise. He'd already spent too many of his twenty-odd years waiting around for his old man in the pubs of south-east England.

'Well, I tell you what. If she's in there I'll stick a copy of the *Racing Post* in the window,' said Ted. It was a deal. An hour or so later Dad was driving around looking for a parking space when he went past the Rose and Crown. No newspaper in the window. Ah well, he thought. Nothing ventured, nothing gained. He was lining up a space in the car park when another car zipped in front of him and stole the space. He was cross. A short bald guy got out, jingling the coins in his pocket. Dad might have uttered a word or two if it wasn't for the rather fetching young woman with him. 'Hmm,' thought Dad. 'Sod the pub, maybe I should see where they're off to.' The car park was full so he had to do another circle around town. This time, there it was! The paper, propped up in the window. So after he finally parked the car he went into the pub. And there, of course, was the parking rogue holding court with Ted and the young woman demurely nursing a Coca-Cola on the sidelines. It was them. They were introduced, and married a year later. 'If the old sod hadn't stolen my space I'd have parked, done my things and then gone home. We would never have met.' So there you go: I only exist because one grandfather was a drunk and the other a car-park bandit.

My mum was placid, gentle and patient, and generally let us get on with it. She loved a few hands of cards – canasta or poker or gin rummy – but would more often be found on a sun lounger in the garden, reading or doing the crossword, or shredding runner beans. At six she would repair to the bath, only occasionally feeling the need to intervene in some violent quarrel. She was chauffeur, cook, mentor and care-giver, a woman for whom the word mother could have been invented. The fact that her own mother died when she was a toddler makes her own maternal gifts all the more remarkable.

My dad spent seven years in the Navy, sunning himself in the Gulf of Aden and learning how to take cover when a particularly savage game of deck quoits broke out. It was an era that coincided neatly with possibly the most warless years Britain has ever had, post-Suez, pre-Falklands. Footage from the time shows dashing uniformed men with fags and big quiffs who don't look like they'd be very good at fighting. My dad got out before he had to kill anyone in earnest. He was marooned for a few months, before getting a job at EMI in London. He would stay there for twenty-five years: an office just off Oxford Street, free records with cool 'Not for Sale' stickers on them, and tons of anecdotes about bumping into Simon Le Bon in the corridor or peeing next to Freddie Mercury in the bathroom. I loved going up to visit – the sudden busyness of London once you'd crossed Hammersmith Bridge, the star quality in the corridors of the Manchester Square building, the kudos to be had from telling everyone how you very nearly met David Bowie's chauffeur. I began to wonder what job I'd do and whether anyone could see their way to letting me do it in London.

Dad never earned anything more than a modest salary, but it was amazing how little we could survive on. The house was bought with the money he inherited from his father after he died in 1966. There was the weekly shop, during which I would try to estimate how much the entire trolley's contents would come to and it would normally be about £8.58 and I would usually be within a few pence of the total. But apart from that, I can't imagine what money needed to be spent on anyway. We didn't go out to pubs or restaurants. Summer holidays were taken in a derelict Sussex beachside hut owned by a family friend. We didn't go abroad until I was almost a teenager. Christmases were fairly frugal, typified by the year when we all got Wombles that my mum had made herself. A tinny camper van would ferry us all around, its 900cc largely inadequate to the task of hauling three adults, four children, two dogs and several arguments around the South Downs.

As a family we did a lot of walking. If in doubt, have a walk was the general approach. We were usually to be found walking somewhere, briskly but pointlessly. I generally couldn't see the point: I don't mind walking as a way of getting from A to B, but there doesn't seem to be much sense in walking as a way of getting from A to A. There was Butser Hill, ten miles up the road, which would have been fun if we had been into flying kites, but we weren't. There was Old Winchester Hill, which was essentially like Butser Hill only it took longer in the car. Queen Elizabeth Forest was a destination which always slightly disappointed me as every time we went there was absolutely no trace of Queen Elizabeth anywhere. We also went to Creech

Woods, sometimes referred to as Hundred Acres in an attempt to jolly us along a bit.

When we weren't walking we were usually having bonfires or mowing or hitting tennis balls around on the scruffy patch of uneven land ambitiously designated the tennis court. In winter we'd huddle around the radio, dad polishing his five pairs of weekday shoes, listening to the Top 40 and taping songs by Pilot and Mott the Hoople. The first song I truly fell in love with was Chicago's 'If You Leave Me Now'. Caro taunted me: 'You only like it cos it's got the word "baby" in it.' We'd squabble about lyrics and who was cooler: Queen or the Bay City Rollers, Ian Dury or Darts, Blondie or Madness.

If the family didn't have much money, I never had *any* money. My parents ran a rudimentary reward system: a merit for doing something good, a demerit for bad behaviour and when you were twenty merits in the clear you got fifty pence. The problem was that you might spend an entire afternoon weeding the vegetable patch or mowing and get two merits, but then Gran would catch you licking a knife or sitting on the swing hammock and dish out three demerits. I was usually in negative equity.

There was dinner money that could be saved, a few pennies a day, which added up to about three-quarters of an LP every term. I sang in a choir that did pay a nominal fee based on how often you turned up. But big money it was not. I had an 83 per cent attendance record one quarter, and was rewarded with sixty-seven pence, all in coppers, a sum that was worth even less by the time I spent it because of a sudden bout of economic crisis that the seventies did so well. Occasionally – but not often – I'd launch some entrepreneurial undertaking to address my penury. I typed up my notes from our classroom translation of Book Six of the *Aeneid*, asked my dad to photocopy it and sold it to my classmates for fifty pence a copy. Unfortunately I missed out a crucial segment that came up in the exam, and had to fend off multiple demands for a refund.

I worked the car parks at Goodwood racecourse in the summers – earning eighty pounds a week – and was almost embarrassed when, from the descending window of a Bentley, a five-pound note appeared in a gloved hand. I put half on an accumulator that came in at ten-to-one. I spent a long time examining the twenty-pound note I won. I'd hardly ever seen one before, apart from in the old shoe-polish tins that my dad used as various floats. It seemed a shame to spend it, so I put it in the bank. As I've never had less than twenty pounds since then, I suppose it's still there.

At seven, it was decided that I needed more of a challenge so I went to Portsmouth Grammar School. It was a forbidding, Dickensian place that still had the cane and divinity, though not always on the same day. In those days PGS was full of sadistic staff and scrappy boys called things like Smudger, Muzz and Titch. Teachers beat pupils for picking their nose or looking at them in a funny way. I was slippered for leaving sports kit at the playing fields and on another occasion for skipping out of turn in a gym class. It hurt. I was lonely for home, an hour-long bus ride away. On one of my first days there was a service of welcome at Portsmouth Cathedral. My mum was there, which made me cry. In subsequent lunch breaks I would mooch over to the edge of the playground and look for comfort at the distant building where we had sung 'Forth in Thy Name, O Lord, I Go'.

It didn't last long. I soon got friends, good marks, and a nickname that some still use today. It was the brainchild of Mr Simmons, possibly the only cool teacher in the school, who unfortunately decided it would be even cooler to go and join the RAF. 'Rice-Oxley,' he said, reading out the register on day one. 'Rice-Oxley ... we're going to have to find something easier than that.' He paused for effect. The class of thirty squirming schoolboys hung on his every word. 'Roxy! Yes, Roxy. Roxy Music! Do you like Roxy Music?' I had no idea what he was talking about so I nodded and shook my head at the same time.

Roxy became interchangeable with the more prosaic Pud (Rice-Pudding), but Pud died in my teenage years, killed off by Mark, who was sensible, serious and keen to make the most of himself. Mark sounded like a grown-up when my friends started using it. He drove a car and passed exams and pretended to be very clever. Sometimes he answered to Marko or Markie Egg, which betrayed an idealist and eccentric below the surface formality. Over the years these characters have battled it out for control, the several different versions of me thrashing it out. I'm convinced this is universal – that, far from being single characters, we are a jumble of personalities and we define our values through the internal dialogue of our various characters:

Roxy: I know! I'll keep a bottle of milk in my desk for a
few weeks, see what happens.

Marko: That's risky.

Roxy: Yeah, but Stevenson and Hughes will think it's epic!

Marko: You'll get caught.

Roxy: How? The teachers never look in our desks.

Or else:

Roxy: OK, why don't I bike all the way into school today?

Marko: Hmm, I'm not sure that's wise.

Roxy: Yes, but I can save the bus money.

Marko: What if Mum finds out?

Roxy: How will she ever find out?

Marko: Remember that time you got a puncture? You had
to walk two miles to find a shop to repair it.

Roxy: I got away with it though.

Marko: Yeah, but at the time it was a cack.

Roxy: I'll manage. Just think, if I do it twice a week, by the
end of term I'll have more than three pounds.

Marko: Mum and Dad have explicitly told you it's too dangerous to cycle around in Portsmouth.

Roxy: Yeah, but what do they know? They've never done
it.

Marko: And it's tiring. You're meant to be going to school
to learn, not to save money.

Roxy: Well just once a week then.

Marko: I don't know . . .

19

I won't bore you with details of my academic record. It doesn't tell you that much. I was quick rather than clever, sometimes a bit too quick. I had virtually no common sense but was lucky to have a brain that retained most of what was poured into it. I liked to get inside new concepts until I understood them from the inside out. When it came to exams, I failed to see what there was to worry about. I was an able student, not the top of the class but never far off it. In fact, something of a pattern began to develop. Roxy was not the best, but a decent contender, a competent player. It was the same with sport, music, most things I turned my hand to. As a child, this was fine. It felt good to be an all-rounder. But as an adult, there was a different word for people like me. And the word is: amateur.

Love was a tricky thing. There were a lot of hurdles to clear. Not only did I have to fancy someone, which didn't always happen at the right place and the right time, and then get her to fancy me (a formidable barrier as I still wore knee-length yellow socks and a side parting), but I would have to arrange something akin to a date, something that no one in our family had managed. We were hampered not just by the insular dynamic of a big happy family, but by pure geography. Glendene was a long way from anywhere. It wasn't just as simple as popping round to her house to listen to records, or meeting in town to snog on the steps of the library. I lived a good thirty-minute walk from anywhere, and forty in the car from Portsmouth. I would have a shallow gene pool to choose from, chiefly limited to my sisters' friends or the girl behind the counter at the newsagent's. Unimpressed by the lot of them, I fell deeply in love with a succession of unattainable girls who lived in places like Gosport or Rowland's Castle, which might as well have been in Tanzania for all their accessibility. I do remember once cycling the twelve miles over Portsdown Hill to Fareham, to wait for a girl I had eyes for only to see her emerging from college hand in hand with someone else. It was a long ride home. Suffice to say that by the time I got to university, where there were several thousand available women all living on my doorstep, I was paralysed with the potential of it all.

2

Where were you while we were getting highly paid jobs?

'Could it be a little bit of depression going on here?'

Dr Nerida Burnie poses the question in the soft Antipodean burr that will become a recurring feature of the drama to come. But she may as well have poked me with a shitty stick. 'Has there been any depression in the past?' she asks.

Depression? I recoil physically at the mention of the word. Depression is other people. People with dark mysterious childhoods, or fatal flaws; people who ate too much or too little, or had no friends, or agonised about their jobs or their loves or both. People from broken homes, broken marriages, broken countries. People with tattoos, piercings, fussy facial hair; people who've needed alcohol or narcotics, triumph or *schadenfreude* to

23

jack up their self-esteem. People beset by tragedy, farce, horror or the vicissitudes of chaos theory. I knew one person who had certainly suffered from depression and she was as unlike me as it is possible to get. Abused as a child, tormented as a teenager, in and out of hospital, unable to override the cruel neurological patterns that still define her today. I looked on her as a member of another species. These are all ideas that come from a different world, as alien to me as Sanskrit or voodoo.

What do I have to be depressed about? Forty years old, a fine home, a wonderful wife, a great job with the best newspaper in the country, three healthy and adorable children. What do I have to be depressed about? Actually, that's the worst kind of question you can ask. It's a question I have since come to despise, as it is normally posed by people who don't understand that depression is not something you do, but something that happens to you. And yet here I ask it aloud, of the GP, of my wife, of myself. It had to be something else. I go home and start Googling my symptoms again. When nothing matches, I enter the word 'depression' and am startled to find three things. First, many of my symptoms match: the loss of weight, energy, patience, appetite, concentration and joy; the panic attacks, rumination, headaches, stomach trouble and cognitive dissonance. Secondly, depression isn't the same as being depressed. The name is a red herring, conjuring up misleading images of people staring through windows at drizzle. Depressive illness isn't like that Sunday-night feeling, or getting back from holiday to find the cold water tank has burst. It's far more pervasive and can't be fixed by a new shirt or a 24-hour plumber.

Thirdly, the illness is far more widespread than I thought. It turns out that it's not just a medical curiosity for preternaturally sad people, but a catch-all that afflicts more than one hundred million people around the world. It may feel like the world's loneliest condition, but depression has become ubiquitous for the planet's unhappiest species. The chances of the average adult getting it are perhaps higher than they have ever been. Or it may be that we are just catching it more often, diagnosing more frequently. The statistics vary depending on who you ask, but it seems that about one in four of us face the risk of some kind of mental health problem in our lifetime. That's someone in your family, at least a couple of your mates, three of you if you play on a football team, ten people in your street, a hundred people in your office, a thousand in your town, one hundred thousand in your city. Antidepressant prescriptions have doubled in the last decade. One in ten middle-aged Europeans are taking the pills, according to research published in June 2011 by the University of Warwick and the IZA Institute in Bonn, Germany. The World Health Organization calculates that depression will soon be second only to heart disease in the burden that it places on society.

So what exactly is it? Two years on, and after myriad conversations with psychiatrists, neuroscientists and fellow sufferers, I can honestly say that no one really knows. The brain is the least understood human organ, which is a bit rich as it is also the organ we use to understand the world. If you speak to two clinical psychiatrists about depressive illness you will get two different definitions, two different physiological causes and two different courses of treatment. Which is very confusing for the wretched sufferer trying to come to terms with the thing. Some psychiatrists and brain specialists believe depression is caused by a collapse of the chemical circuitry in the brain known as the limbic system. This chain reaction of neurological transmitters regulates some of the fundamental things that we tend to take for granted: our moods, our sleep–wake cycle, our appetite, our hormonal system. If it becomes overloaded there can be a sudden drop in serotonin and noradrenaline, the chemicals that keep the circuit buzzing. The circuitry stops working properly. And we become depressed.

But other neuroscientists reject this thesis as fanciful, arguing that the serotonin conjecture is just a marketing ruse by Big Pharma to sell more drugs. 'There is no evidence that there is anything wrong with the serotonin in people who are depressed,' said David Healy, a neuroscience professor at Cardiff University who has spearheaded something of a mini-revolt against the serotonin theory. 'I've worked on the serotonin system since 1980, longer than just about anybody, and I have yet to find anything wrong with the serotonin system.' So what, I ask him, is physiologically wrong with someone suffering from depression? 'We don't know.'

If the science is muddy at best and misleading at worst, there are other more spiritual ways of looking at depression which would argue that, far from being a negative essence, depression is an important warning signal, the expression of something in your life that shouldn't be there. It might be a destructive relationship or an overpowering job. It might be too much travel or a surfeit of stress or a season ticket for Aston Villa. It might be something very deeply implanted, something that you think you want, something that you think makes you who you are. But which is in fact catastrophically at odds with your core self.

How do you get it? How did I get it? The list of causes is equally long: grief, loss, stress, shock, overexertion, viral infections and other serious illnesses, plus any number of more opaque, deep-seated psychological triggers that may take their cue from inner conflicts generated by character tics formed early in life. Suffice to say there are enough causes and triggers of depression to make it impossible to avoid them all as you go through life. Whether you get it or not is really down to genes, luck and character.

The onset varies from person to person. For some, it's as abrupt as a single moment when something cracks, a hurtling, a descent, a shiver, a shudder, a snap, a change as palpable as walking from sunlight into shade. For others it's more insidious, a nagging, cloying essence that gradually builds over time until it can no longer be ignored.

If it's hard to say for sure where and when depressive illness starts, it's even harder to tell people when it's going to end. Doctors and psychiatrists are deliberately vague, careful not to make promises that will discourage or disappoint further down the line. Alan Bennett is good on this. 'How long such depressions lasted no doctor was prepared to say,' he writes in *Untold Stories*. 'There seemed to be no timetable, this want of a timetable almost a definition of the disease.'

Dr Burnie and I have no clue how long this will last. She signs me off for two weeks. We agree to meet in ten days' time to see if I feel well enough to go back to work. I take heart: it would be a short sharp snap, a nasty reminder that I'd been overdoing it. Things would be back to normal by mid-November. But her words linger. Could it be depression?

Has there been any hint of depression in the past?

I left home at seventeen. It wasn't a protest move or an act of escape. It was just that I had finished my schooling (I had somehow ended up in the year above) and thought it would be good preparation for a degree in languages to actually go abroad for a while. Gap years were still quite edgy in those days. Few people backpacked around the world. Of my close friends, one ended up in a bar in Paris, one went to India for a few months, one took an additional A level and a couple of others drifted around in a big pensions firm in Portsmouth which seemed to take on formidable quantities of teenagers.

For me it was to be Switzerland. Dad revived some ancient family acquaintance in Davos, of all places. They owned a hotel and were quite happy to take on a callow English boy who had few skills other than a half-decent outswinger and most of the Beatles tunes roughly fingered out on the piano.

I'd like to say the highlights were all the great people I met, but since I didn't meet any, I can't. I fainted on my first day at the hotel. There was a blizzard of accents and activity, none of which I understood. I wanted to go home. I spent my days off sitting in my attic room, thinking of time and how slowly it was going. Davos in 1987 was less glamorous than it sounds. Yes, it had snow, clean air and expensive clocks. Yes, it had royalty just down the road at Klosters and three different countries within spitting distance (if Liechtenstein counts. I'm not sure it should. And anyway, you're not allowed to spit in Switzerland). But none of it rubbed off on me. It was so totally off season that even the mountains seemed bored.

I had no friends and no clue as to what I was doing. It was the first regular job I'd ever done and I was hopeless. All the Italian waiters called me Desperado, but I don't know why. It may have been because they invited me over to do a little cocaine with them, but the white line I snorted turned out to be talcum powder. Alternatively, it may have had something to do with my table service, which was at best unpredictable. I spilled stuff on people, brought them the wrong food and went about my business with such a baffled air that people would leave the restaurant rather than have me serve them lunch. On one toe-curling occasion I presented an expensive bottle of wine to some guests, showed the label to sir, banged in a corkscrew and pulled out about two-thirds of the cork. Another time, a French waiter called Laurent and I took in orders for breakfast from twenty-four American tourists. But we made a schoolboy mistake and failed to note who'd ordered what, so when each plate arrived we had to walk around the dining room shouting out what was on it.

Then there was the night I shut my fingers in the front door of the hotel. I was walking up to it from the side and the automatic doors didn't slide open as they usually did. There was no one on reception, so I just stood looking in through the glass doors, feeling awkward and stupid. I stood and stood until I thought, 'This is no good, I'm going to have to do something here.' So I put my hand on the glass door to see if it would budge. In the process I must have moved across into the area sensitive to movement, because the glass door slid into the wall, taking my hand with it. The skin peeled away from two fingers. The scars are still there. They are on my swearing fingers.

I was seventeen and so lonely I sometimes went for whole days without saying anything to anyone. I sat in my room and taught myself the guitar, and spent hours and hours trying to start smoking. Then I would scuttle downstairs and rummage around in the hotel fridge for elevenses. I would write stuff – mostly letters back home, but also songs, poems and a diary. I made lists of the things to remember at work, and lists of things to do on days off.

Days off were bad. I quickly ran out of books and guitar strings. I got bored of the same mountain walks. I couldn't ski – it was too expensive and the snow wasn't good enough. I had no telly or radio, just a crappy Walkman and a lot of Lou Reed and David Bowie albums; everything cost money, but I was not being paid – I was just there to learn the language. I tried befriending one of the Swiss chamber maids, but she was already spoken for.

Days off, however, were not as bad as nights off. In 1987 there was nothing to do in the whole of Switzerland at night. So I hung around the hotel, playing on any of the grand pianos that were free. When the resident pianist, inevitably called Toni, disappeared off with his white suit and roving eye to Mauritius or the Seychelles for a month, I quickly occupied his seat in the Stübli, the à la carte restaurant. The Italians breathed easier then. I could do less damage (though plenty enough) from a piano stool.

I mused upon the passage of time. So slow when you watch it, rapid when you don't notice it. I was filled with despair when I kept checking the day and it kept on being 25 September and there were still two more months to get through. Every day I wrote pages and pages about the nothingness that I got up to. My eighteenth birthday came and went uneventfully. A Scottish waitress called Laura took pity on me, took me out and got me drunk at the Chami Bar. It was OK, but we both wanted to be somewhere else. November pressed darkly. The mountains turned white and the hotel started to fill with guests: Americans and Germans and a contingent of people from a local dermatology centre. I read the English papers at the Migros shopping centre without buying them until eventually a manager came over and ticked me off. I almost laughed at him: ha, ha, I'm going home soon. My parents are coming for me next week. This week. Tomorrow. I am waiting at the station for my parents to get off the 4:15 from Landquart.

We spend three days going up mountains and eating well and one night I serve them dinner in the Stübli and play the piano for them. And then, just like that, we leave. We fly back home and I feel about ten feet tall for a month. I was only eighteen and already had some great tales to tell. I also realised an important truth: that sometimes you have to endure in order to progress. It was a lesson that got right under my skin. And stayed there. From now on, I told myself, from now on you must grind out the tough times and the good times will follow.

The good times did follow. Three years studying Russian and German at Exeter University, where I would meet the people I still call my best friends. First there was Debug. We scuttled around in an old VW with mould on the back seat, bang up for anything. We formed a 'band' called 'Interesting Suitcase', because they were the first two words we learned in our Russian class. I called him Debug because that's how you write his name in Russian. He called me Aye-lad, and neither of us were quite sure why, only that Yorkshire accents were very, very funny. Learning Russian together is hilarious, because the word for good is 'horror show' and the word for step is 'shag'. We were in another band together that actually got paid for playing, which was remarkable. Then he got fired for not turning up to band practice because he was going to see the Clash in concert, only it turned out not to be the Clash at all but the Alarm.

They were generally harmless capers back then, and both Debug and I took a relaxed view of our studies. I recall heading out one day in Vic, the old VW, both of us in giddy spirits because it was the first properly warm day of spring. We had an exam on Max Frisch the next day, but neither of us had read *Andorra*, or any other of his works come to that. I wasn't even quite sure whether there was a c between the s and h of his surname. I was confident I could spell Max correctly, but that was about it. In those days, we were hanging around a lot with four girls, fellow Russian students. They were lovely and funny and in the other car up ahead, a crappy blue Fiat called Nift, which had a wearisome habit of breaking down. Sure enough, as we picked up speed on the A38, there she sat, stuck on the hard shoulder, the girls frantically motioning for us to stop. But we were doing seventy in the outside lane and couldn't pull in or go back, so we resolved to come off at the next slip road, double back on ourselves, go back north for a junction and then come up behind them again. We were just picking up speed on the other side of the road when we saw them motoring south again, windows open, waving and hooting and laughing at us and our idiocy. We roared with laughter, thrilled at the intoxication of youth and all the years ahead.

All the young women in our gang were sensible, fun, straightforward and quite lovely. I married one of them. All the guys were dreamers, chancers and rogues, very much into fancy dressing, cross-dressing and, eventually, undressing. We lionised the unfancied seventies folk band Steeleye Span and would sing their more obscure tunes in public places deep into the night. Three out of eight of us have had depressive breakdowns.

I was a typical student: contrary, high-spirited, broke. I decided to let my hair grow. Or, at least, I decided not to get my hair cut. It's not the same thing, in my case, for it didn't really grow, just congealed into an ugly clump in the shape of Norway. I tried a lot of things in the vain hope that I might turn out to be really good at one of them. It turned out I was all right at most things, but nothing special. I knew real talent, real attitude when I came across it. In the cricket nets one day, a left-arm bowler ambled in and sent a few balls at me with an action no more athletic than that of an elderly gentleman removing a sweater. Most spat up at my throat or else fizzed past my myopic grope. It was like trying to hit a bullet with a shoelace. He was a couple of years older than me and gave me a few withering stares. I enjoyed a revenge of sorts when, some years later and from the comfort of my own sofa, I watched the Australian batsmen smoke him all around Headingley in his only test match. In fact, I came away from that practice session with a broken nose, which elicited much sympathy from friends and tales of heroism on my part. No one knew I got hit bowling, not batting.

Another day, another scene. A group of cocky musicians, many with the first bursts of facial hair, were trying painfully to form bands at the inaugural meeting of the Campus Bands Society. I was mostly tongue-tied and in awe of people who knew a) each other, b) what they wanted their band to be called, and c) G minor. So I fumbled around hopelessly until a bloke with side-burns and attitude walked up to me and said, 'I like David Sylvian and the Velvet Underground.' I was too timid to reply that I did too and had pretty much figured out how to play the verse of the glorious 'Silver Moon'. I must have mumbled something dim, because he moved on with the certainty of a star-in-waiting. I saw him again a few months later. He was in a band, a great band, playing a memorable version of a fine tune – 'What Goes On' by the Velvet Underground. They even had a viola player. They literally took my breath away, replacing it with dark poison that I found difficult to inhale. My band was up next, but we played naff, obvious tunes and not very well.

I didn't see him again for years. When I last saw him, it was at the Hammersmith Odeon, where he was singing with a band called Radiohead. They were pretty good.

I found a girl and stuck with her. She was the opposite of me: sensible, grown-up, bags of common sense. I was quick, she was thorough. I was privately educated, she wasn't. She left-handed, I right. She was visual, I aural. She could only play music with sheet music, I could only play without. She had a boyfriend. I didn't. We were fascinated by each other. I spent a few months chasing her, which made the catch all the more sweet. Soon we were inseparable, sharing tiny student beds and wheeling our bikes up the steep hills of the campus. Subtly, we influenced each other. She made me wear blue jeans and watch movies; I made her wear hats and listen to Caravan and 10CC. She made me play tennis; I made her watch cricket.

Most of our courting we did within the easy crowd of friends that surrounded us, playing drinking games and dressing up. That took the pressure off. But it was only when we struck out alone during our year abroad and spent three months sharing a small room in Germany that I knew this was it. We both did horrendously dull jobs in an attempt to learn better German. She performed perfunctory tasks at a local German bank; I worked on building sites, sweeping up mess and drilling holes in the wrong places. At the end of the day we'd curl up and comfort each other. I taught her mind games to make the day go quicker. She picked Rockwool insulation out of my hair.

Terry Eagleton said that, ultimately, we are defined by the things we cannot walk away from. If that is true, then I am defined by Sharon.

Halfway through my second year I had what I now recognise to be a first mini crisis. It was a new decade, and I'd had a raucously good eighteen months, but then suddenly everything seemed flat and stale. New friends were old friends. Magical nights running around south Devon were becoming staid: same people, same views, same anxieties as the academic thing suddenly got a lot more serious. I was dabbling and not excelling. It seemed to me that everything I did, someone was doing it better.

The feeling lasted for several months – the whole of 1990, really. Call it the last full year of adolescence, when I was beginning to wonder quite earnestly what I would be all about. I knew there were options, but I was refusing to knuckle down to one discipline, for fear that it would be the wrong choice and I wouldn't cut it.

The whole thing climaxed in the autumn of that year. I went off on study placements overseas, starting with three months in Voronezh, a monstrous settlement of concrete and mud halfway between Moscow and the Black Sea. I was pitched in with students from other British universities, making me even more aware that there were people more brilliant than I would ever be. Oxbridge students with an ear for a verb ending and an eye for an opportunity; I felt quiet, small and provincial by comparison.

But something was beginning to stir. One day we were bussed out to a collective farm to help gather the potato harvest. It was the last warm day of autumn, during the last autumn of the Soviet Union. The air somehow felt a lot earlier out there, as if it were the fifties. In those end-of-empire days, winter famine was no idle talk. I'd been there a month and still hadn't seen much in the way of red meat or sugar or butter or milk. You could get onions, carrots, potatoes, kefir, the occasional chicken, bootleg vodka and Russian cigarettes named after the White Sea Canal. Oh, and pomegranates. For some reason, there were lots and lots of pomegranates.

It was hard work but the rich soil felt good on my hands. I was stripped to my T-shirt and still working up a sweat. I was reminded that we were not so far from home: Russian soil, British soil; Russian potatoes, British potatoes. Russian humour was very like British humour: ironic, understated, dry. The Russians spat, smoked and swore more than we did, but essentially they were the same as us: two arms, two legs, eager for a good time. We rooted out the spuds and chucked them in an ancient truck tractor piloted by an equally ancient farmer with a face like tree bark and a mouth full of base metal. I wonder if he was around during the Terror. Probably not.

It was the best I had felt for months. I got that strange, sure inkling again: if I can thrive here, just think how tall I can stand back in Britain. It's good to do tough things, I told myself. You come out of them tougher.

On the bus on the way back to the city I was struck by how extraordinary our experiences were. We had just gathered the harvest on a collective farm. We were zipping around the Soviet Union, watching it fall apart. We were being taught by people who remembered Stalin. I began to wonder: maybe, just maybe, it was exceptional enough to merit some form of article. For a newspaper, perhaps, or a magazine. Yes, an article for a magazine. 'How I saved the Soviet Union from famine' by Mark Rice-Oxley. I would need to do more work on it. I had no idea how to go about it. But there it was, the beginning of something. A direction.

For those of you who weren't, it was tremendous to be twenty-something in the nineties. Post Cold War, pre al-Qaeda, between recessions; Eurostar, Britpop, total football, New Labour. Gyms, cable and grunge. Ray Cokes and rollerblades, *Friends* and *Teletubbies*. It was the bottom of the housing market and the beginning of the boom. Things could only get better. There were no killer diseases, at least not in the airport terminals of Charles de Gaulle and JFK and Sheremetyevo. There were no bogeymen, no forbidden ideologies, very few places off the map. It truly was the end of history. Even now I get blasts of nostalgia for 1989 and the European '*Wendepunkt*' when the world was starting from scratch and the Russians briefly loved us and whole countries were reinventing themselves every day. I'd spent a couple of summers inter-railing around Eastern Europe and came to love the tragicomedy of it all. In between the bewilderment and misery there was always something amusing.

In the nineties, I bought (and sold) my first car, received my first email (from a bloke in Prague I'd never met) and caught one of the first Eurostar trains through the tunnel. We started the decade with 5¼" floppy disks and ended it with Google. I went to a dozen weddings, culminating in my own, to Sharon, in 1998. I lived in Moscow, Paris and London, worked in Jerusalem, Sarajevo and Helsinki. It was good to be alive.

The first thing that you had to get in the nineties was work. Oasis asked, 'Where were you while we were getting high?' but it might as well have been, 'Where were you while we were getting highly paid jobs?' There were no jobs in Britain in 1992, so loads of us ended up in Moscow. The Russian capital was an edgy, unfathomable rogue at the time, hard to like but impossible not to love. It smelled of cheap benzene and industrial decay, miles and miles of the same gritty blocks of flats separated by patches of mud and ooze that passed for courtyards. By day, political and economic turmoil made for a burlesque life in which everyone was a black marketeer, a money-changer, a speculator, a chancer; by night, new clubs and bars with names like Sexton Fozd and Pilot opened almost every day, packed with Russian wide boys and Western adventurers. We went everywhere by hailing private cars for small change, and once even flagged down a trolleybus. I had never felt so free.

It quickly became apparent that there was work to be done and money to be made. The post Cold War honeymoon had about another year to run, and Westerners were still in demand. For a while I worked for a British woman whose company installed computer systems for hotels and restaurants. The entire country had run for seventy years on old babushki and little bits of dog-eared paper. It desperately needed a makeover just to pull it into the twentieth century, let alone the twenty-first. Others I knew were making money importing consumer goods or technology.

But the profit motive wasn't for me. I still had a vague idea of working for the press. Fortunately, a new English-language newspaper had just started up in the city. Unfortunately, I had not the remotest idea what I could do for them. The *Moscow Times* . . . I picked one up as I shambled through the airport en route for the rest of my life. But as I read the headlines I had a strange feeling: I'll work there, I thought. That's what I'll do. I noticed the paper had no crosswords so I drew up two or three by hand, cold-called the editor and set up a meeting in the swish hotel suite that the paper was living in.

I've been a crossword fiend for years, ever since my mum gently showed me the mystery of their ways through the long, wet summer of 1986. You must have a quality pen, and fold the paper twice so it's a nice, cushioned quarter of its usual size. There are all kinds of codes and acronyms and double meanings, like solving a murder. It's lovely to unravel an anagram, hitting on a particularly inscrutable clue, inscribing correct letters into small white boxes. Once there was a crossword whose answers were the areas of the shipping forecast positioned geographically around the grid. I like that. I tried to set a couple and found it was actually easier than solving them.

The *Moscow Times* editor was a scary American woman with big red hair and a reputation for a fearsome temper. She would emerge periodically into the hotel corridor and shout something like, 'You gotta tell Igor: that photo violates my rule of the dime!' at nonplussed faces and then withdraw into her office. As I waited, I cursed myself for my stupid ideas. Reporters with ties at half mast bustled around with sheaves of papers, asking runners to 'pull the wires on the IMF'. Cool-as-hell designers were arguing with a proper American newspaperman about leading and kerning. Waif-like Russian girls wafted around looking dreamy. Earlier, I had taken a wrong turn into the political editor's office and come face to face with Marc Champion and David Filipov. Legends! I'd been reading the paper for all of two weeks and already I wanted to be Marc Champion or David Filipov, or even both of them. But what would big serious people like this want with an amateur like me? I'd never even met a real American before. Didn't they use different words to us? What were 'the wires'? What were leading and kerning? And what on earth was the rule of the dime? Clearly I was going to get chewed up badly here.

But when Meg invited me in to her office she was courteous and funny. I think she took pity on me. She must have found it odd: if I really wanted to get into journalism, why wasn't I out covering war in the North Caucasus or Tajikistan, or the thriving Moscow art scene, or theatre or any number of things? Why had I come all the way to Moscow to fill out little grids with letters and make up obscure clues for them?

But if she thought me odd, she never said so. 'I love British crosswords,' she enthused with a toss of her vivid hair. 'I used to do the *Times* crossword every day. It took me half an hour. American puzzles suck.' I didn't quite know what to say, so I sort of laughed, snorted and agreed all at the same time. I'm not sure I've ever completed a puzzle at all, let alone in half an hour. She could probably set these things better than I could. I didn't say that though. In the lifts on my way out I felt a surge of elation. The doors opened to a jazz and marble lounge that had felt intimidating on the way in, but now felt classy and grown-up. I belong here, I thought. The phone call came two days later. I would set crosswords for fifty dollars a pop. Within weeks Meg was on the phone: there was a half-opening on the copy desk. It would basically suit anyone who could spell their own name. Was I interested? I found it hard not to punch the air. 'Yessssss,' I said. Suddenly I knew what I was in Moscow for, and what I wanted to do with my life.

The *Moscow Times* was a great nursery. It taught me not just about newspapers and agencies and Meg's rule of the dime (no face pictured on a newspaper page should be smaller than the American coin), but about Russians and Americans, about summits and elections and wars and coups and the other hardy perennials that keep the news calendar ticking over. I still set crosswords, but was far more interested in learning how to craft news, how to interview sympathetically but systematically, how to write headlines and page furniture. (One of my favourites, a standfirst written by a colleague in very tight space under an uninspiring picture of some Russian skiers said simply 'Skiniks'. I like it because it is a palindrome.)

The rest of the nineties was all about the stories. I turned into a reporter, a foreign correspondent for a news agency, a freelance writer, though in truth most of the journalism I did wasn't so much writing as typing. Journalists are paid to find stuff out and then communicate it to the rest of us. They don't have to be commanding writers to do so, and indeed many of them are not. There are formulae that work and that get recycled. It is essentially the same five hundred words or so, just in a slightly different order each time. For the reporter it is often frustrating, because the extraordinary is often flattened so much it becomes ordinary.

I am in an armoured Land Rover, crawling through the frigid no man's land of northern Bosnia, trying not terribly hard to find Serb military units that are apparently somewhere they shouldn't be. My driver is Odd Andersen, war photographer, lugubrious Norwegian and all-round good egg. We have been listening to the same three tapes for weeks now. Today it's the turn of Jan Garbarek. That's fine. It's Jan Garbarek weather: sky the colour of snot, air laced with snow, ground a mixture of grit, mud and slush. I can smell the sadness in the air.

I like travelling with Odd. Because he is a photographer, he is always in front of me, that one step closer to a great picture, while I am sitting behind a wall or in a car or among some trees, even back at the bureau. If all else fails, reporters can work the phones. Photographers can't take good pictures from inside an office.

We already have good tales to take home. Bosnia in 1996 is an unhappy land, but we have achieved indecent levels of hilarity along the way. We have an ongoing contest to see how often we and our delectable translators can get on to TV Tuzla. We have a fixer with one leg and a cook whose inedible meals we stow in the car overnight and dump in town the next day to avoid offending her. We have smuggled car parts from Croatia in amateurish fashion. We keep running out of money because our phone bills are more than the rent. The heating doesn't work unless you pay the landlord, a filthy old chancer called Krilic, extras, and even then he tends to come at five in the morning to sort it out, clattering through the bedrooms while we are all asleep. Everywhere in Serb-held territory I pretend to be Russian. Everywhere else I pretend to be a journalist. I can't do shorthand, have never been on hostile environment training and give up too easily. The American peacekeepers love me. Krilic hates me.

There were sobering episodes too. During my first week I was briefly taken hostage by the desperate womenfolk of Srebrenica, armed with sticks, grief and frightening dentistry, mouths full of metal. More recently, I stood impotently as an old Serb woman was beaten about the head by a crowd until she didn't move any more. Before that, I stopped for a roadside call of nature and saw a sign on the tree I was watering. 'Mine!' it said. Last week I spent all night in a Humvee for one paragraph that made it into the *International Herald Tribune*. I'm not sure it was all worth it. Before that I managed to crash three different cars on three separate days. The Tuzla police no longer bother taking me in to HQ to fill out forms. Local traffic stops to let me pass now.

That is why I am happy that Odd is driving. It's a long drag. I always think that any outbound journey of substantially more than an hour changes the dynamic of a day, any day, anywhere. It's more travel than actually being there. There is traffic. There is some snow. Odd cranks up the heating. I get sleepy.

I wake with a start, like a small heart attack. Odd has stopped the car.

'I can see them,' he says.

'Who?'

'The tanks.'

'Where?'

'They're behind that farmhouse. Look. They're not even hidden.'

I can see now. A dozen turret guns pointing straight at us, like a Second World War film. Tank movements in post-Dayton Bosnia are a big no-no. It's a story. I wait for Odd to make his move.

'Aren't you going?'

'There's nothing to see here,' he says.

'No?'

'No. Just a row of tanks. That's not a front page picture, is it?'

'Suppose not.'

Odd sits back in his layers of cold-weather gear. Unlocks the vehicle. I sigh and quaver just a little, then reach into my bag for an old Dictaphone and my pen.

And so I find myself walking across a field with some hard-boiled gunners looking through their sights at me. I wonder how fast a round from one of those things travels. Would you see it coming and be able to sidestep it? Is it just like a game of adult dodgeball? How many seconds would I have to react? I see activity atop one of the vehicles and keep my eyes trained on that gun.

I keep walking but voices in my head are screaming that this is nonsense. I became a journalist to lead a full and interesting life; having it cut short at the age of twenty-six would seem counterproductive. We all know I'm a coward. We learned that in Moscow three years ago, when there was shooting all around and tanks on the streets, and crowds of excitable onlookers poured down to the river to watch the White House get shot up like it was a gala sporting event, but I went in the opposite direction, scuttling from doorway to doorway to avoid the snipers. We learned as much when Chechnya came and went, and all I felt was not sympathy for the victims or solidarity for my colleagues who were there on the ground, but great relief that I didn't have to go. We learned as much when I heard a loud bang in Jerusalem during the suicide-bombing spring of 1996 and flung myself under my bed, only to realise it was fireworks.

I approach the first tank. The tracks have fresh mud on them. The gunner looks down at me and spits copiously. I get out my Russian, dust it down and try to think of a question.

Questions! I haven't thought of any reasonable questions to ask, at least none that won't get me killed instantly. What are you doing here? Are you familiar with the Dayton agreement? Have you killed any Bosniaks recently? Take me to your nearest concentration camp, please. I regret being a lazy idiot who fell asleep in the car, instead of someone more organised, who might have jotted down some open questions to put to a Serb gunner. In truth, I honestly didn't think I'd get to talk to a Serb gunner. But I should have known better.

I start with something anodyne, like, 'Good morning, nice day. I'm a journalist from AFP and want to ask if you've just come here this morning.'

He stares at me blankly, mutters something that I don't understand and disappears down his turret. I walk around a bit more, inhale the mix of cheap fuel and ice that passes for air up here. A chicken wanders into view. Weakly I conclude that I have half a story and all of my life and will settle for that. At least Odd seems impressed when I get back to the Land Rover ...

... I am dashing through west London trying to find a train crash. It's out here somewhere, I know it is, somewhere between Ladbroke Grove and Westbourne Park. But if they happen between stations, train crashes can be hard to find. Stations are usually somewhere, but the tracks between them aren't. 'Here,' says a voice from the other side. 'Upstairs.' I scamper with some other journalists into a tower block, up three, four, five flights of stairs and into a flat. 'A tenner,' says a man in a tracksuit. The photographers pay. I do too, even though all

47

I'm going to get is a view. We look down through the bright October morning and there it is, ripped open like a sardine can, the 6:03 from Cheltenham with a lot of dead bodies on board.

The next hours are frantic. The air is thick with burning. Victims are stretchered away. The walking wounded stand in shock, cradling cups of coffee in a local supermarket cafeteria that has been transformed into a makeshift first aid centre. I speak to a police officer who tells me that four people are dead. I call this in to the office – a snap for our newswire and we are the first news organisation to put out the information, ahead even of the Press Association, the national press agency. I feel great, while all around me people are weeping and grimacing and staring blankly at ambulances and paramedics and police-men. Mobile phones ring and ring in the wreckage of the hapless trains and no one answers them . . .

. . . I'm drunk again, but it's not my fault. I am out on a story to investigate the extent of TB in Russian jails. I had to drink all day to ingratiate myself with hardboiled, uniformed types with names like Colonel S. V. Ponomaryov. Just when I think I'm about to escape with my brain still just about upright, I am invited into the prison director's office for several tots of 'pchyolichnaya' vodka, a sticky yellow brew made either by bees or of bees, I can't remember which. I am sure I'm being told state secrets, juicy stuff that will make for a sensational piece, but I have lost my notebook and my mind is slippery with alcohol. I'm just at that delicate point in the vodka cycle: I've already gone through the phases of feeling terrific, and now I'm making wild promises I won't be able to keep. Next will come the sudden collapse into incoherence. Several hours will go missing and I will end up on a bus in Uglich or asleep on a stranger's doormat. I envy the American TV journalist who has come along with me. She doesn't have to do the vodka. She gets champagne instead, because she's a woman.

I have written things on my hand but I can't make them out. They have promised to take me back to Moscow ... but first, dinner! We pull up in front of a restaurant that is empty apart from a long table overladen with food, more food – and vodka. I need tactics. I rapidly drain a glass of water and put the tumbler on my chair between my thighs. I am burbling to the man next to me, who is disclosing some urgent revelations about corruption in the prison service. I try an old memory trick: one is a bun, two is a shoe, three is a ... what is three a ...? The first vodka shots come round. In the commotion of the toast I deftly pour mine into the glass on my chair, then extravagantly mime draining my glass and braying heartily for more. '*Mezhdu pervoi i vtoroi: promezhutok nebolshoi!*' Round it comes again, round and round. I eat about six slices of black rye bread and wolf down some meat in aspic that on another day I wouldn't feed to my cat, if I had a cat. Soon the glass on my seat is full and, worse, I need to go to the toilet. 'Yuk,' I gesticulate, waving my glass around. 'What do I want water for?' I pour the lot into a plastic plant pot and make for the door. In the toilet, I notice that I only have one shoe. But that doesn't bother me. I have had a brilliant idea: I will call myself on my mobile phone and leave a message with all the fantastic details about corruption and TB and the prison service and all the quotes I have gleaned over the day. It takes quite a while and I think I've got it all down. I stagger back to the table.

The next day I check my voicemail. There is indeed a long message from myself, but it's not much good, containing as it does information entirely limited to the whereabouts of my lost shoe.

3

Is Dad all there is?

For the next two weeks I am neither ill nor well. Several symptoms nag away at me like small children in a department store: fatigue, headaches, low mood, pulses of anxiety and those occasional swooning episodes that are so alarming. I envy everyone: neighbours, school-gate friends, my Lebanese hairdresser, SpongeBob SquarePants. Even my children. I envy my own children. As I drag my exhausted body around the streets of Kingston I look at people and think, 'He's not me, she's not me, that man crossing the road is not me, that old woman in an electric wheelchair is not me . . . ' And I envy them all.

But if it's baffling how bad I feel, it's also baffling how well I feel in between times. One day I wake up and feel almost normal. No headache, plenty of energy, no cognitive screeching. I take it cautiously. Could it be all over? I've been here before. I have lost count of the number of times I have congratulated myself for putting this nightmare behind me. There's a haunting Peggy Lee song called 'Is That All There Is?' It's so deliciously ambiguous, jaunty oompah tones suffused with a sad, almost sinister, chord progression that makes me shiver.

The chorus, a gloriously double-edged thing, goes like this:

> Is that all there is?
> Is that all there is?
> If that's all there is, my friends,
> Then let's keep dancing!
> Let's break out the booze and have a ball
> If that's all
> There is.

I've been singing it to myself for about two months, non-stop. 'Is that all there is?' I ask the illness. Is that all you've got? Are you done now? 'If that's all there is, my friends, then let's keep dancing!' Then I wake the next morning with a terrible feeling that that isn't all there is. There is more. And so I feel the negative edge to the question. Is That All There Is? To me?

I'm finding it harder and harder to listen to music. It's a deeply bewildering loss. I am always listening to music, often just in my head. There is always a song that has got me, got inside me, a song that is playing on a loop in my brain. In the past, I would work out how to play these favourites, picking out a tune or some chords on my old piano. To start with, it had to be easy tunes: 'Let It Be', perhaps, or 'Changes'. Jazz changed all that. Now I am endlessly fascinated by half-diminished and diminished chords, which are like dark, mysterious passageways linking up the rooms of a sprawling house of chords. Diminished chords feel like something in the process of disintegration. There are bits broken off them. They sound unstable, as if they're about to fold in on themselves and become something else. Now, when I sit at the piano, none of this seems relevant or captivating. I just stare at the keys. I cannot think what could possibly have made it interesting to play the piano. I cannot imagine what could possibly have been interesting about listening to music. I can't hear it any more. It's all just noise. I am diminished, breaking down, folding in on myself, about to become something else.

I try napping after lunch. When I worked nights at the newspaper I got this down to a fine art. Twenty minutes, less even. Never more, otherwise you negate the restorative effect. Salvador Dalí used to sit upright with a spoon in his hand held over a bowl. As he fell asleep he'd drop the spoon, which would hit the bowl and the sound would wake him up. Just a heartbeat of sleep: it's all you need to feel refreshed and ready for the second half. But now, when I come round I'm dizzy and sick and the room is off-beam. And there's a ridge of low pressure moving through my diaphragm. I'm nervous.

I am most worried about my cognitive and critical abilities. For the first time in thirty-five years, I cannot read. Sharon has got me the second Stieg Larsson out of the library, but I give up after twenty pages. I'm ashamed of my sudden illiteracy, so I slip in my bookmark halfway through the tome. I try to read the paper, to stay in touch with my work, but find it impossible to internalise anything I read. By the time I get to the end of a sentence I can't remember what was at the beginning. It all seems so irrelevant to my current predicament. Suddenly Booker prize winners and Kremlin intrigues and party conferences and Premiership goal-scorers all seem meaningless, incapable of reaching me. The merry carousel of news, once so thrilling, now just looks like plastic artifice, eternally recycling the same old stories. I am becoming like my grandmother. She is 102 and can't really do anything much; I have not been so sympathetic towards her in recent years; now I'm full of sorrow for how her life is petering out.

I can still write, but not for long. I have written a diary for thirty years. It changed, from paper to digital, from dull chronology to illustrated scrapbook, from judgemental commentary to review and essay, aphorism and insight. Now it is a chronicle of my ever-circling symptoms.

Friday 16 October 2009

Stabilising. Symptoms still there – that slack-arsed lethargy in my legs and occasional twinges across my eyes; a fullness in my ears, particularly when I bend down. But no 'episodes' now since Wednesday morning. Milder. I need to keep on this trajectory. More than anything you need to keep on this trajectory, Marko.

For I'm not done yet. The thing that annoys me is that

I've been drifting around saying I've done it all. But there's so much more to do. I haven't even started at the *Guardian* yet; and my kids are just starting to get interesting; the level of interest from my friends in my illness suggests that friendships are fertile and still good for a lot of happy times yet; and, and, and

Yet some people must be cut down, in primes like these, and made to endure the most appalling restrictions and curtailments. This is the essence of the human condition: that we live as though nothing will ever change and we'll be all right for ever, but full in the knowledge that actually something really vile could happen at any moment of any day. How to live with that uncertainty? Make contingency plans, take nothing for granted and enjoy things as much as is humanly possible.

Monday 19 October 2009

When it comes on, it does so in such an insidious fashion; there could be a sudden screw-tightening in the temples, or else a wavering in my diaphragm, or a sudden pulse of anxiety and worry that ripples through my head and torso. I worry: that I might not be able to do my job again; that I'll fail the children; that I'll be marooned here in disability; that this will just drag on and I'll have to show patience and steadiness in equal measure to get through, without even knowing what I'm trying to get through to. So then I say, enough, basta, stop being stupid, pull self together, this time next week it's back to work. And then I say what if that falls apart – I can't focus, can't contribute, can't mix it up with the various stakeholders I have to deal with to do my job. What then?

Just did an IQ test on Facebook. 134. So no real probs with cognitive function then … and no muscle cramps, and no sweats or pain, and no aching glands, sore throats or the like. So no ME. Just a postviral thing. It will pass. Time will sort it out, Marko. Hang in there.

I know I shouldn't but I am always coming back to the internet. To try to find out what's wrong with me. Depression still seems an alien word. I don't feel depressed. I am not crying in the corner. Not yet. And anyway, isn't depression a women's illness?

The statistics seem to suggest so. Roughly three women suffer for every man. Mothers are more vulnerable than fathers. Post-partum depression is of course well documented, but less well known is how many men fall ill during the first years of their children's lives. According to research funded by the Medical Research Council and published in autumn of 2010,* more than 20 per cent of new fathers will experience some form of depressive illness before their first child is a teenager. That's one dad in five. Around 3 per cent will succumb in the first year, and one in ten will have suffered a depressive episode before their kids are at school.

Irwin Nazareth, who led the research, says the findings shouldn't be that surprising. Depressive illness, he says, often

*http://www.mrc.ac.uk/Newspublications/News/MRC007207

sneaks in when you're not looking because you have been upended by a major life episode. And there are few life episodes more major than new life episodes. For the first time in your life there is someone on the planet whom you want to outlive you. 'This is an enormous life event, it changes your lifestyle, you've got to be awake at night, reconsider finances, it's a new person in the house, it changes the relationship between partners,' says Nazareth, a professor of primary care and population science at University College London.

Most at risk are new fathers younger than twenty-four, the poor and anyone with a previous history of depression. I am none of the above. An outlier, then? Not really. During my journey through the landscape of depression I came across plenty of fellow travellers, other middle-class, middle-aged dads bashing away at careers and families, trying too hard, striving to be solid and supportive, trying not to let anyone down, perma-knackered undergroomed types always racing from A to B, cooking while booking business travel, toilet training while conference calling (I once interviewed an MP while bottle feeding), juggling smartphone and saucepan and school run. My rather obvious analogy is the trick of keeping plates spinning. All around me was the sound of breaking china, and it wasn't just my crockery.

There was Alex, an old uni friend who imploded when his sister became very unwell and his employer was giving him no quarter. 'Some days,' his wife told me, 'it was just a question of getting the kids out to school, home again, fed and watered.' There was Bill, who kept going and going until one day he could go no further and he sat in an armchair and stayed there for a month. Recovery took two years. Then there was Nigel, who succumbed when fatherhood took all the fun out of life. I'll tell you more about them later. All of us have seen the impact of our illness on our children: kids with depressive parents generally underperform and run a far greater risk of developing psychological problems of their own.

Nazareth says, moreover, that statistics do not reflect the dads who do not come forward, guys who pound away at work, sink exhaustedly into armchairs at the end of the day, who struggle to switch repeatedly from deal making and report writing to playing build-the-tower-of-cups or push-the-plastic-shape-through-the-hole. Who mask their symptoms with drink and drugs or women and carousing. 'Men often don't come forward,' he says. 'There is this culture of being the tough male who has to be strong and take anything. It is not common for a man below fifty to seek help from a doctor.'

Tim Cantopher, a psychiatrist whose book *Depressive Illness: The Curse of the Strong* helped me turn the corner, has also noticed the subtle change in the incidence of the illness. He reckons the female:male ratio has shifted from 3:1 to 2:1. 'There's been a change in society. Men are being expected to be soft and cuddly and put the kids to bed at the same time as being bread winners,' he told me. Yet there has been little change in the workplace demands on men. The upshot? A feeling that fathers have two jobs instead of one, that there is no let-up, no respite, just unrelenting exaction at work and at home. 'Life is still more difficult for women than men, but men who try to be Atlas and cope with everything seem to be the kind of people who go under.'

Fatherhood is a watershed. The pram in the hallway is the enemy of promise. It depletes. People with small children don't generally distinguish themselves. If they do, it's normally at the children's expense. Powers diminish, potency evaporates. Performers struggle. Look at Beckham, Flintoff, Pietersen, Rooney. Look at Bowie, McCartney, Lennon. Don't tell me any of them were greater at their thing after they became fathers.

The first stages of family life are treacherous. You can tell which parents might be susceptible. They have grey oblongs in their cheeks and look like junkies without the track marks. They seem to be not just thinner, but reduced all round by about 20 per cent, with smaller heads and mouths that turn down.

'It would be surprising if men weren't vulnerable because becoming a parent is a massive change for anyone,' says Rob Williams, chief executive of the Fatherhood Institute. 'It's been peculiar that people have assumed that women would get post-natal depression and men would be immune.'

Williams points out a range of factors that seem highly familiar to me: 'Like most dads, I found the transition to parenthood dramatic and a massive change and trying to separate out tiredness from depression is difficult. You're bound not to feel so "up" for things any more and your relationship with your wife becomes more fraught and difficult.

'The expectation of the father's role in the house with the

new baby has changed. All the housework and nappy- and dishwashing that men do now wasn't there twenty-five years ago; but what hasn't changed is the expectation of fathers' work patterns. Women take part-time work; that hasn't emerged yet in men.'

Dr Caroline Gatrell, an expert in work health and family at Lancaster University Management School, has done plenty of research into the pressures that bear down on working parents. Curiously, she says that parents of one or three children are more stressed out than those with two. 'Men acknowledge that their performance and productivity does dip after the first child and that's where some of the anxiety comes from,' she says. By the time the second child arrives, the couple has adapted to parenthood and knows the ropes. 'But when number three comes along, that pushes the stress levels higher again. It's possible that the woman might have packed in work altogether.'

And this leads on to her second counter-intuitive finding: that parents who both work will be less prone to stress than families in which one partner works and the other looks after the home front. 'If the dad is sharing the income earning with his partner, it is much better – stress levels are lower,' she says. In this scenario, there is more likelihood that partners will split the domestic drudgery, which can become a real bone of contention in families where just one partner works. Nobody wants to do the housework. 'What tends to happen is that women go on maternity leave, the amount of housework cranks up hugely and they can't hand it back.

'Men who do some share of housework tend to have a better

work–life balance than men who don't – and relationships with partners are better.'

But even with a better work–life balance, new fathers are bound to feel that something is missing. They have their work, they have their children, they do their share of the housework, they have their security. But they have very little fun. Rob Williams says that mothers and fathers find parenthood plays very differently on their social life: 'Women find their social circle increases when they have children because of all the friends they make at mums and toddlers' groups, whereas men who go straight back home from the office – what they are missing out on is all the social interaction they had with their mates. Men's social circles contract significantly.'

My social circle began to contract on 30 July 2001. A new life, a little boy, a cute little fellow with an upturned nose, yellow skin and a head in the shape of a cone (they had to use a ventouse to help him out). There are photos of the occasion, me holding this small creature looking acutely uncomfortable, like I am holding an ancient, priceless instrument for a maestro while he goes to the toilet. I am delighted, of course, but find it deeply unsettling at the same time. Some people have since remarked that it must be quite a big step up moving from one to two, as we did in 2003, and from two to three (2006). My response is that yes, these are big changes, but nothing is quite as big as the move from zero to one. Dad. The word seems alien when I say it to myself. Dad. I have become a palindrome.

There are many things they don't tell you about having

children. Things like they won't like beaches until they're about four and they won't like snow until they're eight or nine. They will eat stones and dirt but not their dinner. It doesn't start to get easier until they can blow their own bubbles and wipe their own bottoms. They won't play any games that are remotely interesting until they're three or so, and by that time you'll be desperate for them to play games for six- or eight-year-olds, because there's only so much I Spy and Guess Who you can tolerate in a day. They go through good stages and bad. They will make you laugh by saying things like, 'Dad, do your ears come off?' or, 'Dad, it is extremely difficult to invent your own letter.'

They will change your preferences and tendencies. Hot summer days are no good any more: they just make for irritable, sleepless babies. White Christmases are pointless: even in gloves, little hands will endure for all of five minutes before you have to go back indoors. Late afternoons are to be wished away, a time of chores, mess and fracturing tempers. On summer nights, you go to bed while it's still light.

They will also give you every bug they get, about five a year in my case. You could rewrite Philip Larkin.

> They fuck you up, do your offspring,
> They may not mean to, but they do,
> They give you every bug they bring
> Back home, and then can't care for you.

Until I became a parent I was fairly certain about who I was and where I was going. Suddenly I wasn't so sure. I lost a bit of my edge. It wasn't just the sleep and the nappies. It was more fundamental than that.

My work seemed less important, though the money and security were surely more important than ever. There was something not quite right about our unseemly early morning scramble to get James into nursery so we could both get to work. Some days we'd drop him off in the dark and pick him up in the dark too. Poor little guy. He howled a lot. We were helpless, I more so than Sharon, who had bonded much better with James during her maternity leave. I was turning into a stereotype.

An internal conversation quietly grated:

Roxy: He's your son. He's only young once, and you're
    spending his infancy trotting out meaningless news sto-
    ries for strangers in Turkey and Taiwan.
Marko: Yes, but dads work. It's what they do. My dad worked.
Roxy: Not these days, not necessarily. Some dads really
    bond with their kids, take time out. You could do that.
Marko: I'm not sure. Work is healthy. Brings order to the
    week. The office is a busy, fun place to be. I'm not sure
    that the playgroup is.
Roxy: You're a trier, a trailblazer, a risk-taker, a liver. Yet
    here you're just going through the motions.
Marko: OK, OK, I'll do it. But not for ever.

My company offered an extended unpaid sabbatical. I took a year.

*

At the start it was tough. My generation isn't really hardwired this way. We are programmed to hit short-term performance indicators: an exam, a job interview, a deadline, a pay grade. We are used to being the golden generation, carefree, amoral, cosmopolitan, plugged in. We are used to tasks that last forty-five minutes or a week, not a lifetime. We have been brought up to be goal-oriented, self-centred, impatient, definite, vain, affluent, acquisitive. Nothing that we have been taught can prepare us for something that will require patience, subservience, sacrifice, open-endedness. All that modernity and technology is of little use when it comes to the long, hard yards required to turn tiny infants into proper little people. You can't email your children to a childminder. Twitter encourages you to join the conversation but it won't help you entertain two toddlers who are fighting over a light sabre. Parenting is a devotion that cannot be scored; there are no percentages, grades or promotions (other than that of becoming a grandparent, and I'm not sure that qualifies as a promotion). Payback is years down the line, if it comes at all.

The other challenging thing about parenting is that so many of the answers are counter-intuitive. A baby screams in the night: let it settle itself. An infant falls over: don't make eye contact. A toddler makes a mess of a mealtime: let it, and clean up later. A child struggles with homework: allow it to fail. For the generation used to making things good, taking action, intervening to influence outcomes, these laissez-faire solutions seem all wrong. Equally as bewildering is the switch from work to parenting, a culture shock at the end of even the most straightforward day. I once wrote an article about chessboxing, which is as preposterous as it sounds. The protagonists endure five rounds of boxing in between bursts of speed chess; the switch from one to the other can be a messy affair. So it is with the professional parent. He or she comes home with the bullying affairs of office life still nagging away. Meetings had to be missed, tasks were left undone, in order to get here on time. In the good old days there would be a cup of tea and a dose of decompression. Not now. Suddenly the skills required are different. It's no longer about decisions, mental agility, networking, initiative, but about slow, gentle love, rolling a small ball backwards and forwards, counting bits of chewed plastic, helping young fingers slot the same bit of puzzle into the same hole that was there yesterday and the day before that and the year before that. Yes, the professional parent is like the chessboxer, pummelled and bamboozled at the same time, and never too sure if s/he needs to throw some punches or sit tight and nudge a pawn forwards.

There are the times when you are unwell. I recall an early episode of food poisoning. I was rolling around at four in the morning in agony. All I could do was look at the clock and think to myself, 'I've got four hours to get it out of my system before Monkey Boy wakes up.' You can parent or you can be ill. You can't do both. You can't roll around hallucinating, sweating like the guilty and shivering like a rabid terrier *and* play this is the way we clap our hands with a nine-month-old.

In those early months of homedadding, you could tell how well the day was going by the clock. If he'd already had breakfast, lost patience with everything, had a sleep, woken up, been out for a walk, got bored of all his toys and it was still only 8:23, you'd know it was going to be a tough day. Whereas if we got to ten and there had been no tears – from him or me – things were set fair.

The park was a natural destination for dad and son. Most people there were women, mums. They would give Monkey Boy a sweet smile but look at me with concern. Have I just abducted him, their look said. What is a hatchet-faced man doing leading a small child around by the hand at a quarter past eleven on a Thursday? I would idly wonder who in their right mind would have made these women pregnant in the first place. They had strange, primitive conversation. No one seemed to reply to anyone else.

'Daniel took a few steps on his own the other day.'

'Millie never really crawled at all.'

'We think he'll be all over the place soon.'

'Henry's into everything ... '

'We don't let him have anything with sugar in it.'

'He's really good with his fruit.'

'She's already reading at fifteen months!'

'Delphine just loves music.'

'Millie plays on her own quite happily already.'

At least, I thought, these are people who don't talk exclusively about themselves.

Social activity was pretty thin. The invitations kept on not flooding in. I'd had visions of a home dad standing around in other people's kitchens, effortless in conversation with bright-eyed new mums, offering to pop round to look at a contrary washing machine or to fix a leaky tap, even though I'm crap at DIY. But there wasn't much of that. I'd hang around furtively for an extra fifteen minutes at the church playgroup, just to see if anyone came rushing up to invite me to a coffee morning or a birthday party. I played with the straps on the baby carrier and took an extended interest in the noticeboard so that I became intimately acquainted with the Sunday morning coffee rota and the Children's Act, 1989. A couple of people nodded in my general direction, which made me feel better, until I realised that they were actually mouthing their greetings past me into the room beyond, where the playgroup leader was playing 'Puff the Magic Dragon' on a sitar.

When I did meet other home dads, they were generally as hopeless as me. One poor fellow couldn't even remember his child's name. Actually that's a lie, but he was just about as bad as that, pushing his child on the swing and helping it down the slide, and holding it as it swung across the monkey bars in some vain attempt to enhance its CV. All the kid really wanted to do was sit in the dirt and eat stones next to mine. The eating of stones is something that should cause me concern, but strangely doesn't.

We took the bull by the horns, and when that proved a rather hazardous way to get into central London, we left it where it was and jumped on a train. At least we would have done had there been a train to jump on. Delays and cancellations made the journey an onerous affair. Still we stood on the station, with me showing Monkey Boy where all the trains would have been had any of them bothered to turn up on time. Eventually one rolled in with a languid sigh of indifference, having made the journey all the way in from somewhere not very far away, and it was all aboard.

Kids and trains seem to work quite well, no? There was one alarming moment when Monkey Boy, unobserved for a second, ripped a copy of the *Sun* from the hands of a violently tattooed sociopath and put much of it in his mouth. But we cleared that up with smiles all round and me scolding Monkey Boy that no, newspapers were not to be eaten, particularly rags peddling such indigestible rot as the *Sun*.

We spent the morning at the supermarket. The whole morning. We only went in for some milk and disinfectant. And it was all my fault, I'm afraid. Perhaps, I thought, Monkey Boy would be a happier Monkey Boy if he was allowed to do things at his own pace.

Time to do stuff for him, and him alone. Time to do what he wanted us to. So that meant plopping him on the floor after the lengthy wait at the checkout and seeing where we ended up. It wasn't the most salubrious of scenes.

People I had felt sorry for as they stood at the back of my queue while I packed up the shopping overtook us on the way out. 'Not going to get very far today, are we?' said one chap gaily. 'We don't get very far any day,' I replied.

*

In the park, I noticed that parents rarely introduced themselves but were happy to give out every last detail about their offspring. The name was one of the first things to come out, closely followed by age, current poo consistency and areas in which early signs of genius were already being detected.

Most names took some fathoming. Not too many Johns and Marys any more. Instead a curious mix of monikers: Zhenya, Magnus, Dolores, Xerxes, Gustav.

Gustav! I inspected the bright little chap who has the misfortune to be saddled with such a heavy, mournful name. He didn't look much like a Gustav, but then I suspected few small children would. I rummaged around for a short form, a diminutive to lighten the load, but could only come up with Gu-gu, Gusto and Tavvy. I suspected he was of Central European intellectual stock, perhaps descended from Hohenzollern royalty, but his mother recoiled in alarm when I opened up with some rusty German. I wondered who the poor little mite was named after. Mahler? Holst, perhaps? His mum did have a certain Classic FM look about her. She kept on humming a tuneless refrain that could well have been a segment of *The Planets* that I was not yet familiar with (which is pretty much all of it).

Gustav, I think. Gustav Klimt? I slipped him a crayon when his mother wasn't looking but he showed no sign of producing Art Nouveau friezes.

Carl Gustav Jung? He certainly appeared to be deep in thought as he wandered unsteadily towards four lanes of traffic. Gustav Kirchhoff, Gustavo Kuerten. Perhaps Gustav von

Aschenbach if his parents were ardent Thomas Mann or Dirk Bogarde fans. But if so, why not Thomas or Dirk?

'Thomas, Dirk,' his mum cried. 'Don't push your brother. Come on, help Gustav down the slide.' Yes indeed, or it'll be Death in Little Venice ...

And now there are two! Monkey Boy and Teddy Edward. Gosh, it's hard work. It's winter and it seems to get dark at about a quarter to two. I have developed a tactic of putting them down at lunchtime and then turning the heating up. It seems to make them sleep for about two and a half hours, which is great. But then when they get up, all foffy and groggy, it's already twilight outside and there's nothing to do. We could go and stamp in puddles or collect leaves, but it's so wintry that there are few of either. We spend time in the playroom watching the dusk. There are some nursery rhymes on the cassette player and puzzles all over the floor. Oh look, Monkey Boy is bashing Teddy Edward with a hammer for stealing a corner piece from the Thomas the Tank Engine puzzle and putting it in his mouth. They are both wailing and have lines of snot connecting their nostrils to their mouths and it's getting dark and it's so bleak and empty I think I actually stopped breathing there for several minutes and it's 3:17 p.m., and there are four hours until Sharon gets back or bedtime comes, whichever is the earlier.

The other thing they don't tell you about children is that they grow up. Nothing stays the same for ever. The era of tiny babies lasted about five years for us. It was both hard graft and magical.

It didn't help that everyone else I knew – my sisters, my oldest friends – had the easy perfume of child-free leisure curling off them. I just stank of kid sick. Anyway, at the tail end of the babies epoch I started to think about how I would reconfigure my life, from portfolio parent ministering unto kids and editors in equal measure to a more traditional father who would be a figure of pride for his school-age children. That makes it sound like I had a definite strategy to reinvent myself. I didn't. I was just exhausted by hanging around with toddlers and wanted to hang around with some adults for a while. I pitched myself back into the one thing that has never let me down. Work.

It was exhilarating, picking up the scent of news again. I did shifts on national newspapers and generally tarted around for anyone who'd pay for things to be written down. It really is a doddle, like falling off a log. Anyway, quite soon I was offered a job on the *Guardian*: night foreign news editor, which sounds more glamorous than it was. The role was sometimes exciting, sometimes tedious and always nocturnal. 'It's OK, Roxy,' said Marko soothingly. 'Big heave. Gut it out. Graft it, toughen up. Less sleep, but getting what you want.'

'No,' said Roxy. 'Getting what *you* want.' That's the problem with getting what you want: sometimes it takes so long that by the time you've got it, it's not what you want any more.

There was a further complication. I had built up several very handy freelance relationships. I was loath to give these up as journalism is very insecure: some day, the money will run out altogether and we'll all be volunteers; until that day you take what you can get. My *Guardian* job was three nights a week. It felt like there would be time to keep freelancing during the days too.

And so my days began to settle into an utterly unsustainable pattern. I would wake somewhere between seven and eight, depending on the needs of Sharon, who worked four days a week, and our infants, who were there seven days a week. I would do a school run or a nursery run, or both, then scurry home to knock up a piece or two for publications in the US and Singapore. I would lunch, nap, shower and then race into central London to start my proper job at four. This would go on until one or two in the morning, at which time I would dash home, grab some sleep and start all over again.

Travelling home late at night was tricky: I was heavily reliant on the 1:05 from Waterloo, full of chancers and jokers and drunks and a few people like me; I was equally reliant on my old road bike, which would get me to and from stations at both ends. But if there was a suicide bomb in Egypt at eleven at night, or a government minister resigning or a prime-time US presidential speech, forget it. We wouldn't finish until half past one. I would have my noble steed and fifteen miles of road in front of me.

By July 2005, I was a pretty tired man.

I am standing on the doorstep in the rain, wondering what to do next. I know I should go, but something is stopping me. It's my phone. It's ringing again. So far I've got a plan for the next three hours: dash into central London, interview survivors, nag the police, file to Boston on the laptop. Then I've got a spot with Canadian TV at one but it's not to camera, just a phoner, and they've got a mugshot of me that makes me look quite young so that's OK. There's a radio interview with WBUR at two and then a short hiatus before a quick shower and then starting all over again at the *Guardian*.

I look at my phone. It's a number I don't recognise.

'Hello, Mark Rice-Oxley,' I say.

'Oh, hi!' says an American voice, as if surprised they have got me. 'This is KPFK public radio in Los Angeles, sir, how are you today?' American public radio typically goes by an ugly four-letter acronym, different for every city. It's an alphabet soup of unloved local broadcasting.

'Er, um, not brilliant. There's, er, been a terrorist attack.'

'We know, sir, that's why we're calling. Would you be able to go on our breakfast show in about a half-hour?'

A half-hour. I'm not sure I have that window any more. I'm not sure I have any windows any more. I've parcelled up my time into ever smaller chunks, down to ten minutes here and there. Every second counts. My home phone rings.

'Hang on, please . . . Hello, Mark Rice-Oxley.'

'Hi Mark, it's the *Monitor*.'

'Oh, can I call you back? I'm just dealing with someone on the other phone.'

'Sure, but just to say we have a stringer near King's Cross. He can do the colour. So that should free you up a bit to do the write-through.'

It's been like this since ten to nine this morning. I'd been quietly flatlining on the sofa, congratulating myself on a minor triumph: a twenty-hour day the previous day with a story in two overseas papers on London winning the 2012 Olympics and several radio interviews on the back of it too. Now I was looking at a nice clear day until my shift started. I turned on the telly and saw police tape, ambulances, that dreaded red ticker across the bottom of the screen. It's happened. We kind of knew it would, but it's happened today. I take a deep breath. It will be a month before I can breathe out again.

OK, but now the *Monitor* are saying that DK will do the pavement pounding in London, which makes things a little easier. I can do LA radio, then a rapid ring round – the cops, the home office, see if a *Guardian* colleague will give me a number for the spooks – then update the main story, then do Canada TV and WBUR, then call DK and download all his stuff into the main story. Then grab a shower and go into London . . . no, go into London, swing through Tavistock Square and King's Cross, grab interviews en route just in case, soak up a bit of scene then get to the *Guardian*, *then* shower, then, then, then . . .

It feels wrong, not being there, not being on the scene on the biggest day in London since the war. But that's the way news is going. You can do enough on the phones to make it work. Sometimes more: you can watch TV and the wires and bang the phones, call the usual suspects, just go up and down your contacts book and have more than enough to write a credible story. You'll never do anything memorable, but in my experience of working for a lot of titles all at once it is no longer about doing something memorable, but doing something manageable.

Is Dad all there is?

I'm eating a sandwich and waiting for Canadian television. They were cool yesterday. There were no curveballs. Not like Public Radio's the World, who stumped me last week with a question about Gordon Ramsay. Or was it Heston Blumenthal? I can't remember. It's actually quite fun, radio. You have to think on your feet. It doesn't really work just reading out pat answers to stock questions. It has to feel like a dialogue. US radio hosts are good for that: they always make me sound venerable and esteemed. I wonder if they know what I look like. Sometimes they get my name wrong. It's a bugger to say on radio. Mike Arse-Ruckley here from Lundin.

Pretty soon I'll have to start saying no. CNN have been on: they want me in west London at a quarter past one. In the morning. I'd love to do it, but it's just too much. And anyway, I've come into town without a tie. I'm sitting very still on the news desk at the *Guardian* now, and I'm absolutely finished. My heart feels like it's made of cocaine. I'm jittery and can't really concentrate. Tonight we have two news editors, thank goodness, plus a long cast of seniors who'll hang around for the duration. I'm just doing foreign news. No one's interested in foreign news tonight. I can coast. I can even slip out in my dinner break to do a radio spot with WXYZ radio of Albuquerque or Columbus or Seattle or wherever they're from. I'll get out promptly and get home and sleep and then start over at seven. I mean start again. These Americans have got me speaking their language now. And then who knows. It'll probably be two or three weeks; that's how long a news arc typically lasts. There'll be whodunnits and victim stories, minute-by-minute reconstructions of the morning and big analyses of how this changes the game. It exhausts me to think of ploughing through it all. The things that will help: phone numbers – just get as many as humanly possible. The *Guardian*'s a good place for that. It's like a giant telephone directory of the great and good. My bike – the exercise of getting to and from work will be a good antidote to the exhaustion. My sister's house – I'll crash there a couple of nights, ease the strain. A holiday – we'll go away in August, when the story arc has run its course.

By late 2006 I was warming up for the arrival of our third child with some more impossible schedules, bingeing seven nights in a row at the *Guardian* and then catching up on sleep during days off. But the off days were more on than ever: James was in school and needed picking up at three. I had to compress my freelancing into an even tighter corner.

One night I slept in the office. Put the paper to bed at half past one and sloped off with my sleeping bag to this weird room at the back of the newsroom that has odd-shaped sofas and periodicals on butterflies and restorative justice stacked up against a wall. This will do, I thought. Now, how do you switch off the lights? Answer: you don't really. I found some switches, but turning them on and off seemed to have no effect on anything in my field of vision. Most buildings are now constructed this way, I believe, with a dashboard of switches that do nothing but confuse the staff. Half the place was still smarting with incandescent light as I buried myself deeper in my sleeping bag. I had to be on deck at eight and it just didn't make sense to cycle all the way home only to turn around and come back.

Luckily I'm a good sleeper. I always go out like a light. But what's this? A droning noise elbows its way into my delicious dream. The door opens and a cleaner bustles in with a vacuum cleaner. She doesn't give me a second thought. Maybe it's common practice. I have that sour taste in my mouth which tells me it's the time of night when the body is doing its self-cleansing thing. I look at my watch: it's a quarter past five. I try to get back to sleep but with the hoovering and the lights and the angle of the sofa and the slight tackiness of everything I touch, it's no good. I shower and start work early.

After Janey was born, Sharon and I worked out a pattern. I got in from work at around two, gave the little wiggly one her middle-of-the-night feed and put her down in the spare room, where I slept. Sharon was therefore off duty from eleven to six. Seven joined-up hours! That's luxury, I tell her. I was theoretically spared between three and nine, unless Janey was unsettled or the boys were noisy, or someone rang the doorbell looking to borrow milk or onions or my eternal soul. In practice, I could rarely sleep in beyond seven. There didn't seem much point. Lying in until ten just made me feel jetlagged. I whittled back the sleep still further.

The *Guardian* was a home from home. The backbench is the command deck of the news operation. By day it is populated by important people who decide what is going where in the paper and how it will be presented. But at eight o'clock a mysterious change comes over the operation. Senior staff repair to the

Coach and Horses and the night team materialise from all four corners of the newsroom, like ghouls at Hallowe'en.

It's a thankless job, night editing. We liken ourselves to a very expensive sprinkler system: there just in case something catches fire. It rarely does. There's a reason most of us do what we do by day and not by night. Nothing really happens at night. I can say this after sitting up for years watching newswires tick over with stories like 'Ecuadorian housing minister visits Chile', or 'Study: feeding children crisps could be bad for them'.

After a half-time pause for refreshments between editions, the team would reconvene. The tea would be made and we would soon be cheerfully engrossed in a variety of endeavours, some of them related to journalism. On quiet nights I would think up palindromes involving colleagues (my personal best: for the convivial former night editor Steve Busfield, whose productivity I guessed might dwindle if demoted to the sub-editors' bench. 'Busfield: idle if sub').

Our collective reverie would then be rudely interrupted by the sullen thud of the first editions, which would land on my desk courtesy of a magic tattooed arm that appeared around the corner like one of Mr Tickle's limbs. We would then immerse ourselves in a variety of lurid tales, some of them clearly inventions, from rival newspapers – a gripping court case, or an account of war, death and mayhem in some remote, unpleasant part of the world. We discussed them, ventured our own views and theories, leaned back in our chairs for effect, argued idly about the facts, the basis for any news story. Only latterly would it occur to us that if we found the story so interesting, then perhaps our readers might too and we might want to do something about it, like putting it in the paper.

Sometimes our evenings were ruined by something really quite urgent. Someone would shoot people in America, or the Japanese would have another election. Or there would be an earthquake or tsunami in Asia. I'd like to say that, at moments like these, the night desk would purr into action and earn its money, but it was usually less glorious than that. A flash would scroll across Sky News or the Reuters newswire and I would stare at it for some minutes, hoping it would go away. When it didn't I would slowly, reluctantly accept the inevitable. Night news editing is the art of getting people who don't want to write stories to write stories for people who don't really want to read them. Essentially it was a face-saving, arse-covering exercise to ensure that we were 'present' on all and every spurious story that could snowball into the next Madeleine McCann or MMR scare.

Who to write it? The go-to correspondent who has been awake non-stop for several weeks and never says no but could be about to spontaneously combust in a toxic cloud of innuendo, suggestion and overlapping story contrails? The big-beast specialist who'll complain about you ruining his evening, sniff that the story is obviously rubbish because it's in *The Times* and go on to produce his best piece in years? The casual night reporter looking for her first big break who has already done ten hours at the *Evening Standard* earlier that day, who knows nothing about Zimbabwe and who is in any case clearly busy typing up a freelance piece for *Cement Review Quarterly*? Whoever it is, it'll be a heave. You'll have to grovel, apologise, flatter and sweet talk it out of them, and then when copy comes in late, short, clichéd and plain wrong, you'll have to re-do it, run it back past the writer – making it clear that you have just 'tweaked a couple of things' – and then make sure there's a big enough slot in the paper to ensure that you haven't both wasted your time. Then you put his or her name on top and sigh. All your best work has other people's names on it.

If something big happens after midnight you have an impossible choice: to call the duty editor and explain to him why you've woken him up in the middle of the night to discuss the finer points of Iraqi politics, or to take a punt yourself and stick the piece on page fourteen and wake up the next morning to find it on the front pages of every other paper. I made an early decision: err on the side of splashing stories on the front page. It's a bit like going all-in at poker: usually you get away with it. But when you get it wrong you don't half look daft.

The later it gets, the more you're on edge. Last edition is 1:30 a.m., though you can still make small changes well after that. Once you're done with the midnight edition, it's just a case of waiting it out. Happily, not much really happens, but there were still some very tense nights. Suicide bombers – in Saudi Arabia, Egypt, Morocco – had an unhappy knack of waiting until dead of night before striking. The night Saddam Hussein was executed it really wasn't clear until well after two that he was actually dead. So you wait and wait and leave it until the last possible minute before sending the page. And then there were the Americans. Always leaving their votes, their speeches and their elections until ridiculously late. We would be hyped up to a panic level commensurate with the situations room in the West Wing. The US correspondent on one phone saying he really couldn't call it, the production people screaming down another phone that they needed us to send the front page forty-five minutes ago. In the end, somehow it all worked out. We got herograms the next day. But the problem with doing your job well is that it becomes hard to replace you. I was stuck with late nights for five years.

Finally they promoted me. Two people left the foreign news desk and I was off nights for good. I set about trying to repair my biorhythms after the damage of long-term night work. The body clock and circadian rhythm are extremely important. When the change came it felt good at first. Going to bed at half past ten night after night was a novelty, like moving house. The kids were sleeping better and we were getting close to being something like a normal family for the first time. So it is ironic that, at precisely this time, I started to notice odd things about my sleep.

At first I put it down to the readjustment. There was a night around Christmas time when I was just – *zing* – awake until four. And another in February. Then gradually something different. I started waking up very early, at three or four, and wondering what I was doing, lying there awake. It wasn't unpleasant. I had no pressing concerns to make me worry. Sometimes I'd drift back to sleep but more often I'd just lie there, listening to the new day beginning. You can get an awful lot done just lying in bed doing nothing.

My new job was stressful, very full-time, yet still I'd make time for freelancing, for parenting, for everyone else but myself. I was the man who'd got it all; the only problem with getting it all is that there's so much to look after, so much to keep going, so much to lose. It made for a relentless life: getting up ten minutes before I went to bed to do all the chores in record time before whisking the kids through the morning routines, dashing down to the pool to do fifty lengths amid the breast-strokers and stressed brokers and then on my bike to get the train. Always late. Scrambling around for ten hours trying to do a job that at least one colleague has likened to nailing jelly to a wall. Then home, invariably running for the next Tube to get the earlier train to get fifteen minutes extra time to do lunch-boxes and tidy up and get kids and kit ready for the next day. Then maybe an hour on the guitar or piano to make sure I don't lose it, not that I'm sure I ever had it, but fingers become dull and stupid after a while. Never saying no. Being strong for other people. Never thinking about what's best for me. Never sitting and watching vacuous telly, or going for a quiet walk, or toddling off down the pub with a good book. A lazy person inhabiting the life of a very busy man. Trying too hard.

Oh yes, Marko, Roxy, whoever you are, you think you're the last person who would succumb to a depressive breakdown. But, looking back at that schedule, it was only a matter of time before something snapped.

4

Breakdown

I resolve to go back to work, more in hope than in expectation. But first we decide on a weekend down at Glendene. Dear old Glendene, the house I was born in, the place that nurtured me. I know every squeaky floorboard, every wallpaper pattern, every crack in every coffee mug. I know just how hard to push the lounge door to open it when it's stuck shut. I automatically flip the bolt across whenever I go in the bathroom, without even noticing that I'm doing it. I know how to take the stairs three at a time and how to manoeuvre the shower dial to keep the water somewhere between its two settings, scalding and freezing.

We arrive on the weekend the clocks go back, the moment

in the year when we collectively withdraw from the great outdoors and find small compensations in the quiet things of winter: candles, baked potatoes, last season's trusted overcoat. As we climb through the Butser pass, I feel an indescribable panic rising in my throat. It's getting dark. My right hand is ringing like an old bell dropped on the deck of an aircraft carrier. A high-pitched siren announces itself in my right ear, as shrill and unforgettable as the old BBC Closedown screen.

As we arrive I ripple with unease. My dad has some innocuous Twenty20 game on the telly; I spent half my childhood watching cricket in the front room, but now the motion on the screen is making me jittery and tense and I couldn't care less who wins. I start cups of tea but can't finish them, sit down to dinner but can't finish mouthfuls. Maybe an early night will sort things out, I think. But as soon as I'm in bed I know it won't. It's impossible to lie still. I hear them turning off lights downstairs and it triggers a mild panic: Shit! They're all coming to bed! I'm not getting an early night at all! In fact, they will all get to sleep before me. When Sharon comes in I pretend to be asleep. I don't know why. Maybe I think I can fool myself. Of course it doesn't work. She is soon out and I am alone and afraid, restless and rumpled and unsure of what to do. I think I'm disturbing her so eventually I resolve to move downstairs. But it is no better. I am twitchy and unable to settle, heart hammering in my tonsils, ears full of white noise, a lo-fi buzz in my stomach. I prowl into the kitchen. What to do? I look outside. A moon dominates, white and sharp like a clue to some great celestial puzzle. I watch it. You can see it move, you know.

Slowly, like the hour hand on a clock. The cat wanders in. Koshka. She was my cat. I bought her from a Russian market, shipped her back. She loved me once, brought me skeletons. I would stroke her ears back flat against her head and she would purr like one of those pull-cord toys. Now she regards me suspiciously for several seconds before turning and stalking out. She wants nothing to do with this. I don't blame her. I wish I could stalk out on myself too.

Reading. I'll try reading. Here is an *Economist* article about Latvia. I've been to Latvia, twice I think, but I don't remember much. It was still Communist then. Quite nice beaches, all very Prussian. Lots of amber, full of people whose names all end in s; if I was Latvian I would be called Marks Rices-Oxleys. I read the article four or five times but have no idea what it is about. I pull down a biography of Keith Fletcher from my dad's bookshelf, and wonder if he's been to Latvia. It's cold, so I pull on a dressing gown I last wore when I was fifteen. I stare at my reflection in the kitchen window and ask for the millionth time, 'What is wrong with me?' I've lost two stone. My face, never fat, now looks fraught with angles, a geometric shape that doesn't appear in any maths book. I am shaking and crying and don't know why. I feel it's the end of something enormous, an era: my youth maybe, who knows, my life perhaps. I try some yoga but it doesn't help. All the time it is getting later and later, so late that it's now early. At five, I can't take any more. I knock on my parents' door and soon find myself wedged between them in bed, for the first time since I was tiny. 'What's happening to me?' I ask my mum. 'Am I having a nervous breakdown?'

'I don't know,' she said. She usually has answers to tricky questions. I lie rigid until dawn.

The next day is so bleak it surely can't be a Saturday. Thin rain persists, as though someone left it on and went to the pub. I am constantly on the edge of something. I try telling people but I can't. The feeling is that I feel so wretched I think I'm going to ... what? Going to what? There is nowhere to go, nothing to be going to do. If this was a job, I would quit. If it was a treadmill at the gym, I'd turn it off and go and sit in the sauna. If it was an assignment, I would call the editor and say that it was too hard; it can't be done. But it's not. It's my life. I can't just turn it off. Can I?

We go into town to help my mum with a charity shop she is running. The kids scuttle around display tables laden with rubbish, knocking stuff over and demanding toys. Grandpa obliges. Outside there is a random funfair ride – a House of Horror – run by men with thick necks and rolls of twenties inside their leather jackets. It is not clear why it is there, stuck in the middle of a shopping precinct on a drab Saturday in October. Perhaps a fairground decided it was just too nasty to continue with. Maybe it's an early nod to Hallowe'en. I guess they had to put it somewhere. A painted ghost beckons, but even he looks unconvinced. The thing stands empty, drenched in rain and shabbiness. The kids demand a go. It costs £2.50 and is over in four minutes. It's still only eleven o'clock. What, I wonder, are we to do to make this day pass?

We lunch early and then drive to Portsmouth for no real reason other than to change the scene. It's a city that is always falling on hard times, more mouth than port these days, with ferries just sitting there like fat old men arguing about whose round it is. You always know when a city is finished when they build something very tall and invite the public to pay £6.50 to go up it. Still, the kids play quite happily at Pirate Pete's and I drink tea with Dad and Gran, and stare out to sea. The sun is already packing up for the day. Angry little waves lick and spit at the window, as if they want to get in from the cold. Some football results scroll across a screen but everyone seems to be losing today. 'I think you've got to just try work again,' says my dad. I can tell he's worried. He thinks, possibly rightly, that the structure and companionship of office life will help me find my feet. The first winter night is closing in. We go home.

I go to bed early, but know instantly that I can't even lie still, let alone sleep. Sharon does her best to calm me down, but in truth she's pretty scared too. I look at the window and wonder what will happen if I open it and jump. Not high enough. I've read somewhere that hospital mental-health wards are full of people with broken bones and ruined livers. Killing yourself is difficult. I crouch on the floor and hug myself, trying to squeeze whatever it is out. I drive everyone crazy with my ranging and pacing and panic. I blurt out, 'I think it's all over. I just want to die.' My mum calls NHS Direct and soon my dad and Sharon are off in the car to find an out-of-hours dispensary. 'At least we're making the most of the extra hour,' he mutters darkly to Sharon. He's like that, my dad. A good man in a crisis.

While they're gone my mum tries to settle me. She's been good, very good, at being a mum. Why, she must be thinking.

Why has one of my babies whom I loved so much and nurtured so carefully and encouraged so enthusiastically and raised so brilliantly and with such devotion and self-sacrifice, why has he unravelled so? I played cards with him, canasta and rummy and poker and pontoon. We gave him, all of them, freedom, big open skies and wild country acres in which to roam. We taught them how to ride bikes and mow the lawn and swim and pick up windfall apples without getting stung by inebriated wasps. We helped him to read and write and think. We helped him into good schools, drove him to cricket matches and football matches and plays and friends' houses and choir practice (but never to school). We took him on holiday to the Sussex coast every year, and marvelled at how blond his hair went and how soft his feet had gone by the time it was time to put them back into hard September school shoes again. There was fish on Fridays and roast on Sundays and eating-up Mondays and crisps and peanuts and a biscuit tin (one sweet, one plain) on Thursdays. A lollipop (tuppence) which had to be stuck back in its wrapper while we went to the library. We gave him sisters, three wonderful companions that he still loves now. We let him make some adolescent mistakes but never really worried that he'd go astray. He was more of a dreamer than a daredevil, that one, fresh, cheeky but never too bold. Yes, we pressed him, advanced him a year in school, but he seemed bright enough for that. We allowed him a gap year before university, and we helped him find something to do in Switzerland and visited him and it was like we were three adult friends, not parents and son any more. It's been like that for the last twenty years. We went to see him in Moscow and in Paris, and countless times in London. Dad stayed in his flat in Shepherd's Bush and had to bring his own pillow, only he lost it on the green on the way there, and it was still there the next morning and we all had a good laugh about that.

Why this? If anything, he was perhaps the most easygoing of all four of them, knew what he wanted and where he was going; found the right girl, a little young maybe, but you don't twist on nineteen, do you? Life was always a joyous affair for Mark, so why this? Why now?

Later, together, we will search for some of these answers. She will come to stay every week and comfort me when I cry and encourage me when I start to feel better and talk and text every day. And in my darkest hours I will still know that I am lucky – lucky to have a mother like this, who hugs me and soothes me and says it'll be OK.

After an hour Dad and Sharon come back with pills. No one really knows what they are or what they do, but no one cares. I take two and fret that even that won't be enough. But when I get up to go to the loo I walk into a wall and then drop a glass into a sink. Oblivion awaits. I tip back into bed and get six hours' respite.

The Sunday. It doesn't really seem to get light. I have a bowl of porridge and am desperately nervous about finishing it, because then I will have to face the day with its vast open prison-camp parade ground of time. We go to church with Mum and Dad and I wonder if Christians can get what I've got; if faith can inoculate you against crises of the mind; I think the answer to both is probably yes, to a certain degree. The curate shakes me by the hand on my way out and I think, 'It's so easy for you. You're not me. You will have a comfortable, easy Sunday afternoon with your Jesus and I must go back to my hell.' He nods benignly, but it's impossible to look at my face and think there's not something terribly wrong. There is roast lunch, but I eat little. A walk in the woods is decided upon. I drive. I don't want the journey to end. As long as I am driving this car and don't have to think about anything else, I am all right. The children want to listen to Gorillaz. I am struck by how I can't bear listening to music I used to love. When we stop we must jolly along with the kids on an obstacle course. I hold my daughter's tiny hand and feel like something has opened in my diaphragm. It's like I'm winded, hollowed out, and need to catch my breath to stop caving in on myself. Eventually we go back. Sharon drives, talks of how things will be and how we will cope and how we'll get through. We've done tough stuff before, she says, and I look at her and think if anyone can get me through this it is Sharon. We go home, to another night of medically induced oblivion.

I lie on the bed, watching the sun attempt to squeeze a little happiness on the world. It's fighting a losing battle, scurrying low across the sky like an elderly shopper with an Asda bag trying to get home before it gets dark. The back garden gets no sunshine at this time of year. The shadow from the house comes halfway up the Leylandii that separate our garden from the one at the back of the house. We will have to wait until March for our suntraps.

I am already looking forward to March. My dad says I'll be well by the spring. 'Six months,' he says. 'It'll be six months. It'll go faster than you think.' If I can just grind out the winter. I'm good at grinding. If you could only see how I have been grinding away, year after year. I would applaud my own grinding, like a footballer celebrating a goal: 'Really good graft there, Marko,' Roxy would say after another eighteen-hour day. I'm a cockroach: you can dump on me and crush me, but I won't give up. I will grind it out.

I've been on antidepressants for two days now. Dr Burnie wasted no time in dispensing them and a sleeping pill called Zopiclone, one of the best-named medicines I have ever come across. It doesn't just do what it says on the box; it does what it says in the name: it zops you until you're a bit of a clone, upends you into one big fat juicy warm zop of sleep, which you then clone night after night. There are a couple of hitches – the GP won't let you take them for more than ten days, and they make everything taste like mint steamed in mercury – but those are worries for further down the line. For now it's all about the antidepressants: since I started taking them I have if anything been feeling worse.

I have been warned. This is no miracle cure, no magic bullet. In fact, nobody seems to know why or how antidepressants work at all – if indeed they do work. There are unanswered questions, not least of which is why don't they work immediately? OK, here's the sciency bit: the theory goes that people with depression suffer from a drop in serotonin, the chemical that transmits messages from one nerve cell to the next. Nerve cells normally reuse serotonin by reabsorbing it. Antidepressants known as selective serotonin reuptake inhibitors block this recycling process, leaving more serotonin sloshing about to do the neurotransmission job. But if SSRIs do indeed successfully inhibit the 'reuptake' of serotonin so that there is more of the stuff readily available, why does it take weeks or even months to notice a difference?

I sneak on to the internet. Strictly speaking, I shouldn't be here. For the sick, Google searches are far more likely to alarm than reassure. And I know that I only have five minutes before I will collapse, exhausted, back on to my bed. Five minutes is enough to type in SSRI and Citalopram into Google, enough to find a couple of chat rooms and follow a thread or two. But what's this? People on here speak of being depressed for five years, for ten; they talk of long, harrowing battles just to get up in the morning; people speak of mental illness. I'm not mentally ill, so this can't possibly apply to me. There is one woman who has tried to commit suicide three times, and is talking about it again. Others are urgently trying to reach her, telling her throw open the windows, breathe in the air, listen to some Chopin, find some birds or flowers. But it's useless. Reason doesn't work on a depressed mind. It's a form of madness.

I stagger back to my bed. Once I was a glorious person, once it was a golden age. Now I am in the same small dark pool as people who think of suicide, people who have been depressed for years and years and years, who cannot break the cycle, whose lives and livelihoods have been ruined for ever, who have lost their one chance at living through no fault of their own, but through the arbitrary intervention of circumstance, a sudden catastrophic misalignment of chemicals.

I read the patient-information leaflet from my box of Citalopram. Another mistake. Do not read these things. They are just legal self-protection by Big Pharma. The sheet of dense, six-point text tells me that common side effects include difficulty sleeping, weakness, sweating, dry mouth, feeling sick, constipation, irregular heartbeat, dizziness, headache, tremor, agitation. Those are most of the symptoms I had in the first place. Less common side effects include problems with concentration, memory loss and anxiety. And, writ large on the first page:

> Thoughts of suicide and worsening of your depression: If you are depressed you can sometimes have thoughts of harming or killing yourself. These may increase when first starting antidepressants, since these medicines all take time to work, usually about two weeks, but sometimes longer.

At regular intervals the sheet tells me that it may take several weeks before I feel any improvement. For about the millionth time I ask, where is the bottom? How far off? And how far down?

DEPRESSION

5

The shrink

I am face to face with a psychiatrist. A psychiatrist. From the Priory. That's where I've ended up. It is the slenderest of silver linings that my curiosity has been pricked. 'At least I'll get to see inside the famous Roehampton Priory,' I think. 'Who knows, maybe I'll get to meet a fallen sports star or a seventies glam rocker without his wig.' It's a small consolation. In fact, it's no consolation at all. As I am to find out, there is nothing glamorous about the Priory whatsoever. The main building sits in smart parkland, like a National Trust home, but on the inside it's a bit shabby and unloved. It doesn't seem suited to the task of caring for people with psychiatric problems. (I still don't count myself in that group. Yet.) There are too many corridors, and large empty rooms with chairs in circles, which from my point of view does not look good. One corridor has a row of bedrooms on it, and some doors are open. Inside them, nurses and cleaners bustle around scrabbled bedclothes. I don't know why I'm surprised. I didn't think people came here to stay. But then, at this point I am still at the stage where words like 'therapy', 'rehab' and 'sectioning' denote abstract concepts, things that happen in other people's lives.

The sun was low over Richmond Park when we left home. It is that week, late in the year, when there are suddenly lots of leaves around, banked up against kerbs and borders or else scurrying across open land trying to escape the onset of winter. It was only three miles to Roehampton, but it felt like quite an outing. My horizons are rapidly narrowing. Soon, just going out through the front door will feel like a big journey. We've left my sister at home in charge of six children. 'I don't envy her,' Sharon remarks. I say nothing. I do envy her. She is not me.

We wait for ten minutes in a reception area. You can tell the hospital is private: appointments start and end on time. There is a tea and coffee machine and a large fish tank. I watch fish. Several undernourished adolescent girls come and go, chaperoned by mothers with blonde streaks and relentless faces. I'm finding it impossible to believe that I'm in the same boat as underfed adolescent girls. And yet here I am.

The psychiatrist is avuncular, matter-of-fact. He has a revolutionary's beard and red socks, and looks well maintained. It's an enormous relief to be able to spill the whole story to someone who offers to make sense of it all. I lay before him the shambolic carousel of my life, and start to list the symptoms in the order they appeared: headache, lethargy, bowel problems, panic attacks, anxiety, muscle tremors and shaking, tinnitus, black moods, insomnia. When I choke on my words or get bogged down in a soup of self-pity, Sharon calmly finishes my sentences, gives the more objective view of what it's like to watch someone fall apart. She's out there, right on the edge, too. I can tell. Her face is blotchy, which happens when she gets upset or angry. It's clear she's been crying, though I don't remember seeing her doing so. And I should know: I've been following her around like a small dog with internal bleeding for the past week. She squeezes my hand every now and then. I get little blips of reassurance: if there's anyone on the planet who can get me out, it's Sharon.

The psychiatrist, Dr Wilkins, scribbles in fountain pen. He has done this a thousand times before. I am just his Monday, 2:30 p.m. There will be people after me, people tomorrow, an endless procession of misery. Someone will come in at 3:30 with haunted eyes and hands that shake. There will be a 4:00 p.m. who needs a new prescription, a 4:30 who thought she was in the clear but is now worse than ever. There may even be a 5:00 p.m., a feisty one adamant that psychiatrists don't know what they're doing and that modern medicine only makes matters worse.

Despite this wearisome afternoon ahead, Dr Wilkins has a pleasant manner and a sense of humour, which helps. He asks good questions. How have I been sleeping? How is my concentration? Temper? Appetite? All gone to hell, I say.

Any family history of depression?

Normally, whenever there are those little forms to fill in that ask about historic family illnesses, I'm lucky enough to be able to tick, in rapid order, the boxes marked 'no'. There is no history of angina or high blood pressure or glaucoma or rabies; no one has even had cancer, as far as I'm aware. My grandmother is 102 and tough as teak. We have lucky genes. But there is a smear of depression. Twenty years ago my dad succumbed. Out of the blue, the last person you'd suspect of vulnerability. It coincided with most of us leaving home on virtually the same day. Julianne had already gone at sixteen, for London and to dance for the next thirty years of her life. Carolyn moved to London to start up with a law firm. I went to Moscow. Kerry had always hated being left behind, so she moved to London too. My dad calls it ticking-fridge syndrome: suddenly, after twenty years of mayhem, the only noises left in the house were the appliances softly going about their business, quietly blinking 0:00 into the empty rooms.

My own personal medical history is pretty straightforward. Not even a broken bone. A tonsillectomy three years ago, when the kids' illness kept getting through my defences and settling in my throat. Since then, nothing. More 'no' boxes; more ticks.

Then, after some genial banter about how business is booming, Dr Wilkins turns to softer questions: how is our marriage? Do we still make time for each other? When was the last time you had a good laugh? We look at each other and actually laugh. It's a tacit admission that neither of us can actually answer the question. We can't remember.

There used to be laughter, lots of it, one long conveyor belt of the stuff. There was the time when we were in Peru playing I Spy on a very long journey across the Altiplano, and one of our company said, 'I spy with my little eye, something beginning with double-l.' Or when we were buying ice creams at Newlands Corner and I got an ice lolly so cold that it stuck to my tongue. 'Look,' I said. 'Two hands, one hand, no hands!' I pranced around a bit like a fool, the lolly jutting from my mouth. Then I pulled it off and half my tongue came with it. I was in agony. Everyone else was doubled up. There was an inter-railing episode when a French restaurant thoughtfully provided my old friend Lisher and me with a small heater for our table. I loved inter-railing with Lisher because he never finished his meals and I got to eat his leftovers (he always finished his wine though). The food came – vegetables, new potatoes, sauces and some raw chicken and beef. Hmm, we thought, strange French custom. Never mind. We tucked in, chewing the rare meat. After a while we got to wondering: it really was quite a mild evening and the heater seemed a bit unnecessary. So we asked the waiter in our bad French. 'Er, *excusez-moi*, but *pourquoi celui-là?*' He looked at our empty plates, aghast. '*Mais pour faire cuire la viande!*' We laughed all the way to Belgium.

Small children have inevitably brought laughter along with the drudgery. All my children like to draw and have a favourite television programme which shows them how to draw stuff. 'Quick,' said the eldest, on seeing that it was about to come on. 'Let's go and get our pads.' After a stampede of little feet, they all re-emerged from their bedrooms, the boys with notebooks and Janey with a pair of knickers. 'What do we need our pants for?' she asked.

But with a young family, the laughter often comes through clenched teeth. There is simply too much serious stuff going on to let go. It's a very different release from the unfettered hilarity of laughter with friends, but when children are very small friends tend to stay away. The life of a new parent melts down and reconstitutes itself around the new arrivals. I used to love the banter and conviviality that accompanied a savage group hangover. Endless cups of tea through another timeless Sunday, mercilessly lampooning some substandard mid-afternoon movie. But with small children, mid-afternoon movies are the same old cartoons and hangovers are to be avoided at all costs. I dimly recall a New Year's Day hangover when James was just a baby. He cried and cried. We passed him back and forth like a live grenade all morning. Not for the first time I found myself thinking, 'How will we get through this day?'

Wilko clears his throat.

'It's clear to me that you have a stress-related condition, a depressive illness. It will take time to get over it.'

There is a pause.

'But you will get better.' Note how he doesn't tell me when I'll get better. This thing has no timetable. It will certainly be months, but no one can tell me whether it will be three, thirty-three or three hundred and thirty-three. 'It's different for everyone,' Dr Wilkins says. He does give a few vague indicators. When we discuss work, he suggests that I'm unlikely to be back before Christmas. When we mention plans for a New

Year's Eve party he says, 'Do it next year.' When we talk about antidepressants, he says I'll be taking them for a long time – at least six months beyond the point at which I'm properly well again. There may be no fixed timetable, but it's a long-term thing all right. Later I figure out why no one will be drawn on timings. First, they just don't know. Secondly, if they give you a ball-park figure – and it now seems to me that you won't be properly well for at least twelve to eighteen months – then you might give up. And thirdly, if they do give you a well-by date and you pass it with little or no improvement, then you lose all trust in them. And trust in them is vital.

Dr Wilkins tells me not to worry, that I am not alone: it's not uncommon for people in my line of work. I am an assistant news editor at a national newspaper, a gruelling job with a lot of pressure and responsibility. You only get noticed when you make mistakes. Dr Wilkins says I have a perfectionist streak, which Sharon seems to find darkly amusing. 'He's not a perfectionist when it comes to tidying up the house,' she says. Dr Wilkins laughs, but says this is a different kind of perfectionism, where an individual sets himself unrelenting standards and then drives himself ever harder to achieve them.

I am relieved. I think he is spot on. He says the Priory can help, and we arrange some further appointments. Then we go home.

It's half-term. The kids fill the house with their squabbles and go-gos and sicknesses. This autumn break is the worst holiday of the year, a prison term of ten long days indoors, waiting for it to stop raining. The TV is on too much. The kids take it in turns to be up half the night. Sharon looks tired, doesn't know whom to look after next. I think she is desperate to go back to work. James is the most poorly, limp and feverish. I sit in the house with him, on our own, for a couple of hours one afternoon while Sharon gives the other two a last bit of daylight in the park. It's hard to describe how hollow I am, scooped out and on the verge of folding in on myself. Even breathing is done with effort. But I have to be strong for James. He asks for a game. We erect a rather shoddy, dog-eared board game and go through the motions. After five minutes I just have to say to him, my son, 'I can't do this any more. Would you like a bath?' I run him a bath and sit in the dark while he plays feebly with some plastic boats. I have him in bed by six.

Finally, after an interminable inset day, half-term is over. It's back to school. The house is silent, cold. The rooms are empty. It is then that I notice the lemon tree. It has been shivering in my back garden since it arrived on my birthday, soaked by the rain so that the card of care instructions hanging off a branch is soggy and hard to decipher. I can just about make out that I should have brought it in ages ago. I find a spot for it in the bedroom. I can watch it there. It will keep me company.

Am I going mad? Is this what it is like? Mentally ill. How strange and terrible that term sounds when applied to me. Depression, mental illness, bipolar, schizophrenia: how dark and sinister are the words we use to describe people we have written off as mentally unreliable. Does it help us understand them any better? I'm just as guilty as anyone else. Before this happened to me, depression was for losers, mental illness was for the weak, schizophrenics were people who got let out of jail to knife someone fatally in a north London park. And as for mad ... Mad and crazy have come full circle. Mad and crazy are people who are scatty and cavalier and fun to be around.

Have I always been a bit mad? I hear words, sounds, as if left dangling from another era. I wonder where they come from, these fragments that write themselves almost without my input. I jot down what is heard in my mind and suddenly there's a piece of writing, a burst of notes, half a song, right there in front of me. I'm not even sure it's mine. I almost have to look around to check if anyone has seen through my sleight of hand. I talk to myself too – but then you know that already. Sometimes it's Roxy and sometimes it's Marko and sometimes even mro, a crisp professional sign-off that I have made my own. Is this mental tail-chasing unique or universal? Do you address yourself in the third person? Argue with yourself? Or is it just me? Am I mad? Dr Wilkins says that in order to get shot of this thing I will need to find out what made me ill and cut it out. But what if the thing that made me ill is me?

If this is madness, is it a good or bad thing? Perhaps it's just a rite of passage. I've read that in order to truly find yourself, you first have to lose your mind. Is that what is happening? Maybe I haven't been true to myself, all these years. Maybe I've been denying myself something fundamental and now this is me trying to allow it to express itself. But if so, what is it? Is it Roxy, clamouring for a more playful, more carefree, less earnest life? Or Marko, dutiful son, husband, brother and father, doing what others expect? Or is it mro, impatient and infuriated at my inability to commit to anything for more than five minutes?

I am momentarily heartened. I will beat this thing. I will work out where I went wrong and put it right.

It's not easy. That's an understatement. It's really, really difficult.

I sit on the floor surrounded by jigsaw pieces. It's a Tuesday morning in the middle of November. I'm never off work on a Tuesday morning in the middle of November. I've just had to turn the radio off because I just can't listen to music. I've tried and tried, because there would be nothing better than just spending months and months listening to everything that's ever been recorded, making notes on it, storing up ancient lost chords for future use, reading that Alex Ross book I'm supposed to have read. But I still can't read, still can't listen to music.

The rooms are cold and filled with that emptiness that mid-morning does so well. I am still functional, just about. I got up when Sharon went to work. I managed to get the three children dressed, though it's hard even being in the same room as them at the moment. When they shriek it cuts through me like news of a death. When they take exception to something as innocuous as a pair of socks, I find it insupportable. We idle through breakfast. I'm not so hungry. These days I'm virtually never hungry. But I realise I am thirsty. I get up to get myself a drink.

'Can I have a drink?' one child asks.

'Same,' the second one says.

'My have drink,' says the little one.

I fill a jug, find three cups, plonk them on the table and sit back down. About thirty seconds later I realise I am thirsty. I get up to get myself a drink.

The clock crawls towards eight-thirty. I walk them to school. We are very early. Though they are brutal on my nerves, it makes me cry to leave the children. I am all alone. I walk home slowly, out of breath. By the time I get to the front door I am shuffling like an old man with someone else's hips on. I close the door and hear the slam echo around the vacant vectors of the house. The heating is off. It's an utterly unremarkable day, perhaps the day Stevie Wonder was droning on about in his sell-out tune about calling someone to say I love you. But the phone does not ring in my house. The hours of the day start to revolve.

I open a puzzle. My sister bought it for my fortieth. It's a thousand-piecer, a picture of all the different kinds of sweets we ate as children in the seventies. The puzzle's got them all. Double Deckers and Spangles and Tooty Frooties and Curly Wurlys. Fruit Pastilles and Lion Bars and Matchmakers. My favourite trick was to eat the crunchy shell off the outside of a Minstrel and stick the softer chocolate back in the bag; once I'd done it with all of them, I'd squeeze the little balls of chocolate together and then eat the whole lot.

I'm stuck on Maltesers at the moment. I like sifting through the little pieces, examining their different shapes; in a good puzzle, few shapes are the same; there is a moment of light exhilaration when I find one of the jigsaw's four corner-pieces with the capital M that lets me start my box properly. I estimate that if I do around fifty pieces a day it will take me about three

107

weeks to complete the puzzle. What then? Will I be well in three weeks? Unlikely. I work slower. While I am puzzling, I am successfully diverted from my thing.

When I stop it edges back in. I sit on the bed, look out of the window. I have no idea what to do with myself. I water the lemon tree, but that's enough exertion for at least a couple of hours. So I sit some more. I look: at unread books on the bookshelf, at cracks in the cornices, at time on the clock. It is still earlier than I think; it is always earlier than I think. There is no one around. Just me. I have called my mum and Sharon and told them it is not a good day. I don't know how much more of this I can do; how long will it be? I can hang on for a few weeks, but if this is how it's going to be for ever, I can't. What do I do with myself? There comes a point in conversations like these when you sense the frustration, the impotence on the other end of the line. Then you know it's time to hang up. This is something you just have to do on your own. No one can help. They have to get on with their lives. You have to work out how to be.

Patience, Marko, patience. I deal the cards again. The heft of the deck in my hands is somehow reassuring. Playing cards are an agreeable size and weight. They are packed full of data, not just information about the present but cryptic messages from the past. Why are only two jacks shown in profile? Who was the queen of spades and was she victim or vixen? Why are aces high and low, alpha and omega?

Three cards face down, four face up. J, 7, Q, T. Cards and me go back a long way. We played for buttons, matchsticks, pocket money. When there weren't enough of us we'd use a cardboard box as the extra player. He was a demon at pontoon, that cardboard box.

Three cards face down, four face up. K, 2, 2, 3. Kerry used to wear glasses, so we'd get her to hold her hands up high so we could see her cards reflected in the lenses. Carolyn always won, Caro and Mum. Gran would struggle to deal because of her arthritic hands and would blame it on the stickiness of the cards. 'You kids and your sweets,' she would moan. Dad would tot up the winnings and losses from a week of playing solo on holiday and establish that I owed 81p, Ju 56p, Kerry 28p, himself 17p. The others were winners. And my dad would say 'unlucky in cards, lucky in love' and I would think, 'I don't want to be lucky in love, I want to be lucky at cards.'

Three cards face down, four face up. J, 6, K, 9. Another king near the top. That's good. We played a lot in Russia too, mostly the Red Army game *Tysyacha*, sitting for hours with Sasha and Oleg, learning how to swear and add up in Russian and flicking out court cards with an emphatic *'eta on!'* or *'eta ona!'* every now and then. I took delight in the fact that the Russian words for the suits are not the same as ours: what we call diamonds they call tambourines, our hearts are just worms to them.

Seven cards face up. Q, 9, T, 9, 4, Q, Q. All those queens, but no queen of spades. For a week or so in May 1991, before Communism collapsed, we trundled around the Soviet interior on Russian overnight trains with a bottle of vodka or two, some kolbasa, a knife and a deck of cards. We chased the lady, and if you caught her you had to down a finger of vodka. By the end of the week the alcohol barely affected us. We dried out on the Black Sea, drinking Russian champagne in empty restaurants, knowing that this was time we would never have again.

Seven cards face up. 7, 5, A, 8, 5, 5, 7. What a hold 'em hand that would make. But would I play? 7, 5 in the hole, it's highly unlikely. But if I'm big blind I might get lucky and limp in. But then I hit bottom pair and someone else bets his ace and I probably fold. Too bad. Note to self: when I get better, I will play a lot more poker. Oh, there is so much I will do when I get better. I will laugh again and read and take nothing for granted. I will go to the Cheltenham Gold Cup and Lord's and the Old Vic and a summer festival. I will do things I've never done: fly a kite; surf; volunteer; parachute; sail. I will spend an entire September living bare-chested in the woods. I will notice the sky, small creatures, advertising billboards, the faces of com-muters. I will go to countries I've never been to: China, Algeria, Iceland. I will make love again, buy Sharon flowers and champagne and surprise her like I did on her thirtieth birthday, when she thought we were going to Cambridge and we ended up in Florence. I will live again. I want to live.

Seven cards face up: 2, J, T, 4, A, K, A. The ace of spades. I'm reminded of the Saddam deck, the one in which the Iraqi leader's sons were aces and Tariq Aziz was the eight of spades. I wonder, if I was a playing card, which one I would be. Kind of depends on the milieu. As the only boy in a big house-hold, I was the jack of clubs, playful, a little dark at times, always up to some skulduggery but ultimately rather inconsequential.

A jack of all trades who never really applied himself to become a master of anything. At the *Guardian* I'm probably something like an eight of hearts, not a bad card but not one that's going to frighten you, unless hearts are suddenly trumps and you've got nothing with a face on it. At home I have been playing at being a king for a while, even though I can't grow a beard. That's OK: the king of hearts generally doesn't have a beard. But isn't he the one with a knife at his back, the one they call the suicide king? I've never much liked the king of hearts. Give me diamonds or spades any day. Anyway, it's clear from my current condition that I'm nothing like a king any more. Now I'm a deuce, two of clubs, something to throw away. In the ever-expanding universe, where the earth is a grotesque aberration and people a fragile accident, I suppose that we are all deuces, weak and ephemeral, unless and until we pair with another deuce.

Last seven cards face up: A, 4, K, 2, 3, 8, 6. Right, now we can play.

I play patience for hours, picking up cards, moving them about, eyeing up moves further ahead down the line. About one time in eight it will resolve itself, but the game becomes slightly less satisfying after each resolution, slightly more compelling for every time that the cards will not align. It is always more enjoyable to be solving a conundrum than to have solved it, to travel than to arrive, to be absorbed in a problem than to have dealt with it. Depression is an exception to the rule. Depression is no fun as a process. The long act of resolving depression is agony, the resolution itself bliss. I can only put up with the misery because I know that the outcome will be immensely satisfying.

I'm starting to tell people about my thing. I hate the D-word. People don't understand it. It's such a confusing term that I choose not to use it at all. I couch it in different ways, depending on who I'm talking to. So for the footie guys, I'm suffering from a 'stress-related illness, like Marcus Trescothick'. For the professional parents at the school gates, it's a kind of overexertion burnout. For the kids it's just Daddy's quite ill and will not be going to work for a while, and please stop fighting over that plastic lizard. In general, I just call it my thing.

Only with those in the know, who've had something similar, can I talk about clinical depression. These are the people I really want to talk to. People like me. People who can tell me what I can expect. People with whom I can compare symptoms, discuss tactics or just hang out with, dully inspecting the wreckage of our future. People more ill than me, who can make me feel grateful again.

Alex is one of my oldest university friends. He has been suffering for three years, which scares me. I'm not sure I want to hear from people that far ahead of me. Their stories make me nervous about what lies in wait. But Alex is great. He tells me I have my thing and he has his. He tries to demystify it in a lovely email:

> It sucks, fella. I have a couple of hints. Be very kind to
> yourself. I kept on beating myself up about it – it doesn't

help. Involve Sharon – I found it hard to talk about it all. Helen found it hard to understand. Be very kind to yourself – I can't overstate this.

Your shrink will probably tell you about this bit. But you may have good days and then bad days. If it is depression then it is not a single entity. As an example, I have hit a bad low over the last couple of weeks. But I have had loads of energy but no enjoyment. The recovery is not uniform – some days you will be plain knackered but feel content. On other days you may feel really down but have a desire to do loads of things that keep you busy, but there is no enjoyment. For example, last week I did all my filing – that took me two days.

Other than that, it is bizarrely a good life experience. If you fancy some company let me know. I can pop over if it would help. If you don't want me to then no issues, sometimes I can't bear to be around anyone so I won't be at all offended.

Finally be very kind to yourself, order lots of nice food from Waitrose or similar. Don't fight what is happening and be very very nice to yourself.

You are in our thoughts.

My boss calls. I'm terrified about missing work, about somehow being classified as a reject. On the one hand, I don't want to make light of this: only a serious thing could keep me from doing the job she entrusted to me. On the other, I don't want to make it sound so horrific that she writes me off for good. As it turns out, she seems to know quite a lot about this. When I say I hope to be back by the end of the year she says, don't make any promises, concentrate on resting and getting well, don't rush back into action and don't for a minute think that anyone thinks badly of you because of this. She says a friend of hers suffered similarly, and made a full recovery. I like stories like that. I need more stories like that. I feel good for five minutes after putting down the phone.

A nurse calls. More and more professional medical types are taking an interest in me. This is an occupational-health call. The nurse asks how I'm doing and what I'm taking and whether I'm taking what I'm supposed to be taking and whether I'm getting up when I'm supposed to be getting up and how I'm sleeping and what I'm doing hour by hour, day by day. We speak for forty-five minutes. I always feel better after talking to medical people. She repeats what others have said: that it will take a month at least for the medication to start working properly and that in the meantime I should rest but not ruminate, go for short walks, see people a bit but not too much. She is the only one who uses timescales. 'We wouldn't be looking at a return to work until January,' she says. It seems a long way off.

I have another meeting at the Priory. This time it's with a psychiatric nurse to assess my case. She and my psychiatrist are drawing up a three-week rehabilitation programme of group therapy and one-to-ones and classes and practical courses designed to help me out of the house and into a caring, nurturing recovery process. There are sessions called things like 'men's support group' and 'cognitive behavioural therapy/depression' and 'stress management' which all sound intriguing. There are others – 'dance movement therapy' and 'assertiveness (Green Room)' – that I'm not so sure of. At the end of our meeting the nurse and I decide that I am a negligible suicide risk, which is nice. I go home and do more sitting.

Suddenly there is a hitch. Health insurance people ring to tell me there is a problem with my cover. Apparently it was downgraded a few years ago and does not now cover psychiatric care. If I'd known that I wouldn't have bought it. Or maybe I would. After all, no one thinks they are going to need psychiatric cover. We are all mentally sound until we're not.

Anyway, now I am on my own. Dr Wilkins's secretary calls me: 'We're not very impressed by this,' she says. 'They told you that you were covered and now they've changed their minds. They shouldn't be doing this to you. You're not very well.' I mumble assent and brace my shredded nerves for an argument with a disembodied voice in a call centre somewhere, who agrees that a mistake has been made and that as a result the insurer will pay for one more session with my psychiatrist.

I go back to the Priory. Dr Wilkins is shaking his head, which is never a good sign. He has also shaved off his beard, which is curious. I have become a problem case. I am no longer a triple-A-rated patient. My three-week rehabilitation programme will have to be axed as I can't afford it. Looking at the five-figure price tag, I'm not sure any health insurance provider could either. 'It's annoying,' he says. 'I often think with busy people like you that it helps having a programme like this to just get you out of the house and keep some structure in your life.' I shrug. Either way, I will still be feeling like death warmed up.

Treatment for depression is a very different ball game for the uninsured. The NHS can't afford to offer much more than pills and a waiting list for group therapy. Only those considered a serious risk to themselves or their families will get fast track access to the psychotherapy that is so vital to assuring recovery. The rest must wait months. My GP shakes her head. 'If we offered psychiatric treatment to everyone who needs it, it would bankrupt the NHS six times over,' she says. Another Priory psychiatrist told me, 'You only get specialist treatment for depression on the NHS if: a) you have a high risk of suicide, b) if you are thought to be a risk to others, or c) if you are prepared to go on an enormously long waiting list. But it's now that matters.'

Out of the turmoil a resolution emerges. I will book a dozen or so sessions with a psychotherapist to try to do the work on 'psychological flexibility' that might help me through the horror of depression. If it goes well, it will also help prevent relapse in future: I'm told that relapse rates for those who don't undergo psychotherapy can be as high as 80 per cent. That's like playing poker against someone with pocket aces.

I will also need to fork out for a few more sessions with my psychiatrist, who does not feel he can wash his hands of me. But for the rest of the time I will have to do this alone.

6

The thought police

Time is passing. Days repeat themselves, deathly still, colourless. Hours drag by so slowly, but weeks seem to multiply. The sick leave is piling up. I've never been off work for more than a few days at a time. Now it is two weeks, four weeks, seven and a half weeks. I can hardly remember anyone being off work for more than six weeks. There were some people who got RSI at the news agency I worked for, including a good friend who was off for more than a year. How much better I understand his predicament now that I am marooned. These barren months are unsettling me, so I am finding different ways to measure the lost time: in haircuts, doctor's appointments, *Countdown* octochamps.

The trouble with all this time and nothing to put in it is that, fairly soon, you start thinking. And that doesn't help. Mostly I think about work, and how I'll ever get back there and whether it was work that put me here in the first place. National newspapers are not for the faint-hearted. It has been a tough year in a tough operation, but I'd have put money on someone else falling over before I did. Everyone works long hours, particularly on the news desk, with rapid-fire pinballs of news pinging around. It's enough to drive anyone ... mad. But I didn't think that anyone would be me.

I Google 'lemon tree care'. The internet is better at lemon trees than it is at depression. First take one tree. Find a sunny spot indoors where it can winter. It will die if you leave it outside. Lemon trees aren't really meant to grow at these latitudes. Stick it in a large pot with some gravel or sharp sand for drainage and John Innes No. 2 compost. It can be quite satisfying to wedge in the rootball and build up the brown stuff so that it holds it in place. Don't worry about getting your hands dirty. Fingers can be cleaned. They are always cleaner than when you started, after you wash mud off them.

Be watchful. Don't overwater or underwater. A good soaking of rainwater about every fourth day should do it, but that will depend on the plant. Don't overfeed or underfeed. Get some citrus feed for winter and summer and apply accordingly. Don't fuss over it, move it too much or pot up too often. The soil should be slightly acidic, roughly the same pH as urine, which is helpful. Keep it away from draughts and radiators. Don't be tempted to put it outside too early. They don't like frost. When it is warm, find a position in full sun or partial shade. Try adding grass clippings to increase nitrogen in the soil. Prune feeble branches in the autumn.

Alternatively, stick it in a room, lie on the floor and stare at it for hours. You've got the time.

Sometimes I wonder why I am writing about my thing. What's there to say? I have secretly hoped for something dramatic to happen in this quiet little life of mine. But this is anti-drama. Day after day, it's the same. How many different ways are there to say: woke up from medically induced sleep; ate breakfast cheerlessly, dodging the children and their bright, jagged speech bubbles and *exclamation marks!!*; sat in empty rooms, lay staring at the lemon tree, waiting for something to change; looked out of windows; shuffled about; tried to find things to break up the hours: patience, the sweetie jigsaw; a break (from what?) for camomile tea; shuffled about some more; observed the dusk, felt mildly better (you do in the second half of the day); hid away when the kids got home; looked forward to bedtime and the struggle to get to sleep. Outside the weather is still as a photograph. Nothing happens again. I just about am. That's all.

I try lying still. It doesn't work. It's like that feeling you get when you're quite drunk late at night and the room is spinning. You have to sit up. I sit up. I try the radio. Ken Bruce is doing *PopMaster*. But the effort of trying to remember the name of Go West's second single is just too much for me. I turn it off. I put on a meditation CD. I last five minutes. I call my mum. We say the same things over and over to each other. I say I'm not going to make it, she says is it really that bad? I say I can't get through the day, and she says it's really going to be such a short amount of time in the large expanse of a life. Each time she speaks I feel calmer for three or four seconds. Then the panic returns. I will die. I will not make it. I definitely will not make it. My dad comes on the phone. He talks sense. Do I want them to come up? Well, no, it's OK. The outlaws are coming later on. No sense in coming just for an hour or two. I hang up. I sit in the front room. The sun half lights the room, like the smile on the face of an old person. I sit in the sun. I pick stickers off the windows, stickers of Shrek and Spider-Man that the kids have plastered everywhere. But it's no good. I can't stay in this room. I'll try upstairs. I go into Janey's room. There is the giraffe puzzle. It's one of those chunky wooden ones; it's made of twenty-six pieces and each piece has a letter on it and they all fit together alphabetically. The head is A and the legs are W, X, Y and Z and the neck is B, C, D, E and F. I can just about do it. Once you've done it, you can turn it over and do it all again, only using the numbers on the back. If you haven't given up the will to live.

I look at the box. It is made by a company called Bits and Pieces and they offer 'clever puzzles' and 'intriguing gifts'. Good for them. It's actually called 'alphabet giraffe with tail', which leads me to wonder whether they also do an 'alphabet giraffe without tail'. This one is actually an 'alphabet giraffe without two front legs as someone has lost W and X'. In our house, someone has always lost important bits and pieces, like W and

X. It would be a fine idea for all those parent–inventors dying to get on to *Dragons' Den*: a machine that would hoover up your entire house and return all the little atomised fragments of stuff to their original collective. Only it would need a setting to avoid it taking apart the shepherd's pie.

The bed. I sit here for twenty minutes, hounded by evil thoughts. I look at the wall, the garden. The sun has gone in. It is 11:07. Five hours until the kids get home. Eight or nine until Sharon does. I call Sharon. It's a short call. Neither of us knows what to say. I sit on the floor, do a bit more of the sweetie puzzle. Nearly finished now. I sit on James's bunk, look at his books. I make a hot drink, drink it on Janey's bed. The front of the house is definitely better. It's south-west facing. The back of the house is so dark. Anyone would get depression if they hung out there for any length of time. I shuffle downstairs, rinse out my cup. Think about making another hot drink. Decide against it. I slowly tidy a few things in the kitchen, then sit down for a rest. I eat some mackerel for lunch because it's there. Then I have another rest. The sun is going down. I do more of the sweetie puzzle. Then sit on the bed for a long rest. The phone rings but I can't find the energy to answer it. Even though I'd love to speak to someone.

How long would it take to go mad if you just sat and did nothing? Days? Months? I think of people who have endured solitary confinement. John McCarthy and Brian Keenan. How come they didn't go mad? They had each other, I suppose. And I'm guessing they had the strength of mind to come through it. I think of Tony Judt and Jean-Dominique Bauby and Peter

Apps and others whose bodies can no longer serve the lively minds that inhabit them. Judt told my colleague Ed Pilkington that he was 'a bunch of dead muscles, thinking'. With nothing to do, we are reduced to the summation of our thoughts. And that is a truly terrifying prospect. The ultimate nightmare isn't being alone in a shower when the mad knifeman comes calling, or waking to find mankind has gone and you're alone with the night and the nuclear winds. It's realising that you do not recognise the person that your thoughts are turning you into; that there is nothing conscious you can do to stop the process; that, in fact, the more you try to 'think' your way out, the tighter you wind yourself up in it.

Today, there will be a merciful break to the monotony. Sparky is coming over. You'd like Sparky if you met him. At first, the tendency is to think, 'Oh my God! Why is there sixteen stone of Englishman in front of me, telling me what to do?' But after a while Sparky becomes pretty indispensable as a friend. He was always there, looking out for us, challenging orthodoxies, doing bold things. When we were lost and afraid during the first weeks of university, there he was, cooking spaghetti Bolognese for us and laughing richly. During the scary days of October 1993 in Moscow, he was cooking again: chicken cumin with cashew nuts, I think it was. When, suddenly and frighteningly, we found ourselves with a baby that we had to keep for ever, Sparky brought his frying pan and served up a treat. Sparky is older than us and taller than us and feels like a big brother. He always has a plan. At uni he kept on organising things like a

Blues Brothers night that lost loads of money and a run to London for an Albanian kids' charity that may or may not have existed. And then he gets cross when things aren't all shipshape. In a cosy pub in the heart of Wiltshire one night, we were playing that drinking game in which several people have to be the theme tune from *Hawaii Five-O* while miming paddling a canoe. Only everyone kept getting it wrong. 'Stop!' ordered Sparky. 'This isn't working. It has to be bang, bang, bang.' We have teased him about that ever since.

True to form, Sparky brings ... lunch! My spirits perk up instantly. It's a thick soup with loads of hearty stuff in it – potatoes, leeks and some of that dark gamey meat that turns your poo black the next day. We go for a walk and I tell Sparky how it is. It definitely isn't 'bang, bang, bang'. He's been through a bit of mental agony too, it turns out, a combination, once again, of work, dadding small children and utter uncertainty about the future. He has two great kids and a wife who works and his own business and a terribly busy time juggling the lot. It sounds familiar. I talk to him about depression, about how crappy that word is; that I'm not depressed, I just have depression. He understands.

I also talk to him about something new, something I have just learned, something that might start to make a difference for me. I talk to Sparky about how to stop thinking.

I never really thought too much about thinking; it's just always been there. But when you start to think about the act of thinking you discover what a very odd, unreliable thing it is. Normally it doesn't let you down; you have a wide range of inputs, perceptions, data, which then provoke thoughts and most of these you can rely on.

Thinking is a positive word. It's what we do, *Homo sapiens*. Words associated with thought are almost always positive: thoughtful, rational, clever, perceptive. The 'knowledge' economy favours those with know-how, acumen, ideas, superior thinking. On the other hand, people who are 'thoughtless' and 'unthinking' are frowned upon.

But is thinking always good? It hasn't always served me well. Many of the best things I ever did – a first kiss, a slinky goal, an unexpected chord – I did without thinking. The best journalism I ever produced wrote itself in five minutes. The pieces I agonised over often read like it. Difficult phone conversations were easier if I didn't think them through first. As a teenager I would think endlessly about girls I wanted to ask out, plan the entire phone conversation. Then dial the number and find she was out or ill or on a date with Andy or Steve or another of those schoolyard rivals who were already shaving and played for the first XV. When my career headed towards a dead end in the mid-nineties I thought about action for months and months before finally following my initial instinct. I'm not saying thinking is always unwise. It certainly has its place. Over the years I have thought hard about subjects and it has paid off. I like to bring order to complex subjects. It makes the universe seem less chaotic. But it's important to recognise that it doesn't make the universe less chaotic.

I've also discovered that you're not always who you think you are. Our thoughts often construct a narrative about ourselves that then goes on to define our behaviour, so as to become a self-fulfilling prophecy. People think of themselves as tough, brilliant, proper or else tired, defeated or shambolic, and it nudges them into behaving that way. Few of us are actually that straightforward. Thoughts are not always an accurate reflection of the truth. They often rely on just one point of view. They may be fuelled by subjective perceptions, skewed data, value judgements. They may resonate loudly just at the moments when they are least reliable. We may get caught up in them, lost in thought, and lose all objectivity. We may fall prey to the same circles of pessimism and lock ourselves away in unbreakable cycles of innuendo, suggestion and misinformation.

As it turns out, this is one of the defining characteristics of depressive illness. Bad thoughts mount a hostile takeover of your broken brain, broadcasting a repetitive loop of unhelpful, judgemental and quite apocalyptic propaganda that is only likely to lead you deeper and deeper into the maze. For weeks, months on end, as you sit on the floor and contemplate how far you have fallen, the cycle of bad thoughts feeds on itself, sending pulses of anxiety down frayed nerves, making impossible the very things that will make you better – rest, calm, acceptance. At times like these it is vital to be able to see thoughts for what they are: a projection of one version of reality on the silver screen of the mind. Not an unimpeachable truth, just a film. Seductive, persuasive and quite plausible, but also subjective, twisty and wholly unreliable. But achieving that objectivity is easier said than done. When you are in it, you need to be told a thousand times a day that the terribly sticky-black thoughts you are thinking are not the truth, but just the surreal footage of a mind trying to heal itself.

This is the single most destructive thing about depression. With most other illnesses, at least you still have your mind: to think about recovery, to plot a rehabilitation programme, to distract you from your agonies in books, or music, or film or daydreaming. With your mind intact there's a lot you can still do, however ill you are. But when it is the mind that is ill, thinking can't come to your help. In fact, the opposite. Thinking is like quicksand; the more you do, the deeper you descend.

Mark Williams thinks a lot about thinking. As a professor of clinical psychology at Oxford University and the producer of a series of CDs on how to cope with depression, he argues that it is our ability to develop an 'inner language' that gives us a paramount advantage over other animals. 'We can work "offline",' he tells me later, once I'm well into my recovery. 'We don't have to be there and present. We can remember, imagine and anticipate. We can bring to mind the past even though it's long past and process it and anticipate the future. It makes us better problem solvers; even though we are not the strongest animals on the planet, it gives us an evolutionary advantage. So we don't consider that it might have a downside.'

But a downside there is. I have been a prisoner of my thoughts for two months now. That internal conversation between Roxy, Marko and mro has dwindled to a monologue, dominated by a single, sober, solemn voice that I don't recognise: 'I can't make it through this.' 'It's too hard.' 'I'll never get back to work.' 'I'm finished.' Negative thinking has begun to colour everything. 'Sharon will have a breakdown herself, trying to cope with me and the kids.' 'The kids will go stir crazy cooped up in here all winter, with me unable to take them out.' 'The sleeping pills won't work for ever – and then what?'

'Negative thinking is very adhesive – it doesn't let go,' says Williams. 'Once language gets involved in something it can't solve, we redouble our efforts to solve the problem of our mood and wretched feelings. And when we only feel worse, we think it's naturally occurring. We don't realise that the rumination is contributing to the problem.'

Williams says that the penny often drops for people like me when we meet fellow sufferers. When we hear them talk about the negative thoughts in their head. It helps us to understand that the negative thoughts aren't specific to the sufferer; they are specific to the illness.

There is another tool that can help, but it takes a lot of mastering. I must learn to see my thoughts for what they are: a powerful piece of agitprop, not an absolute truth. I need to pull back from my thinking, examine each thought with a detached curiosity like a scientist studying a turd. When I have negative thoughts I must stop myself, tell myself: 'Oh: I've noticed I'm having that thought again – you know, the one in which I'm washed up for ever and lose the house, the family, everything and die miserable, that one.' That moment of detached curiosity, once properly cultivated, will help me by stopping me from buying into the thought itself. And the thought will pass and another will come and I will try to do the same thing again.

This is what I tell Sparky: that I am trying to learn to detach myself from my thoughts. It's easier said than thought.

I sit on the bed. I'm usually there. I am breathing, concentrating on the breath. My thoughts tell me stories, most of them unhelpful. So I tell my mind, 'Thank you, but not today,' or else, 'Hmm, I'm noticing I'm having that thought again.' Sometimes this works, sometimes it doesn't and anxiety results, so I breathe deep into the hollows and try to get inside that feeling and see it for what it is: a feeling, not a reality; not a threat, just a reaction. This is the way forwards, and I need to practise. Stop thinking about days and weeks to come, start thinking just about now, about this moment, this breath.

Outside the world is using up the last of its light for the year. Some days the sun shows up late for work, doesn't hang around long, has a crafty fag behind the clouds and then is gone before four. And that's when there is sun. Mostly it's grey and dull, like we've run out of weather. It doesn't help. They say that twenty minutes of bright light on the retina each day can help lift depressive symptoms. Where am I going to get bright light from on a day like this?

The boiler man comes, drinks sweet tea and clanks around for a bit, then has to come and find me to tell me something dull about my hot water system. I'm on the bed again, staring at the ceiling and trying not to think. Listening to him talk about my flue and my hot water tank gives my mind something to do, but soon I need him to go, so I write a cheque. It's exhausting. I flake out again and try not to think.

The thought police

These are some of the negative thoughts that chase themselves around my head like children on an ice rink:

I'll never get back to work – I can barely do the school run without exhaustion and I still can't read. How will I ever recover?

I'll lose my job, the house, everything. We'll have to sell up and go and live at Glendene. The children will be for ever defined by their father's madness, which shall pass from generation to generation.

Sleeping pills. I've been taking them too long. I'll get addicted and then won't be able to sleep again.

The kids. My nervous system simply cannot support them being in the same house as me. Will I have to leave and recuperate somewhere else? In hospital?

Sharon says, 'We can get through this.' But get through to where?

I am learning to notice what happens when these thoughts announce themselves. Usually, after several seconds, there is a pulse of anxiety from deep within, a bit like thunder after lightning. If it rolls around for too long it will trigger another negative thought: 'Oh God, here it comes again, I can't take this, I need to move around, oh I wish it wasn't here.' Of course, that's not a terribly positive thought, so it triggers another rumble of anxiety, and pretty soon there's a veritable thunderstorm developing out of this lowest of low pressures. How destructive it is depends largely on whether you can hold your nerve and tell yourself the most important truth about your thoughts: 'It's not me. It's just the illness that's speaking.'

I lie still, not quite awake, not quite asleep. I don't know the time, but it's earlyish. The guy next door is moving around, showering and shaving. His daughter is having a tantrum. The milkman has come and gone. Sharon is stirring. She is not getting enough sleep either. She says I have been asleep, but I'm not so sure. If I lie really still I think I can pretend that none of this is happening. Right here, right now, I'm comfortable, warm and safe. The children are silent. A car fires up outside. A door bangs. The world can't get me in here.

The alarm goes off. Sharon has never been one to hit the snooze button. She is up and off, enticed by the distraction of work. I vaguely tune in to the impatient cadences of Radio 4. But I don't move. I'm not sure I can move at all today.

Sharon brings me toast. I gag on it, but some of it goes down. I am nervous of the impending moment when she says, 'Right, I really have to go and catch the train.'

'Right,' she says. 'I really have to go and catch the train.'

A spasm of thought jerks in my head: 'Don't go! What will I do all day? Will I ever see you again?' I have been in love with Sharon for half my life. It ebbs and flows like the sea: sometimes we are more into each other than at other times. We are quite open about this. In a stupidly male way I love her most when we are saying goodbye. When we lived in different countries it was thrilling to be meeting in airport lounges and railway stations. On Monday mornings she would leave me in my little flat in Paris and catch the first Eurostar to work, and I would go back to sleep and dream of loss and treachery and betrayal. I love her most at moments like these, when I can see how strong, how admirable, how utterly determined she is never to throw in the towel. I'm not sure she would even know where to find the towel. But I hate that she is leaving me. I don't want to be on my own. I know I have to do this thing on my own, but it's so lonely, like I'm the last hostage left to be released.

'Can I call you today?'

'Of course you can. You can call me any time.'

'When will you be home?'

'Well, we've got drinks with clients tonight.'

'Oh.'

'You will be OK?'

I nod, but we both know I won't be. Not today. Not any time soon. She leaves to go and earn the money to pay my psychiatric bills. I get up.

Later, much later, I ask her: how did you get through it, those terrible weeks? 'When you're in it you don't realise how bad it is,' she tells me. 'You just put one foot in front of the other and do what has to be done. It's only afterwards that you look back and your heart lurches and you think, "God, how did I do that?"'

*

131

Bleak midwinter. It is still. Trees, river, grass, all motionless, stunned by the suddenness of the frost. Frigid curtains of low-hanging mist give the riverfront a surreal edge. The yelps of excitement from my children are the only bursts of warmth.

There had been some debate about whether to go out. In the eight years since we became parents, blank days have to be partially filled. Any parent will know that children, particularly boys, are like dogs; they must be walked. And so we fold ourselves reluctantly into the seven-seater and watch Granddad scrape off the ice while Sharon fiddles with the dashboard, trying for the combination of dials that sometimes results in hot air. I am inside my head, chasing up horrid thoughts.

Number one, my current favourite, is that there is no way out: I can't kill myself because that will deflect this terrible illness on to one or more of my children; it will also invalidate any life insurance policies I have, leaving my family destitute. So I can't do that. And I'm not sure I would know how to. Hospital? It seems tempting at first: time and space away from home, where it seems I can't get better amid the hurly-burly. Hospital seems like the option I am after when I say to myself and Sharon, 'I want to stop; I want to abdicate; I want to get out of my skin and my head.' But I think it through and realise that, even if hospital turns things around, I will have to leave and will be right back at square one. I don't want to go to square one. It was cold and wretched there. So number one thought keeps revolving, around and around with no resolution. I could keep chasing it for ever and get nowhere. But I don't have time because number two thought is jostling for attention.

I'll never sleep again. The sleeping pills have stopped working; so has everything else the GP has prescribed. Without sleep, the anxiety and mood problems just get worse and worse, making sleep even harder. Then number three thought edges in. This is the work thought: how, I ask myself, how will I ever be able to function in a stressful workplace again? There is a voluntary redundancy package on the table in front of the *Guardian* staff at the moment. Surely I should take it and recover at my own pace? After all, thoughts of work generate anxiety and that sends me into these terrible descents. But then, I ask myself back, if you quit work you'll have nothing to get better for and also you'll then have to look for a job at some point and that won't be easy for a recovering depressive. Oh, I reply. I hadn't thought of that. (Actually I had, about a million times.) This conundrum has no resolution either. So round and round it goes, enjoying itself at my expense. Then there are thoughts numbers four, five and six: will I get better (everyone says I will, I don't believe them), will it take years like the case I read about on the internet last week, and how can I cope in the meantime with three young children and a wife with a business to run? I wrestle with these thoughts as the car slowly warms up and eventually we get on the road.

In the pits, it's always better going somewhere and doing something. It stops the thoughts rotating. They take a breather, waiting for the next opportunity to strike. I can look out of the window and try some tactics I have been taught to make things less dismal. I try to concentrate on the moment, the beauty of the shivering trees, the deer, the frozen parkland, motionless and brittle. I enviously imagine the lives of the joggers: one, a twenty-something woman with very red cheeks, is, I fancy, going home to a shower and then to pack up her VW with presents and overnight bags before heading out to Bibury for Christmas with her parents; two middle-aged men will part at the gates to get back to their homes and their children with shiny faces and delusions of Santa. Only an older woman makes me feel relatively lucky. She is not moving fast; she is not running well; she is only out there because to her, in her loneliness, the day seems long, even though it's one of the shortest of the year.

We arrive. Now the thoughts get in line, waiting for their moment. There is a messy two-minute interlude of buggies and mittens and children and boots and the tucking in of trousers and socks, and sulks at what we've forgotten, and a near miss involving a car and a cavalier child. We head off, going nowhere. Ham House is shut: too dangerous, apparently. I want someone to rule that I am too dangerous and need to be shut down. So instead we shamble through the whiteness, the children inevitably finding great entertainment in the frozen puddles that are both skating rinks and frontiers to be cracked open. I must hold hands with Edward and to be honest it saves me from a tortuous forty-five minutes. I take interest in his hopeless inability to stay upright: lean forwards, I say, like you're picking pens off a small table in front of you. I don't want any pens, I'm skating, he replies, keeling over backwards, saved only by the lifeline that is my right arm. He digs his heels into the ice face and creates a fracture, then a hole. Black water shows through. We skim along to the next puddle.

In any other year this would be the best Christmas ever. It has snowed, for God's sake! Great fronts of the stuff for several days. Suddenly everyone from Bing Crosby to Greg Lake is worth listening to again. Only I can't get hooked. For me, it's all about me. Everyone else will have a brilliant Christmas. I miss it already, even though it hasn't actually arrived. We used to call this day Christmas Eve Eve. Now it's just one of the darkest days of the year.

After lunch I plunge again. Sharon makes frantic phone calls and we have an emergency appointment to see Dr Wilkins. On the way in I want to be everyone, anyone I see. The guy opposite me is reading a book. Oh the simple pleasures of reading a good book on a train. I want to be a guy reading a book on a train. On come some revellers. It's Christmas, after all. I see parents with their little ones, and lovers swapping their first Christmas secrets. There are tourists and shoppers and people with cakes and bags from Hermès and lost backpackers pointing at a Tube map, looking for Bayswater.

It is almost dark when we edge up into west London. I am momentarily distracted by the address and an A to Z. Normally I see Dr Wilkins at the Priory. But this is his Wednesday venue, a rather grand practice in a Georgian terrace just off Sloane Square with a fish tank, lots of corridors and Christmas music (carols from King's of course, not Slade and Wizzard). Sharon sits. I pace. Sometimes, at moments like these when the horror of my predicament seems akin to a film or someone else's nightmare, I simply cannot believe I am me, that all this is going on in my life, that I can't turn off the television or put down my book or bury my head in a cuddle that will make it all go away. Wherever you go it goes; no antidote, no palliative medicine. Just it and you and an awful lot of time. Two hundred years ago they would have thought me possessed and I would have been subjected to a spot of bleeding. Four hundred years ago they would have tied rocks to my limbs and dropped me in the Thames. I wonder if they didn't have the right idea.

When Dr Wilkins calls us in I feel the first flicker of relief.

Psychiatrists know that their patients hang on their every word and so are careful about what they say. Even so, after Sharon recounts the horrors of the past week, how weak and sleepless I've suddenly become, Dr Wilkins says: 'I'm very sorry that it's turned out this way.' What way, I wonder. What way have I turned out? Whichever way it is, it doesn't seem good. The plummeting, the hurtling sensation, my hands ring like they are thawing after a thousand-year frost. I gulp like Scooby Doo. Sharon tells Dr Wilkins that she wants me in hospital.

'Well,' he says, in a manner that indicates he is about to disagree. 'If he'd been like this on the first day you came to see me I would have admitted him.' The 'but' hangs in the air for a while. We all know that it concerns my lack of insurance. A week in the Priory would cost about five thousand pounds. It's money we just don't have. 'The alternative, of course, is the NHS ...' He doesn't need to finish the sentence. A friend has just spent two nights in an NHS mental-health ward. It wasn't pretty.

'Instead, I'm afraid that the only course of action I can recommend is ...' I hang on his every word. There's another course of action? I thought we'd pretty much exhausted every avenue. Maybe it's a spa cure? A few weeks on a Caribbean island. Perhaps they still bleed hopeless cases after all. Something that might enable me to hibernate for a few months while the worst of this thing rages.

'Tranquillisers.' Dr Wilkins stops, as if expecting protestation or at least scepticism. When we show neither, he seems a little surprised. He warns me that they will make me feel dull and a bit sluggish. 'Great,' I think, 'can I take them for ever?'

We are both stunned by the horror of our lives as we surface into the midwinter twilight. Everywhere is lit. I focus on a Chloé storefront and an upscale men's couturier with a bored young salesman standing in the window. How I long to be him. He will stand for another hour or two, dealing with some list-less shoppers who enter the store by mistake and stay just long enough to make it appear that they aren't totally appalled by the prices, and might still buy something. He will count down the minutes until closing time, then he'll be off, meeting two friends on the King's Road and after that anything, literally any-thing, is possible.

In the pharmacy, the third we have visited in two days, the tweedy saleswoman is cheerful enough, wishing us a happy Christmas, though surely she must suspect that all is not peace-ful within, given the parcel of Lorazepam she is handing over. 'Happy Christmas,' she hails after us. I just grunt.

On the way home Sharon is calling everyone – her dad to come and pick us up, friends to reschedule holiday events. I call my dad. 'It'll last eighteen months,' he says in a well-meaning but unhelpful fashion. Someone else who's changing the goalposts. 'Mine did.' I am about to explain that we are different cases, but I can't be bothered. I watch a raindrop make its way down the pane. Some droplets are racing in the opposite direction, as if the first has got something badly wrong. 'I may be in hospital if this doesn't work,' I say.

'What, hospital? Well yes, maybe in the new year. But you've got to get through Christmas and New Year first. For the family.'

For the family. That's my problem: always putting everyone else first. I never learned how to look after myself. You would understand that if you saw me. I'm nondescript in height and weight, mangy dog hair that could do with a good groom; no potions on my face, cheap glasses on my old eyes, thin clothes on my back. I don't buy stuff and I don't get out much. I rarely have a drink after work any more. Weekends revolve around the kids and their schedules. I don't have a schedule any more. But there I go again – thinking. Negative thoughts. They have got to stop.

7

Lethargy

My mum and I have done the school run and are now having coffee, only I'm having it without the coffee. Caffeine doesn't agree with me any more. Nor do alcohol, sugar, salt, flavour. In fact, my appetite seems to have entirely deserted me. Meals stick in my throat. They seem no more appetising than a pile of wool. Mum is driving back home this morning, leaving me alone with the derelict winter day. It is seriously quiet, like the moments before a bomb.

'Are you sure you'll be OK?' she asks. She looks tired too. She has been up and down the A3 a dozen times over the past two months. Sleeping on the pull-out bed. Playing with the children like there's nothing wrong. She's a calm, unflappable person, but now when the kids are really noisy or argumentative or just plain unreasonable, it gets to her. I have a good weep and say I'll be fine. She doesn't look convinced.

I have a shower, make it last. It is quite simply the best time I'll have today. Afterwards, I don't know. I'll sit. I'll sit in my room and watch the lemon tree. There will be a weed or two I can uproot. I'll sit in the boys' room and look at their books. I'll sit in Janey's room, on her bed, and stare up into the milk-of-magnesia morning. Maybe the giraffe puzzle, see if I can assemble it in a grotesque way to suit my mood. I'll sit in the playroom and watch the comings and goings of the close; you can sit there all day and just observe: the breathless parents and their anxious schedules; the builders, with their mugs of tea and teddy-bear arms; the baby boomers taking their *Daily Mail* opinions out for a walk; the leaflet guy with his homesick gait; the delivery vans dancing a paso doble in the narrow confines of the lunchtime traffic; the gardener with his diesel-powered blower that rounds up leaves like a sheepdog; the schoolchildren, ragged and wayward, thrillingly alive; the blind woman from number 8 and her yappy little dog. I'll sit and watch it all.

Of course, if I can watch the entire close, the entire close can watch me. I am ashamed of myself, my sudden frailty. We are a talkative community and people ask after each other. I am running out of answers. They must have noticed me shambling up to the shop in the jobless midmorning. They will be asking themselves, what's happened to him? A victim of the recession? They will soon be asking me. A neighbour accosted me a few weeks ago, when I was on the steep descent into the pits. It must have been a slightly better moment, because I told him I'd been poorly but was on the mend. Now I'm not sure what to say. You can tell from people's faces, the instant you start talking about depression. They put you in a pigeonhole that is dark and deep, with something rancid at the back. They put you in there and never bother looking in it again.

Some people ask if I am on medication. I don't understand why they ask this question. What are they going to do with the information? What does it tell you? Not much. GPs put you on antidepressants at the drop of a head these days. Everyone from postnatal mums to sad septuagenarians are on them. Everyone on the depression spectrum is on a prescription, from those at 1 or 2 who feel mildly out of sorts to those at 9 or 10 who are languishing in mental-health wards (I consider myself a 7, since you're asking). Better questions – the kind of things we ask each other – would be: Going any better at the moment? Are you seeing anyone? What sort of thoughts have you been having? How are the other symptoms?

This lethargy, treacle-sticky and oppressive, is my all-enveloping symptom. It's not as acute as the rumination, the insomnia, the black moods. But it takes a superhuman effort to get up and do anything. My heart is constantly racing, but its horsepower is diminished. I've almost forgotten how to walk. My feet feel five times heavier than usual. We have twenty-eight stairs over four flights in our townhouse. I used to take them two at a time, 2-2-2-1; 2-2-2-1; 2-2-2-1; 2-2-2-1. Now going up the first two sets of seven wipes me out. It's like 1-1-1-1; 1-1.

1

1-1-1

1-1

1-1.

The old woman next door had to move out because she could no longer handle the stairs. I know how she felt.

I observe my lemon tree. It is looking improbably well. I move it into Janey's room because that's at the front of the house and there's more light there. Small pink buds are forming and look particularly pleased with themselves. There is a pungent smell of May about the place, and three fruit on the lower branches. They look ancient, dark green and a long way from resembling a lemon. I mix blue citrus food crystals with rain-water and soak the compost. Then I spray the leaves, watch the water trickle to the tips and drop off slowly, plop, plop, plop. It takes my mind off things. I wish there was more to do to look after a lemon tree. I wish I had something to do.

Depression sucks. It's not even a proper word. A heavyweight affliction like this, and they couldn't even come up with an accurate way of describing it. The reason? No one really understands it. There is something ironic about the fact that we have all this brilliant brainpower at our disposal, and yet we still don't understand how the brain itself works. You'd think that one of the first things that great minds would want to understand is how great minds work. But no, we're clueless.

'Depression' is meaningless. It's a dent in the ground or a nasty weather system or sharp economic contraction, but not a human condition. I am not depressed. It's far more serious than that. I wonder how other languages, other peoples deal with this affliction. Maybe somewhere else in the world they have thought of better terminology, a more purposeful phrase that captures this family of conditions. '*La dépression nerveuse*', '*depresión*', '*die Depression*' (I wish it would), 'Депрессия' – the great European languages have little to offer on the subject. Yes, the French have their Romantic *vague à l'âme* and *mélancolie*, but they seem a bit too wistful and fey and don't get the grittiness that is central to my thing. The Germans have *der Zusammenbruch*, which sounds more dramatic until you find out that it just means collapse.

There is a more promising line of enquiry from the East. The Chinese – and yes, prevalence is considerable in China – use a term, *shenjing shuairuo*, which equates to 'neurasthenia', which I look up. This diagnosis dates back 150 years and literally means nerve weakness, which I can wholly relate to. A nineteenth-century American neurologist, George Beard, coined the term and said the condition was a result of the atomisation of modern life: the bewildering confluence of steam power, newspapers, the telegraph, scientific advances, the rise of women and the erosion of faith. The symptoms are familiar: weakness and fatigue, rapid often irregular heartbeat, restlessness, muscular aches and pains, tension headache, sleep disturbance, inability to relax, inability to recover through rest, low mood.

In short, me right now. I like neurasthenia as a term. Most Western psychiatrists don't, but parts of Asia do. Sonya Pritzker, an academic who has researched mental illness in China, tells me that neurasthenia 'is considered much more socially acceptable as both a complaint and a diagnosis in China'. Japan, it would appear, has a similar term that connotes neurasthenia: *shinkeisuijaku*. There's a lot of it about. More than thirty thousand people kill themselves in Japan each year.

When it comes to treatments, I'm disappointed, depressed even. I hoped that a more spiritual Asian approach might be discernible. But Pritzker says that Western medicine predominates in Chinese treatments. They even have Prozac. It's known as '*baiyou jie*' which means 'one hundred problems resolved'.

I have nothing better to do, so continue rooting around in dictionaries looking for terminological clues. 'Suffering' is a more fruitful source of enquiry. It's a curious beast, suffering. None of us would ever invite it upon ourselves, but it's strange how often people say how much they learned, how much they gained, from a period of great torment. The French '*souffrir*' and German '*leiden*' are narrow equivalents. But the colloquial Russian word for to suffer is '*perezhivat'*', which literally means 'to live through'. As if suffering and being alive are somehow equivalent. Which of course they are – it's impossible to be alive and not suffer. Everyone from Aristotle to Nietzsche agrees on this: that to be alive is to suffer, that greatness comes through dealing with suffering, that suffering is the greatest teacher there is. 'Wisdom comes alone through suffering,' said Aeschylus. Horace went even further: 'Suffering is but another name for the teaching of experience, which is the parent of instruction and the schoolmaster of life.' Fine words. But none of them tell me how long I must suffer for.

*

You don't want to be me. Not. right now. You know how sometimes you think to yourself ooh I wouldn't want to be him or her. I wouldn't want to be in their shoes. Well I'm that guy. The one you look at with pity and horror and think, 'Gosh, that could've been me, but I'm *soooo* glad it wasn't. Did you see how he trembled? Burst into tears when we just asked how he was? He used to be such a livewire. Must be terrible for his wife.'

A few years ago, you'd have liked being me. Just for a while. It was entertaining and occasionally thrilling. But not now. Now, I'm the person who makes you shudder, like the cancer sufferer or the guy in a wheelchair. You don't know where to look or what to talk about. All you can think of is why do some people cop really nasty stuff, and others get off scot-free? Well it's my turn to cop some nasty stuff. And it's really nasty. So no, you don't want to be me. If you see me, nod a cursory greeting and then walk on by. Try not to think of me for the rest of the day. It won't do either of us any good.

There is a troubling emotional inflation that governs our recreational life. Once upon a time, exercise was a stroll at the weekends or a jog in the park. A bracing seaside swim or half an hour with a trowel. Men were wiry, women were lumpy and both were out of breath if they ran for a bus. Then came gyms and personal trainers and amateur events and size-zero models. Nations got fitter. The shapes of people changed. Now people are pumped and psyched and sculpted and ready to give 110 per cent to achieve their personal best. And for what?

Recreation no longer seems to be about decompressing, but about achieving. People are no longer content with letting off steam. Instead they want to create more steam, to reach new records of, er, steaminess. Higher, faster, further, stronger. The runner doesn't limit himself to a jog three times a week; he must do seven marathons on seven continents in seven days. The amateur golfer keeps his score, nags away at his handicap, winds his putter round a tree when he misses the three-footer that would give him the birdie that would set his new record. The adventurer cycles across Siberia or windsurfs across the Pacific. So many people spend their spare time rowing across oceans that I wonder that there's room enough for them all. Exercise is no longer a means to an end, but an end in itself. Recreation has turned professional.

I confess I'm guilty. I played a lot of sport in my youth, was always naturally fit – if a bit weedy. When I returned to Britain in 1999 I took up football. To start with it was just a joy to play. Summer Mondays in the armpit of Wandsworth, we played for hours until we couldn't see the ball for the dusk. Then the emotional inflation thing began to bite. Why did I play well some weeks and not others? Why was I invincible in the tackle one minute and a featherweight brushed aside the next? I was no longer content just to play football; I wanted to improve as a footballer.

It was the same with other sports. I learned how to swim properly, then entered a triathlon; then I wanted to do the triathlon quicker. I joined a gym and did a weights class; then I wanted to put on heavier weights, and even heavier weights, until I felt my body really protest. I cycled to work, then wanted to cycle quicker. My record time was thirty-eight minutes. I was cross with myself if it was over forty. Then I invented a game: I would score my ride in to work in terms of the number of people I overtook and the number of people who overtook me. On days when I was 20–14 I would walk tall. But I'd be fuming if I was 14–20 and would get cross when 'stokers', as I called people on ancient bicycles, would cruise past me. On summer holidays it wouldn't be enough just to splash in the shallows and buy ice creams all round. There would be a buoy to swim to, a distant lake shore to attain, some laps of the pool to get through.

It's the same at work. There are personal bests here too. There have to be. Share prices have to go up. Economies must grow. Professionals must pull all-nighters. More must be done with less. We measure our lives in the narrowest possible way, obsessing about GDP which goes up if we sit in traffic for an hour with the engine on, but not if we stop in to chat with a sick neighbour. All of this is second nature to Thatcher's children. We must make the numbers go up. We must drive ourselves hard. Hard work is good work. What doesn't kill me makes me stronger. We are addicted to numbers on a screen: 17 minutes 48 seconds! £4.59! 2m33! 79! They are just numbers. But they have the power to tell us a different story about ourselves and our experiences. A story that says 'that experience was exhausting and unpleasant but it made me a better person'. A story that says 'I am better than you, better than I was last week, faster, stronger, tougher than a year ago'. A satisfying narrative that goes: 'Yes, I am a better person and I'm moving forwards, in the right direction, ahead of the field, out in front where it feels good and I can feel exceptional.' Except that these are just stories, only one version of events, one skewed, narrow version based on a single over-extrapolated dataset. There is another way. We can feel good without constantly driving ourselves to excel. And as for direction, well it's sad to say that no amount of personal bests will deflect us from our ultimate course.

Exercise may have delayed the onset of my depression – it is a very good antidote to depressive illness because of the effect it is thought to have on brain chemicals. But I think it is instructive that my decline through the late summer of 2009 was characterised by an overwhelming lethargy which made exercise all but impossible.

Striking the balance is one of the many hard things I have to do in my spell in the doldrums. Too much of anything and I will regress. Not enough and I won't progress. A five-mile run today would kill me. In three months it might be a virtue, part of the recovery programme. But how will I know if I don't constantly try it out? Dr Burnie's advice is to establish how much I feel capable of each day and do half of it. At last, an excuse for leaving half the washing-up undone.

The occupational-health nurse calls and we talk about it. I tell her I used to be a fit guy. Now I'm shocked by how little I can do. 'Don't give in to the lethargy,' she says. 'Don't overdo it, but keep trying. You'll find you can do more and more.'

'Exercise is an antidepressant, but you've got to pace it in the early stages,' Tim Cantopher tells me. 'To begin with you have to leave tasks half done. Don't try to complete things. Be gentle with yourself. Once you are better, then you can be more active. But then it's about recognising the basic fact that if you keep putting eighteen amps through a thirteen-amp fuse it will keep blowing.'

I lie on my yoga mat. The room is quiet, apart from the gentle hum of an air-conditioning unit and that bleeping sound that indicates that a large truck is going backwards somewhere. I'm the only man in the class. The instructor, Tony, is walking among us, correcting a posture here and there. He kneels beside me and asks in a South African twang, 'Have you done yoga before?'

'Er, yes.'

'What type?'

'Hmm, hatha?'

'That's not what I do. I do iyengar yoga. How long have you been practising?' This guy is not like normal yoga teachers. Usually they waft about and wear dreamy smiles and tell you to listen to your body and empty your mind.

'Um, a few years. On and off.'

'I don't do on and off,' Tony scolds. 'Now, unless you are very good this class will be too much for you. Is there anything wrong with you?'

Well, gosh, where to start? I thought yoga was for everyone, spiritual cleansing regardless of state of body or mind. That's why I chose it. That's why I pulled out my yoga mat this morning and made a superhuman effort to actually do something at last, despite every part of me shrieking 'no!' I made the effort because yoga is probably about as much as I can manage right now.

'Erm, I've had a nervous breakdown.'

'Oh, well, be very careful then.' And he backs off like I've got leprosy.

He's right, of course. Other people are always bloody right. The class is too much. I'm doing downward dog when the pressure in my ears seems to invert and I think for a brief moment that I might just turn inside out. But I can't give in. There are ladies present. And no one seems to abide by the cardinal rule of yoga: only worry about what is happening on your mat.

Now we must pair up. Tony plays the yoga-pimp.

'Now, Mark, which one of these lovely ladies are you going to choose?' I am awkward, pick the woman nearest to me. We use belts to pull each other around. It hurts but in a good way. Tony steps out of the room for a moment and immediately the women turns to me.

'Don't worry about him. He's like that with all the new people.'

'Yeah, especially guys.'

'The last guy didn't come back after the first week.'

Smart fellow, I think.

'Don't be put off. You're doing well.'

I don't quite know what to say. I fiddle with the yoga belt and bit and put on one of my faces, a half-grin, half-grimace that says something like 'all's well that ends well'. I feel like I've stumbled into a *Monty Python* sketch. In a minute Tony will return with a bunch of loganberries and ask us to re-enact the sinking of the *Titanic*.

After the class I am exhausted. I spend the rest of the day on my bed, staring at the garden, wondering if it is boring to be a tree, more boring than it is to be a depressive. The exertion takes its toll. Three rotten days ensue. I'm not just lethargic. All the wicked symptoms are back – the anxiety, the sleeplessness, the black moods. I have overdone it. By lying on my back in a roomful of women, I have overdone it. But there is a small sliver of silver lining the cloud. While I was in the class, being taunted by the teacher and reassured by the ladies, and while I was doing the postures and noticing my arms and legs and the way they moved, I almost forgot how tragic I've become.

'I know!' Roxy declares. 'Why don't we just give up work! Hole up. Devote a gentle life to the raising of confident, par-ented children who will know they are loved and nurtured and be kind, warm, popular people as a result.'

'Won't work,' mro says.

'Oh! Why?'

'Because a) you need the money, b) you're good at your job and c) you're not cut out to be a full-time home dad. And d) and e) There you go: five good reasons why it's a bad idea.' mro is in no mood for compromise.

'But I'm good with them. We'll invent games, a hundred ways to while away a winter. I'll write a book about it.'

'You can't afford to. You need the income now. And it

might look attractive today, when the sun's out and everyone's happy, but it won't make you happy.'

'I would bake! Teach them all the stuff that schools don't teach, like about fires and spring and how musical chords are like rooms in a house.'

'You'll be too busy packing lunchboxes and picking towels off the floor.'

'I could sit and read for hours while they play in the close.'

'Stop it. We've been here before. Work is part of the solution, not part of the problem. And stand still when I'm talking to you!'

'What if I can't ever work again?'

Ha, that got you, mro. He doesn't have an answer to that one.

Today is a bad day. A bad, bad day. It's actually been a bad old week. There had been a little respite, a few days around the turn of the month when I surfaced and got out and asked the world is that all there is? And now this. Monday was bad, Tuesday started bad and then got a little better through the afternoon. Wednesday was flat but I did too much, clearly, because the decline in the evening was stunning. We were playing cards with the kids, something I used to love, but now I just don't care. I just wanted them in bed so I could steady myself in a quiet place. And then today ... I was gloomy in the morning and it was as much as I could do to get the kids into school. I tried yoga and couldn't finish the class. So now I am beached in the bedroom again, can't do anything except inspect the lemon tree and wait for time to pass.

It always starts with the fatigue. It was the fatigue that told me something was definitely wrong back at the start of all this. It's the fatigue now that tells me I've overdone it: yet how can a school run and a day sitting around be overdoing it? I wonder if I need to be quarantined, isolated, utterly removed from any sources of stress so I can rebuild. I wonder for the nth time whether I'll always be like this.

The vigour of youth: it was my strong suit, my ace in the hole. And, now it's gone, it makes me weep to see the energy coursing through the world, the spectacular health of my companionable lemon tree, nature's endless capacity for regeneration.

That triggers something, something small and distant, like a bell ringing in a mountain-top monastery. Nature's endless capacity for regeneration. Things break, breakages mend, illnesses come and go, there is a dynamic to everything. A human being is constantly regenerating. Like the paradoxical Ship of Theseus, I am the same person I was last year only every atom of me has changed. And in that change lies all my hope. I thought time was against me; actually it's my biggest ally. Nature regenerates. Surely the same thing must happen to me.

8

Mood-doom

Depression cannot be a black dog. It's not external. A black dog you could feed to a tiger or tie up in a sack and dump in a pond. A black dog you could tether to a bus stop while you skulk in a betting shop. A black dog you could bury in a shallow grave, making that 'job-done' gesture with your palms brushing against each other once you'd filled in the last of the earth. Of course, if it was affable and soppy, and didn't shit everywhere, you could keep it and it would provide company while you make your lonely way through the darkness on the other side of the fence. It would scamper through unpromising parks under lowering skies, sniffing for clues while you find a suitable branch to use as a walking stick. It would bark at seagulls while you amble across wintry sands at low tide, wondering at the sea. It would pretend to listen as you unburden yourself, would lick your face if you got a little too sorry for yourself. No a black dog is not depression. A black dog is external.

Depression is internal. It's a virus, a spirit, invasive, depleting. It's not even black. It's less substantial than black, a vacuum that plunges to the diaphragm, sucking away breath, creating the conditions for implosion. Depression is a radioactive substance too elusive, too unstructured for the periodic table. Depression is anti-matter, no-thing. And it's trying to make me no-thing too.

Who is winning? It's hard to say. I flailed at first, didn't know what hit me. It wasn't pretty, like a one-sided boxing match. Yes, if depression is to be external, then it's a flyweight pugilist, infinitely light on its feet, deceptively powerful in the punch. It landed blows all over and down I went again and again until I came to love the canvas, hugged it close and drank in its musty scent that smelled of a locker room from 1977. I don't mind admitting that I came close to KO on a couple of occasions, but I think you know that already. Now I'm playing rope-a-dope, which hurts but gives me hope. Eventually my opponent will tire of his ferocity, will blow himself out, will not even be able to fart for exhaustion. And when he's in retreat, when he's grimacing from the exertion and is trying to find a new line of strength from the stale, barren air that surrounds us both I will tiptoe up to him. I will tiptoe up to him and lean in to his evanescent form and whisper, 'Is that all there is, my friend? Is that all there is?' And finally he will concede that it is, that that's all there is, that he has nothing left up his sleeve. He doesn't even have a sleeve. He will slouch, he will melt away like the Wicked Witch of the West in *The Wizard of Oz*. I will peel off my gloves and spit out my mouthguard and bandage my wounds and call my friends and say, 'Then let's have dancing! Let's break out the booze and have a ball!'

Yes, I will not be crushed so easily. You can tell from my face – which is by now all acute angles and dark smudges, like Karen Carpenter singing Kurt Weill tunes – that I'm in the fight of my life. But I'm coming to understand the essence of depression, reduce it to its constituent parts. There is rumination: hyperactive, filibustering, the symptom that only ever stops to interrupt itself. There is anxiety, with its wires and live circuitry giving you a pulsating buzz like in Operation when you're clumsy with the tongs. There is insomnia, velvet-cloaked as a Victorian villain at a séance.

And there is mood, the most volatile of them all, slippery and unpredictable. Mood is the centrepiece of depression, the black cherry on the cake. It's the bit of depression that most people think they understand, because most people have been a bit low at some point in their lives. But this low is something else: it is the wretchedness of the addict, the emptiness of the widow, the loneliness of the homeless, the helplessness of the refugee; it is losing more than you can afford on a blackjack table and facing your losses alone; it is finishing a cigarette that was the only thing you had to look forward to. It is that sinking feeling in the chest, the abdomen when you wake up and don't know what you're doing. It is saying goodbye without knowing when you'll say hello again.

It's an odd word. Mood. It doesn't seem to belong in the English language. And, like goalkeepers and bass players, you only really notice it when it goes wrong. When you have a depressive illness it doesn't just go wrong, it disintegrates. It lets in nine goals and breaks an E string. With a quick pirouette, mood very quickly becomes doom. Mood was the last of the unholy quartet to announce itself, but is the nastiest. For when mood plummets there is no telling what you might do to yourself. Mood feeds the rumination that feeds the anxiety which feeds the insomnia that drives mood ever lower. And so it goes on. And so it goes on.

Today I am taking this little coterie of malefactors to see Sacha Khan, a psychotherapist. There, now I'm in therapy too. Now I can actually start sentences with, 'Well, my therapist says . . . ' Sacha is going to help me understand why I became ill, and how I am to get better. He will help me find out what is wrong with me, although as Ruby Wax memorably put it in her stage show *Losing It*: 'You are what's wrong with you.' Needless to say, I'm pretty pleased to see him. I sit in a leather chair and look out over Putney Hill as the dusk goes about its desultory ways.

Sacha shows me a diagram. It looks like this:

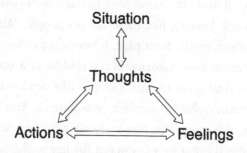

It looks like something I never quite got to grips with in reme-dial economics, but basically is telling me that situations can make you have unhelpful thoughts which then affect your mood and your behaviour. Which can then have a feedback effect on your thoughts and your mood. And so it goes on.

We try to find an example for me. He asks me when I have negative thoughts.

'Well, at the moment, pretty much all the time.'

'What about before you were ill?'

'Well, not often really ...'

Well, OK then, yes. There have been times. Occasions when thoughts have turned in on themselves and mood has plummeted as a result. I don't really like remembering them ...

... an old schoolfriend is doing well. Writing music for TV shows and has a play on at the Whitehall Theatre. We see him during the interval, and feel small by comparison. I wonder when I'm actually going to do something with my life.

... New Year's Day and I have a hangover. We are in the middle of Herefordshire, I think, or Worcestershire. I'm not sure. But it all looks the same on 1 January. Everywhere looks the same on 1 January, like there are no people. We buy the paper and there, on the front page, is one of my oldest journalist friends. Writing from Grozny, in the middle of a war. A fantastic piece. And again the realisation is like swallowing a fatal dose of mercury: she has made it, you haven't. You have sold out, feeble, safe, cowardly. She is doing what you want to be doing. There is not a jot of concern for her well-being, nor a burst of pride for the fine achievement of a friend; just a nasty yellow sulphurous smouldering that takes months to burn itself out . . .

. . . I buy *The Times*. A former colleague has been promoted to transport correspondent. It's a good job. He's done well. He's a nice bloke, but something needles me nonetheless. I feel heavy.

What is it in us that makes it hard to delight in the success of others? Where does it come from, that toxic logic that someone else's success must mean our comparative failure? Life is not a zero-sum game. Surely the success of someone in your network will enrich that network and reflect well on your world? I don't know why, but I have never been too comfortable with the idea that there are people out there who are more brilliant than me.

Sacha helps me to stand back a little. See this stuff for what it is – unrelenting self-torture. A little later we will try to figure out why I do it. But for now he sets me a more simple task: a little thought diary. Write down the negative thought when it comes, write down the reaction that follows, any behavioural tics, and then write down the feelings that ensue. I go home. I write for a long time.

I am walking. It is my eighth walk of the week. I should be grateful: for a while back there I couldn't even do this. Now I can. I can trudge up the hill at dusk and observe the silhouettes of the trees, so still and perfect like rips in the sky. At the top I veer through the trees to the clearing where the mist curls off the grass like a horse race just went past. I didn't feel much like walking today. Actually, once I'd watered the lemon tree and done the washing-up, I felt like doing nothing. But I know that doing nothing is the worst thing I can do. So I pull on my walking boots, with every impulse from my poor old brain urging me to do nothing of the sort, and I tug the front door shut and breathe in the air. Immediately I feel 10 per cent better.

It's extraordinary what our brains get away with. There is all the stuff that we know, deep down, is good for us, will provide us with long-term satisfaction, things like reading books and building Lego with our children and exercise and being neighbourly and polishing shoes and fixing things that are broken. Then there is all the stuff we know is just a short-term hit, that in the long run will not do us much good – might actually do us harm – things like biscuits and watching telly and getting drunk and gossiping and supporting a sports team. And we opt for the latter every time.

Why, I ask Peter Rogers, an experimental psychologist at Bristol University. He's a bit baffled by the question. The answer is, after all, obvious. It's human nature. It's what we do. 'In part it's about short-term and longer-term perspective,' he says. 'There's a short-term gain and reward from eating chocolate cake which, in certain situations, may outweigh the long-term concerns with that. Smokers are often caught in that dilemma; in the short term there is the pain of withdrawal versus longer-term risks from continuing smoking.'

I ask Willem Kuyken the same thing. He seems a good person to ask as he is the co-founder of the Mood Disorders Centre at Exeter University, my Alma Mater. We have a bit of a chat about the south-west and the city and how it's changed since I was there, paying twenty pounds a week for a room in a house and sloping off down to the beach to 'revise' and earning twelve pounds a pop for the early morning shift at Circle K. I think I take him a bit by surprise; one minute we are discussing how the campus has changed and how my old hall of residence doesn't exist any more; the next I am asking him why people are so stupid and always seem to ignore, subvert or otherwise overlook what is in their best interest. 'The mind is a powerful thing when it comes to constructing reality and impulse control,' he says. 'When you feel dreadful, the mind has this hibernation instinct to get under the duvet. You know that if you get up and go for a walk now you will feel better but it's not powerful enough a notion to become an intention.'

In depression, it's even harder to be self-disciplined. The things that will do you good – moderate exercise, a little socialising, some gentle housework, a small project like painting a fence or digging a potato patch – mostly seem repugnant. The things that will not do you good – chat rooms, thinking,

Google, Mars bars – are almost irresistible. The mind will have its instant fixes, and it's only after much trial and error that you learn that sometimes it's best not to trust your instincts.

And so I walk. I never feel like it, I've never been much of a walker, but I walk, twice a day sometimes. There are different loops of Richmond Park: either through the gate and straight on, turn right at Ham Gate and up through the Isabella Plantation and back across the top; or through the gate and turn right, up past Ladderstile Gate and down through the plantation. Or you can just keep going straight on at Ham Gate until you get to Petersham Gate and then you can stop for lunch at the Dysart, if you're feeling wealthy, or you can just get the bus home if not. Or you can yomp straight through the woods, past this old people's home which always strikes me as odd, like some kind of social experiment on people living in a different time, and on towards Pen Ponds and, for a really long walk, the Sheen Gate a couple of miles further on. For this you will need sturdy boots. I have sturdy boots. Sometimes I drive in and park at Pen Ponds or Pembroke Lodge. I stand on the hilltop on the edge of the park, looking west and trying to find Terminal Five out there amid the redbrick sneeze that fans out from west London. I have a peek through the telescope on King Henry VIII's Mound and chuckle about the time James appalled his grand-dad when he looked through the sighter at St Paul's and said, 'Wow, you can see a mosque!'

I nearly died in Richmond Park once. It was when rollerblading was suddenly rather fashionable and I had a decent pair and had just arrived back in England from one jaunt or another. I had a spare day knocking around that I didn't quite know what to do with, so I got those rollerblades out and took them off to Richmond Park for a spin. The park might be good for walking, but it's rather severe on rollerbladers. The paths are too stony, making you judder so much that your jaw goes numb after a while. So I thought, 'Why not take the road?' I didn't really know the park very well in those days, but was managing quite effectively, digging into the uphills and coasting merrily along. After a while I became aware that I'd been climbing quite a bit and was fairly tired. A gentle downhill emerged, which was nice. Then it suddenly disappeared away in front of me into a 1 in 4 descent that went on for about five hundred yards round a sharp bend. I could either throw myself on to the verge and certainly break something, or go for it and risk a quite appalling injury involving me, a few vehicles doing twenty miles per hour and quite possibly several deer. I went for glory, tucked everything in, even things I didn't know I had. I didn't really appreciate what an absurd risk I'd taken until I was down at the bottom, whooping like a gold-medallist ski jumper. Note to self: that's another thing to do when I'm well – get those old rollerblades out and get back in the park for a proper spin. This time I'll stay on the paths.

I eat. I've suddenly discovered an appetite, a hunger. Dr Wilkins says it might be the Mirtazapine. I don't care. I'm changing shape, heavier than ever all of a sudden. I eat three meals a day: always a lot of porridge at breakfast, more than all three bears put together; a family meal at night; and now I'm hungry at lunchtime too. I hoover up anything in the fridge. Big soups; fishy stuff; bacon; pasta.

After lunch, with a full stomach, I sit in the front room, under the lemon tree, and lap up the heatless sun; I can get to feeling almost stable for an hour or two. I wonder if diet is important. Some sufferers swear by their EPA-heavy fish oils, caffeine-free Wulong tea, their proteins and superfoods. Peter Rogers is something of an expert on this, and is unconvinced. 'My own feeling is that diet itself is unlikely to have a big impact,' he tells me, rather wistful that his years of research haven't teased out anything more sensational on the links between food and mood. It's oddly counter-intuitive, he says, but when it comes to mental health, people actually do pretty well on a wide range of diets. 'The body is designed to be resist-ant to changes imposed from outside by physiological things like consuming a meal. There are fine physiological processes that ensure that sufficient amounts of nutrients are extracted from the foods we eat. There is rather little scope for diet to dra-matically influence the brain.' All I know is that a great big bowl of pasta at lunchtime settles me nicely into the afternoon. As the second half of the day is almost invariably better than the first half, it feels like a watershed. It starts to become a self-fulfilling prophecy.

I meet people. Mostly because they insist on visiting: I don't set stuff up. Last week my sister came over from Bromley and we walked through the murky January thaw to Petersham Gate. I had lunch out for the first time in months. We caught a bus home and were still talking three hours after she arrived. That wiped me out. Before that, Tim-Bob came over and we did a power walk: one hour, four miles or so. That also wiped me out. Today, I'm walking to Pembroke Lodge to meet Alex, who has now been suffering from depression for three years. That frightens me. I'm not sure I can do three years of this. We are both forty, working dads with working wives, lively kids, busy jobs. But he quickly puts me at ease:

'I've got my thing, you've got yours. I'm not letting you have mine. I'm jealous about it,' he says.

Alex was another dad who had it all. A good job. A lovely wife with her own growing business. Two terrific boys who love kicking a ball around with my lads. Then his sister became seriously ill, and he started to unravel.

His breakdown was made infinitely worse by his employer, who insisted that he stop malingering and come back to work. Eventually the doctors diagnosed PTSD. His sister died. A lengthy legal case ensued in which he argued that his employer had aggravated his health problems.

'I have long phases when I'm well, when it's like there's nothing wrong. And then it hits me.' Matters were complicated by the long legal battle. 'Every time the court case came up, I got worse again.'

What we both really want to know of each other: was there any precursor, any sign that this was in the offing? We tell everyone it's all out of the blue, we are normal healthy people who have just had the misfortune to be the one in four. But were there any tell-tale signs? Alex thinks not. I am not so sure.

I fiddle around at the computer, scouring chat rooms and trying for the millionth time to see if there is any data out there that might indicate how long I will be ill. It's the open-endedness that I find so abhorrent. If it was six months, nine months, even a year, then I'd happily give in and hole up to sit it out. I can be patient like that. But I'm no good at holding on indefinitely. I check my emails. I'm deeply ashamed of how static my inbox has become. Like a compost bin in winter, cold and dead. Just a trickle of PR puffs and circulars. When a personal message of support lands, I cherish it, read it several times until my ears ring and my vision swims and I have to lie down for a bit.

I miss work. There's a reason why offices and organisations and companies and newsrooms will always exist, however the twenty-first century redefines the world of human endeavour: we are good in company. We are uplifted by contact, real human contact, with our fellows. Having another face to look at, watch, interpret, can act as stimulant and antidepressant. Isolation is hard to bear. We lose our anchor and are more likely to float off into dangerous currents of hyperbole, overreaction, indolence, extremism. Socialising normalises. Our more out-landish and unpleasant lines of thinking are soon extinguished by a quick exchange with a sensible colleague.

Now, in the depths of my thing, I sometimes don't speak to anyone for hours. My voice surprises me when it is put into use after such a long lay-off. November is the worst month to be ill. Nobody is about. My colleagues are fine people. They send DVDs and books, encouraging messages. They relate news and gossip: headcount to be reduced by 10 per cent; so and so is leaving for *The Times*; *Guardian America* to close down. My job is safe. Above all, I'm not to worry about being perceived as a skiver. I say I feel hopelessly out of touch. Nonsense, comes back a reply: news is like pop songs. Same stuff just in a slightly different order. You'll pick it up soon enough once you're back.

I go to meet my boss for lunch. It's the first time I've been into London on my own since it all started. I feel jittery on the train, like an escapee from an asylum. I buy the paper but cannot read it. There is a fluttering sensation as I near King's Cross; my teeth begin to chatter uncontrollably. We meet in an Ethiopian place and I eat like a horse as she fills me in on all the comings and goings. I try to pretend I care, but it's all negligible given my preoccupations of the past few months. I find myself watching her mouth as she carries on, but not much sticks. I try to talk about what happened to me, but can't really nail it. It all comes out bland. 'It was quite tough at times,' I say, like it's all over now. 'I think I could be back in a few weeks,' I continue, making promises I can't keep.

The unspoken question is who is to blame? We are a blame-worthy species, always seeking scapegoats for our misfortunes and setbacks. Chief executives and government ministers must fall on their swords when something happens on their watch, even when it is something so random, so utterly unpredictable that no human could ever have prevented or even predicted it. Football managers are sacked when someone else (the team) does badly. We expect people to be accountable for what cannot possibly be in the control of any single individual. We must find others to reproach for the things that go wrong in our own lives – a teacher at school, a former lover, a despicable boss, a cavalier motorist – when, actually, if there is anyone at all that should be blamed (and often there isn't) it is ourselves.

This is why I am starting from the position that I am principally to blame for what has happened to me. Something in my own attitude, outlook, instincts and reflexes wrapped me up a little too tight until I snapped. In order to get properly well, I will need to find out what it is about my values and attitudes and instincts that makes me like this. Essentially, I must find out why I am what I am. For now, all I can think is that I hate to let people down. I love to be needed. In my employer, my children, my wife, I found people who were all prepared to need me. And I hurtled around trying to make sure I catered to those needs, just in case they might decide they didn't need me so much after all.

I don't know why I am like this. But I will need to find out.

9
Sleep

It's about 3:20 a.m. I know this not because I've checked the clock. I'm not meant to check the clock. Checking the clock is not helpful. It always says bastard things like 03:38 or 04:29 and never 22:17. No, I know it's about 3:20 because I've added it up: went to bed at 10:30, read for a bit, lights out, turned over a few dozen times (midnight), moved to the spare room to avoid waking Sharon, sat up for half an hour (approximately 12:45), tried again, turning and turning (01:45), went to look at the sleeping children, turned the pillows over to find the cool side (02:15), tried thinking of nothing, twice jerked awake as I came close to sleep, put pyjamas on (02:45?), over on to my front to try to squash myself to sleep ...

So that would make it well after three. I try to remember the position in which I usually drift off. I think it's my left side, but when I lie on it I can feel my heart pounding away like it's providing the soundtrack to a horror film. I try to stay calm. Rational. I know that in a while, a few days perhaps, maybe a grotty week or two, I will suddenly emerge on the other side and ask what the fuss was all about. Then I will approach my bed and my pillow with a shrug, climb in and go out like a light. You go to bed, you sleep. It's easy, right?

I never had any problems with sleep. There was a strange week once. It would have been in 1982, because the Falklands War was going on and I think I was quite troubled by it. I wouldn't have wanted to fight. There was a song going round and round in my head, something quite unlike anything I'd heard before. It was called 'Ghosts', and it was quite an ugly thing, but fascinating at the same time, in the same way that an unusual face is fascinating and draws you in until you realise, after a while, that you might be a bit in love with it. I think it was the first song in which I could hear the notes that *weren't* being played as well as the notes that were. Anyway, 'Ghosts' was playing on a permanent loop in my head, making me wonder if the world might not necessarily be so pretty and marvellous, and the Falklands War was rumbling on, and I was twelve and starting for the first time to feel a bit unsure about things. I lay in bed, night after night, and just couldn't sleep. Until one or two in the morning. I would call out to my parents, and my dad would come in and explain that it really didn't matter. Lots of people, he said, had to stay up all night to do their job. He used to be in the Navy, and so used the example of a duty officer on deck through the night watch. I thought of ships sinking in the South Atlantic, and was more awake than ever.

But apart from that time, sleep was a neutral presence in my life. I have calculated that I have had twenty different homes since Glendene. There was a wide variety of beds in that time: student mattresses on creaky floorboards, Soviet sofabeds with envelope sheets into which you folded a blanket; a nasty specimen supplied by a cheap landlord which felt like it had been fashioned from a box of spanners tied up with string. I slept like the dead in all of them. Not any more. It was one of the first things to suffer during my long descent. And now, when I'm starting for the first time to think I might beat this, my sleep is the last holdout, the stubborn pocket of resistance that will not be tamed.

For the insomniac, different times of night have different qualities. The time between ten and half past eleven is the golden age that you want to hold and cherish and keep for ever. This is the time that you feel nostalgic about when it is twenty past three. For at this time, there is still a chance that you will disappear suddenly into the void and the next thing you know will be birdsong and milkmen and dawn lifting itself up and over the windowsills. Still a hope, still a chance.

The second phase is unsettling and takes you up until the streets are quiet and the house is cold. Here the feeling is that if you do manage to drop off, all is not lost. The next day will be OK; you will have cause for mild optimism in the morning.

And the longer you are insomniac, the more you recognise that this is your real window. The mind and body, no matter how ravaged, still need sleep and they'll take it if you let them. As I've got better at this I would say that as much as 50 per cent of the time I get to sleep during phase two. But it's difficult. Loneliness and restlessness edge in. Now I know what Thelonious Monk meant when he wrote: 'It begins to tell / 'round midnight.'

After two, things get wretched. This is when, if you've been doing this night after night, you ask those unanswerable questions: why me? What did I do to deserve this? What is happening to me? The questions, the lines of thinking, are disproportionate to what is actually going on. It's just a little bit of sleep, that's all. And yet in the small hours (such a misnomer, they rarely feel small) the tendency is to feel like it's the end of the world. By now pretty much everyone in the entire continent is asleep. The bed's in almost as bad a state as you. In theory, you're supposed to get up and read. In practice, you can barely finish a sentence without the worry barging in and demanding your undivided attention.

Apart from anything else it's a great sadness how those romantic hours have become disgusting to me. Once upon a time, two, three, four in the morning meant something very different. Fat basslines, thick friendship, plastic pint glasses and bedraggled party dresses, barefoot through the streets of Paris or Petersburg or Portsmouth, excitable, awake. Or else snug in trains deep behind the Iron Curtain, with a packet of cards, a bottle of vodka and three of my lifelong friends. The small hours are too few, too elusive when the going is good, when there's a dawn on the Neva to admire or a fairy-tale ride through the streets of Budapest or Zagreb to be had. In those days, not sleeping was a badge of honour, a whole event in itself, and one to anticipate and cherish and recall fondly in the prosaic light of a Monday morning. There's a lovely little song by Cherry Ghost called '4 AM': 'Oh 4 a.m. is the time when you were mine'. I'm not sure who the 'you' is that inspires the song. In my version, it is time itself: 4 a.m. was once my dream. If I was awake to greet it, it had to mean the very best of times were being had. Not any more.

Funnily enough, my parents and the outlaws are all sleeping badly at the moment too. Mum gets up and plays bridge against a computer. My father-in-law lies still, trying not to wake his wife. If he gets up, she will get cross and tell him to 'snuggle down'. She tells everyone to just 'snuggle down'. It works with the kids. It doesn't work for me.

I should add that this insomnia is not the wakefulness of the busy executive with his deadlines and to-do lists or the furious restlessness of the self-employed churning over how to get tomorrow's money today. This affliction is all in the passive mood. It all happens like some capricious reflexive verb that has yet to be invented. In Russian they don't say 'I can't sleep'. They say 'It isn't sleeping to me'. I like that. For a long time now, it hasn't been sleeping to me. Not properly anyway. From two to four you will really fight the thing, like it's actually in the room with you. That's exhausting. After four things could get truly horrible, but by then you're probably so bereft that you'll drift off at some point into thin dreams about empty cities and lost causes. But not for long. By now you're desperate for morning so you can move on, write off the night, hope for better luck next time. A few nights of this and it becomes bewildering. Your bones ache like cold rods of uranium. You can feel the shape of your skeleton. You have startling moments of sudden realisation that plummet to your stomach like a sword: this is really me, I am in deep trouble, this is a vicious circle that, like some diabolical spreadsheet cell, will not be resolved.

There are two reasons why insomnia is such a tell-tale feature of depression. First, as sleep expert Kevin Morgan told me, there is a 'hardware' issue: common neurophysiological mechanisms that underpin both mood stability and sleep. If you like, the sleep train must shuttle down the same mental pathways that have been chewed up by the physiology of depression. But Morgan says there is a 'software' issue too: the rumination that is generated by depression is precisely the kind of thinking that frustrates sleep onset.

'What do people do when they wake up at night? They think. Why? That's what brains do,' he tells me, warming to his theme. 'It's four in the morning, you wake up, you're struggling to understand how to interpret feelings and circumstances of life, you're probably a bit tired, resources are low. Ideally you'd get out of bed and do something. But people don't. They stay in bed, thinking or hoping that they'll go back to sleep, but instead they embark on thinking. For people who function normally it might be thinking about what's happening tomorrow, what you're going to cook on Christmas day. After a while they bump into worry-thoughts that will frustrate sleep.

'But when a depressed person wakes up they rapidly reach the worry-thinking stage.'

The first weeks of insomnia were deeply unsettling. My organism was just too wracked to be able to sleep: hands vibrating, anxiety churning, a restless genie in my legs. There was my new friend Zopiclone, which did a job. But in the pits of the illness, when I could barely keep still let alone allow my mind to wander into neutral, the pills were fighting a losing battle. In the worst phase I would go to bed heavily dosed up, get a few delirious hours and then wake suddenly with a hypnic jerk. The first instinct would be to bury my head in a pillow in the vain hope that, like a normal sleeper turning over for a new cycle of slumber, I might be carried off again. No chance. I would then be on the lookout for signs of dawn, hoping that I'd made it through six, five, even four hours. When you're struggling to get to sleep you always want the numbers on the clock to be earlier than they are; when you suddenly wake up in the middle of the night you always want them to be later than they are. On the darkest night of the year I lifted my head to look at the digital clock. It said 00:08. It was a long treacherous night thereafter.

There is, seemingly, nothing that you can actively do about insomnia. Falling asleep is one of those perverse things, like writing or love, that are harder to do the more you try. We have largely become conditioned to thinking that the more effort we put in, the more we will get out. That's clearly not the case with sleep. Trying to drift off just doesn't work. Sleep is a reflex and needs to happen effortlessly. When it stops happening and you start trying, problems begin.

'If you ask people who don't have a sleep problem what they do to fall asleep they say "nothing",' says Morgan. 'Sleep rests on automaticity. Attempts to override automaticity impair performance. If you want to do it properly don't think about it.

'If you ask a person who is having problems sleeping what they are doing about it, they'll say "I've tried everything". But that's just it: people who don't have a problem don't try anything.'

I've tried everything.

Some things do help.

1. A second bed. It may not be possible for everyone, but perhaps the single best practical step that we took to prevent our household from becoming consumed by this was to start using the pull-out sofa in the spare room/playroom. We'd done it before, during those parlous days with a tiny infant in the house, when it made sense for at least one of us to be getting some sleep. Sharon and I both felt a gentle kinship for the spare room, a largish bed, not uncomfortable, all to oneself. It was the chamber of sanctity, the inviolate redoubt, a place one could go to be alone and untroubled. We resurrected it. Some of the time Sharon slept there while I tossed and turned and ambled and shambled through the night. More often than not, I would use it as a safety net. If I didn't go to sleep in my own bed, I could always try the spare room. I'm not sure why it worked, but on many occasions the change of scene was enough. There were,

of course, many nights when it didn't, but the spare bed made bedtime feel not so dreadful.

2. Pills. Why do we hate medicine so much? What is it that has turned the simple, effective pill into a small capsule containing all that is bad with modern life? Sleeping pills must not be abused but, deployed smartly, they can make the difference between a rough ride and utter capitulation. Cartons come with long warnings about overuse and dependency. In my experience, if you take them for two to three weeks *when you really need them*, they work well, buying you time and space to get over the really difficult patch. Addiction doesn't really come into it: when you feel well again you are no more likely to take a sleeping pill than rob a bank. I can sense when I am vulnerable. Using sleeping pills for three to five nights, just until I feel I'm over the worst of it, has helped enormously. There is a psychological game here: you don't want to use pills when you don't need to. If you have a bad night, wait for a second before succumbing. Then resign yourself to it: you'll use pills for several days, just until, just until ... well the world will feel different in a few days' time. You might be really suffering, in which case you'll have to go on for a few more days. Or you might be feeling stronger. Then you say to yourself, 'OK, no pill tonight. I know I won't sleep brilliantly, but I will be able to congratulate myself on moving forwards.' That little fillip, the feeling of having coped without a pharmacological crutch, can help you put the bad spell behind you.

3. Pills treat the symptom, not the cause. That is why you need other tools to help settle the mind. Meditation helps in

two ways. First, a half-hour session in the middle of the evening – after telly but before bedtime reading – can really slow the heart rate, calm you down and make you feel sedate. I'm told that, after a few months, meditation can actually induce neurological change. So it's not total hippy nonsense. Secondly, when you're lying there, wondering how to get off, some breathing exercises in which you fill your mind with observation of the breath coming and going, filling and emptying, curling and sighing.

4. Exercise. Strictly speaking, the conventional wisdom is to take quite vigorous exercise and make yourself tired, but don't do it too late in the day. I have consistently found that a game of football in the early evening vastly improves the quality and duration of my sleep.

5. Acceptance. The hardest, but the most valuable lesson of all, and one that is crucial to lasting recovery. Essentially it boils down to this: bad things happen to us, but they are as nothing compared to the bad things we do to ourselves. We make things worse by our constant judgements (I should be asleep), our ceaseless comparison of ourselves to others (the wife and kids are asleep, why aren't I?), our unrelenting standards for ourselves (if I don't get eight hours' sleep, I'll be a wreck tomorrow). Acceptance is about seeing those statements for what they are: unhelpful interventions in what is already a tricky situation. We are who we are and no amount of fretting, particularly at half past one in the morning, is going to think our way out of the problem. What if instead we were able to say, 'I'm not sleeping too well at the moment, but it won't hurt me. My body will

sleep when it needs to. I can always catch up.' I can safely say that every time I lie awake agonising that if I don't sleep it means I'm not as well as I think I am, I will not sleep. Whereas each night I think I am what I am and there is little I can do about it, sleep comes more easily. Stop thinking. It's really hard to do, but if you can just stop the mind from broadcasting its peculiar mix of propaganda, impression, recollection, projection, apprehension and sedition, you invite in a nothingness that is a close cousin of sleep.

There's another clever little trick that I was taught by Colin Espie. As a clinical psychologist and director of Glasgow University's Sleep Centre, he may know more than just about anyone else in Britain about sleep and insomnia, and is a reassuring man for the insomniac to talk to. Espie likes to cite the example of soldiers in the First World War who were executed for falling asleep on duty. Bombarded by enemy shells, scared rigid in trenches and sentry posts, terrified at the prospect of going over the top, dozens of young men nonetheless could not prevent themselves from dozing while on duty. 'The ultimate reassurance for the insomniac is that sleep is irresistible,' Espie says. 'These people had shells exploding all around them but still could not remain awake. You cannot resist sleep. You can resist eating, you can choose not to drink. But you can't choose not to breathe and you can't choose not to sleep.'

Thus even during a wretched night, the wakeful will probably clock up a few micro-sleeps. In fact, they may well sleep for longer than they think they have. Exaggeration is a nocturnal animal. When someone reports that they 'haven't slept a wink', don't believe them. Unreliable narrators. And when it's you yourself, definitely don't believe. The first person is the most unreliable narrator of all.

Tied up with this unreliability is a remarkable piece of negligence: few of us really know how much sleep we need. We baffle ourselves by going for days, weeks even, on low volumes of sleep – boast about it even. Then we are perplexed at the way we can slumber for nine or ten hours and awaken more weary than we went to bed. Scientists report that we are, on average, sleeping more than an hour less than our Victorian forebears, but no one really knows what this means. Averages are no good with sleep. It's like walking into a shoe shop and asking for an average-sized shoe: there is no one-size-fits-all.

'The fact that people don't actually know how much sleep they need is quite interesting,' says Espie. 'Most people would know within a half-size what their shirt collar is or shoe size. People know the dimension of many of their physical measurements. We don't live our lives according to group average, but we share our waking and sleeping lives with others and this is where we have to compromise.'

And so to Espie's trick. If we don't know how well we are sleeping, and we don't really know how much sleep we need, we should experiment a little. Start by going short, 'tightening the sleep window', as Espie calls it. That is to say, go to bed very late and get up early. Sit up and read and do gentle puzzles or watch quiet documentaries until you are really, really tired. This may seem counter-intuitive. The hard-of-sleeping tend to go to bed promptly to give the best possible chance of getting off in good time. Bad move, says Espie. This can only increase the pressure. If you go to bed at one you will undoubtedly spend less time punching the pillow and may in time come to trust your bed and your sleep once again. Regardless of when you fall asleep, get up at six. Do the same again the next night and the next, until you start to find it harder and harder to make it to one o'clock. Behold: your sleep drive. This is why insomnia is not sleep deprivation. The sleep-deprived would fall asleep standing up if you let them. They have the instinct but not the opportunity. The insomniacs, however, don't trust their sleep. They have the opportunity, but not the instinct. I have been through both, as a father of young infants and a post-breakdown depressive. I know which one is easier. 'Trust your sleep drive,' Espie says.

I try it. On night one, it feels pretty wretched. I am still up and about after one. I have done two-thirds of a crossword and dipped in and out of books about maths and swallows. Now I am watching my children sleep. It's calming to watch their little O-shaped mouths sucking in air. My daughter is on her back, pixie face nestling in between pillows and duvet like she was placed there by angels taking a cigarette break. My middle child sleeps in a reckless position, arms and legs splayed like a slaughtered fawn. My big boy is so deep beneath the bedclothes I can't see him. All three are buried beneath layers of teddies and soft toys. No matter how much I bang and crash around, they will not wake. They are in dream sleep, twitching occasionally, and sometimes my daughter will yelp 'Don't scratch it' or else 'This is fine' and then disappear back under the thick eiderdown sleep of the innocent. I lie on my daughter's floor and wait for something to change. Within a few minutes I am calmer. I move about some more, slowly, like a Soviet bag lady. I try again, lying, staring at the dark, watching its quality, waiting . . .

I surface. It's not morning, but it's definitely not one any more either. You can tell by the silence: it's not new, it's been there a while. And the darkness is deeper (does a room get darker the longer it has been dark? Or is it the same dark as if you'd just drawn the curtains?). From somewhere distant, a siren. But I am not here for sirens. I turn over and sleep a little more.

I wake at six. About four hours' sleep. There are times when four hours' sleep would have pitched me into despair. But now I feel triumphant. The next night I am very tired at eleven. It's really still outside my sleep window. But I just try lying on the bed for a while, to see what it feels like. I sleep for eight hours.

Underneath the lemon tree a single leaf lies bleached in the sun, curling slightly at the edges. I pick it up, examine it with a deep curiosity I have not felt for a while. All the other leaves remain in their place, waxy green in the morning daylight. Why did this one drop? There is nothing about its shape or hue to suggest vulnerability. Its stalk seems perfectly adequate. Thin veins of life radiate perfectly from the midrib. It is a fine leaf. And yet it fell. And everything carries on as before. The soil looks dry. I must have neglected it. I water it slowly, mist the leaves, clean the plate on which the pot sits. And then I lie and wait. I lie still, here, in the wintry sunshine, underneath the lemon tree.

RECOVERY

RECOVERY

10

Mindful

'To begin the mindfulness of breathing meditation practice, we begin to gather the awareness around the breath flowing in and out of the body, not altering it, not straining or forcing . . .'

I sit on the floor and listen to the dreamy voice on the meditation CD floating around in the space between my headphones. She has a nice, gentle intonation, like a mother telling a small child about the death of a hamster. But it's not really making much sense. I've never really 'got' meditation. Sometimes my yoga teacher would end the class with five minutes of meditation and I'd be itching to race out of the class, get dressed and do stuff. As far as I was concerned meditation was not only pointless, but it also introduced the Beatles to the sitar, a match made in hell.

I have been persuaded that I should try. There are at least three reasons for this. The long, dark days between now and the day when my life resumes need filling and there are still not many things I can actually do without overtaxing my system and falling back into the pits of the thing. Sitting on the floor doing nothing is one way to fill an hour. Some people say that, in time, maybe after a few months, meditation can actually be an enjoyable experience. But that, like pretty much everything else, it takes practice. Mindfulness and meditation can also help with the rumination. I have already been dabbling with the idea of suspending one's thoughts, not buying into them, seeing them for what they are. Mindfulness is apparently precisely that – bringing an intentional awareness to thoughts and feelings and examining them deliberately and dispassionately so as not to get carried away by them. Lastly, I have helpers who are actively pushing this stuff. A friend who runs meditation sessions has emailed me some tips; a colleague from work has sent some CDs; and Sacha Khan, my psychotherapist, is keen for me to try some mindfulness-based cognitive therapy, a programme that is gaining increasing credibility on the margins of the National Health Service.

'Mindfulness is a particular quality of awareness that comes with paying attention in a particular way, on purpose, moment by moment, and non-judgementally,' he tells me.

It takes a while for me to buy into it. Awareness is an alien concept to the Western mind. It is, apparently, a much bigger thing in Eastern philosophy: presence of mind, the 'third eye' that sees our being selves as quite detached from the breathless fury of our thinking selves. At first I look for my awareness in the dark floaters behind my closed eyelids, as if it is a physical place. I think I find it somewhere just above my left eye, but I spend so much time looking for it and trying to find it and thinking that I've found it that I forget that what I'm supposed to be doing is not looking, or finding, or trying, or thinking, but just being.

The CDs help. The suggestion is to focus on the action of breathing, to give the mind something to do. You can feel the air cool in the nostrils, or expanding in the chest, or even right down in the diaphragm. It is rather pleasant. I watch the breath come and go for a while, thinking as I do so that it is a precarious reflex that keeps us alive. How many times do we breathe in a lifetime? Say ten times a minute (unless you're exercising or hiding from a burglar): that's six hundred times an hour, or 14,400 times a day. Call it an even five million times a year, give or take a few heart-stopping moments; and so more than four hundred million times if we get to live beyond eighty, which I've decided once again that I would quite like to do. That's a lot of breathing. I wonder if there's anything else we do four hundred million times. Blink? Probably not. Heartbeats? Perhaps. Move, feel, think? And then I realise I'm not meant to be thinking about this at all. I'm meant to be meditating. Watching my breath. What happened to that?

The hypnotic CD voice suggests counting at the end of each outbreath, to give my busy little brain something to do. The suggestion is that every time you discover you have wandered off and lost your count, you go back to one again. I struggle to get beyond three. I'm all right at the first one, I count it all in and I count it all out again. I am halfway through sucking in number two when my mind does a dainty shimmy, wriggles away through the barbed wire and dances off into the distance. It hears a police siren and imagines a car chase, the capture of villains with contraband; or maybe an ambulance or a fire engine hastening to the scene of some minor disaster – an inferno in a tower block or a traffic jam swallowed up by a giant sinkhole. It hears hooves clipping past and wonders when it was that horses branched out from the primeval swamp and became horses; it hears the yelps of small children and I wonder what my own children must think of me. The other day, James asked me how I was feeling. 'A little better,' I said. 'Good,' he replied. 'The little blue pills are doing their trick.'

He's smarter than I think. The little blue pills ... I wonder about Lorazepam, the drug that has locked me away in a golden sheath of chemicals so that I am protected from the sharp edges of the illness. It's not a high, or a buzz or a thrill, just a deep calm, a shudder of serenity, a welcome detachment, like I am crudely superimposed on the background of my life. I want to marry Lorazepam, take it for ever. Dr Wilkins says four weeks max. I wonder what will happen when I come off it, whether it will be back to the horrors of Christmas all over again. A bolt of anxiety fizzes across me, glancing off the Lorazepam shield. When I told my occupational-health nurse that I was taking benzodiazepines, I could tell she was dismayed from the silence at the other end of the phone. 'How much are you taking, Mark?'

'One milligram, three times a day.' Further silence.

'Well you'll have to come off that fairly quickly, or there can be problems of withdrawal.' Of course, then I looked it up on the internet and joined the chat rooms and the forums teeming with benzo-addicts and long-term users. I read about tolerance, dependence, withdrawal syndrome and ominous-sounding 'cognitive impairments'. Withdrawal symptoms can include anxiety and insomnia and depression – the very things it's meant to be treating. And so I think, what the hell? I've come into this thing with one problem and I'm going to end up with two.

'Where are you now?' the CD voice admonishes, as if she knows that I've wandered off. Where am I now? Oh, yes, I'm supposed to be meditating, counting my breaths, not thinking about all those things that just make me feel worse, not trying to think my way out of this corner because that just doesn't work. I'm meant to be trying not thinking for a change, and all I've done is think, think, think. Where am I now? Well I'm right slap bang in the middle of the circular 'what will become of me?' argument once again. And I'm no closer to a resolution. Where am I now? I'm sitting on the floor, staring at the wall, where do you think? Where am I always?

Where am I now? I wish I knew.

I go back to the counting. I try to picture the numbers, big, fat and square; three-dimensional; black and white; blown up by a foot pump; etched into a cornfield; sitting on a clifftop; flipped over on a calendar. But it doesn't help. By two, I'm off again, spooked by the dates on the calendar, dates that tell me I've been ill for more than three months, fourteen weeks and four days to be precise. That's more than a hundred days, or about 0.6 per cent of my life. This time I notice my preoccupation quickly, and come back to the counting. One ... two ... three ... when you have your eyelids closed, are your eyes still open behind them? Why is my local Sainsbury an anagram of the street it is on? Is it sunny on the sun? Why do sneezes come in pairs? Who is the most famous Ian in the world?

'Whenever the mind wanders off, as it will do from time to time, without judging, without giving ourselves a hard time, just taking the breathing to whatever it is that has interested us, noting, being aware and breathing.'

The voice continually pulls me back and reassures me: the art of mindfulness is not about scoring well or outperforming a rival. It's all about what happens on your mat. The moment of noticing that you have lost count, or that your mind has drifted is in itself an occasion of mindfulness, a moment of pure awareness. It's a paradox: the worse you are at it, the better you are doing it.

Mindfulness is often presented as a new cure, a universal balm to deaden the effects of all the white noise of the twenty-first century. In fact it's an old idea rediscovered. Put simply, mindfulness is paying attention to stuff. It's the opposite of that car journey when you drive from A to B but can't remember any of it because you were lost in thought. It's the opposite of when time flies because you are so absorbed in something. It's the opposite of fury, hysteria, immersion, turbulence, passion, emotion, bewilderment. Mindfulness is being there, watching, observing, noticing that you are you and now is now. It's detachment, distance, objectivity. It's a sight for eyes jaded by the world they think they've seen a thousand times. Mindfulness sees it all as if for the first time.

Take a raisin and eat it. Now take it and eat it mindfully. Observe every wrinkle, every seam and fold. Put it down, then pick it up – feel its heft, however slight. Hold it up to the light and evaluate its colour, opacity or translucence. Put it to your nose and inhale. Rub it against your ear lobe and hear the noise it makes. Put it to your lips and feel its texture. Drop it from a height and listen to the sound it makes on impact. Pop it in your mouth. Roll it around on your tongue; toy with it with your teeth. Bite. Chew. Taste. Move it about a bit. Feel what it does to your saliva glands. Observe how it disintegrates, the sensation as it passes the oesophagus on the way to the stomach.

This is a fairly well-rehearsed example of doing something mindfully. There are lots of other things that can be done in the same observant, deliberate fashion: the washing-up; a shower; brushing your teeth. And, yes, watering a lemon tree. I take a watering can, examine its colour, study the rose which is silted over with neglect, observe the muck on the underside from where it has been left in the mud along with Janey's magnifying glass and a plastic Batman that looks suspiciously like it has been thrown from an upstairs window. I move slowly to the water butt, peer inside to examine the quality of ancient rainwater, mouldering for months, cold, still and dark, a little like me. I position the vessel under the tap. I turn the water on, watch the startling escape of fluid, sparkling like diamonds in the shrill winter sun. I put a hand in the current and shut my eyes, feeling through stiff fingertips for the dull ache of life that water brings. I let the can overflow and watch the patterns and movement that water makes when left to its own devices. I mount the stairs, one at a time, and address the lemon tree, which is in Janey's room. I begin to soak the roots and watch for the tell-tale trickle through to the underplate. I mist the leaves and fruit. I pull up a few idiotic weeds that have chosen, for their one great chance at life, an ornamental tub in a northern hemisphere December. I turn the pot around, so that growth will be uniform and leaves ambidextrous. I inhale the perfume of the flowers, a scent that takes me back thirty years to Mays and haze and holidays ...

At first it's not apparent to me how this 'being in the moment' will cure my depression. Sacha Khan explains that, by paying attention moment by moment, we can change the relationship we have with our inner experience. Instead of getting caught up in it all – and dragged down by it whenever it turns negative – we sit on the edge and watch it.

'Often it's the case that we can see where someone else is going wrong,' he says. 'This technique allows us to see ourselves with the same detachment, perhaps in the way that others see us. People with depression ruminate a great deal and those thoughts can be overwhelming. This gives us breathing space; by doing this practice, we cultivate this ability to look at the problems with a degree of objectivity.'

Typically, I want meditation to work right now, like a mobile phone or a soft-drinks dispenser. Atypically for our times, this is a rare case of deferred gratification. Meditation takes time to pay off. It is no quick fix.

I do not find it easy at first. Sometimes it's a turbulent, even queasy affair. My thoughts will not settle down. I will lose track of myself for whole minutes at a time. I will give up after ten minutes and say, 'No Marko, not today.' I will become sad or agitated. Sometimes I see black and red behind my eyelids, shapes that do not belong in this world, like a scene cut from *Rosemary's Baby* for being too graphic. I must be patient. Like ice skating or learning the tuba, it takes several months of practice to get to a place where mindfulness and meditation really can start to make a difference. It's not for everyone. People with really severe depression, or psychosis or addiction problems may not benefit. Likewise patients who are not prepared to suspend their scepticism or to practise regularly. But Sacha adds, 'If people commit to it, they tend to benefit from it.' That's good enough for me.

The first thing I notice is that the worse I feel the better I am at meditation and mindfulness. If it's a lousy day I really look forward to my hour-long session, putting it off again and again so I still have it to look forward to. Sometimes I practise twice, three times a day. I still rarely make it to a count of ten but I notice improvements, changes as the months pass. When I am in a good patch – and I've started to have one or two – meditation is all but impossible. My mind is racing away with itself, eager to get back into all the things I want to pick up again. On days like these it's as much as I can do to sit for twenty minutes. Some days I skip it altogether. Later I will come to regret that.

For now, though, I am practising. One exercise is to focus on each part of the body in turn, noting all sensations that are there. Sometimes, when you sit, you can't actually feel certain body parts. You have to assume they are still there, but if you try to detect any sensation in, say, your little toes, or your forearms, there is nothing there. This is particularly true of my shins. I'm not sure I can ever actually feel my shins. Except when they have been kicked. What's the point of that, a body part that you can only ever feel when it hurts? I peek to see if my shins are still there. And then I recognise that I've been diverted, so back I go again.

Another exercise simply concentrates on the breath. You can choose which part of the breathing body to focus on: the nostrils or the throat, the chest or the abdomen. I quite like to feel it in my nose; it is odd how sometimes one nostril is a little blocked and other times the other one is. I also like to feel it deep in the diaphragm, where it swells and ebbs like the sea. Other exercises invite you to listen out for sounds without judging them good or bad, irritating or reassuring. They are just sounds. You can't change them, so don't fret about them. At other times you are encouraged to watch your thoughts as they come and go like fish in a stream. Again, there is little you can do about these thoughts. You can push them away, but it is the nature of the mind that, if they involve something that really does bother you, you won't be able to banish them for long. They will seep back in. So just watch them. No thought lasts for ever. They come. And go. Sometimes I nod off, which I know I'm not supposed to. But I take heart. Usually if I can nod off in the middle of a day it means I will have few problems getting to sleep at night.

For a couple of months I am truly immersed. Sacha is pleased. When we first met he took a bit of a punt that this mindfulness-based cognitive therapy would be helpful for me. 'You're a journalist and we live in a verbal, left-brain society,' he recalls later. 'Sometimes we can overvalue that. One way of dealing with our problems is talking about them and using language. But it occurred to me that it would be good for you to step out of that mindset and try using your brain a different way, get to know your experience differently.'

There is more and more about mindfulness in the public space. I wonder if it's an idea whose time has come. 'It's actually thousands of years old,' Sacha gently corrects me. 'It was popular in the sixties and I think the reason it is becoming popular again is that science is starting to validate some of the claims that it can physically change the brain.'

As a result of this scientific seal of approval, mindfulness-based cognitive therapy is now recommended for people with three or more episodes of depression under the UK's NICE guidelines. In reality, provision is patchy. 'In the south-west, or Bangor, Oxford, places like that, it is much more substantive provision,' notes Willem Kuyken at Exeter University. 'But in other parts of the country there is not much going on at all.'

Kuyken believes mindfulness has come of age. 'Somehow society has become goal-driven in terms of achievement: we have lost the space for people to be present and be and there is something very appealing about it within our contemporary society.'

Kuyken points me towards some research – a study of sixteen parents who completed a course of mindfulness-based cognitive therapy. The results were instructive. Most found the practice made them more easy-going parents, less angry, more able to detach themselves from the chaos of a young family. The course helped the parents see that getting worked up over trivial episodes was pointless. Small children are exuberant, irrational, sometimes utterly ungovernable. Getting agitated over their behaviour is often counterproductive. Mindfulness helped the parents stand back and understand: They are just children. Children make a mess. Children argue. Children screech. It's what they do. No point shouting at them for it. Many of the parents taking part in the study said that their calmer response had helped defuse situations.

The course also helped the parents get down on the children's level, make themselves emotionally available, submit to their pace of life and their interests, rather than imposing adult sensibilities on a confused child. One father told the researchers: 'When she was at nursery and ... counting ... I wouldn't bother at all. Even drawing pictures, I couldn't be bothered. But I make things with her now. Whenever we go out, she has a treasure bag, a plastic bag, and she will put bits of wood in it and when we get home, we make things ... with it.'

Mindfulness is not only useful for the bad times. It helps in good times too. Think of a perfect day. Me, I see a beach in

Asia: soft sand, lively surf, warm air. There'd be a hearty breakfast, some surfing, definitely coffee, a game with the kids, a large lunch with a big group, siesta, some cards maybe, or just banter. But such is the power of anticipation that I'm often wishing most of it away. At breakfast, I'll already be picturing the surf. In the sea, my thoughts turn to cappuccinos, but when I get there I don't savour my coffee, but wonder what I'll do when I've finished it.

Years and years have passed by like this, my time gone by far too quickly. It physically hurts me to know that 1976, probably the heyday of my childhood, is now thirty-five years gone, so distant in fact that almost half the human race will have no recollection of it at all. What has become of the intervening years? I lost them in a hurry. Mindfulness – being in that blissful moment rather than hastening on to the next – is a powerful antidote. It slows down the acceleration of time.

I'm to end my dreamy relationship with Lorazepam, before it turns from a brief affair into something altogether more serious. Loraz – my bright blue pill, my little darling who gently intervened when things got nasty and provided me with a secure passage through the whirlpools and rocks into my future. She has been kind and sweet to me, reliable, steadfast, unsung. Like all jilted lovers, I expect her to complain; I expect her to complain a lot and I'm not sure what my answer will be.

In truth, I didn't feel too dopey or stoned or dull on Loraz. Just serene. Sleeping like the dead and moseying through the day like a canal boat through Gloucestershire. The children's shrieks bounce off me at a tangent that takes them harmlessly into outer space. Conversation is easy, a script I've read ten times before. I'm not sure anyone notices that I'm drugged up to the eyeballs. We go ice skating with a family from around the corner. In my slow, blissful state I can glide smoothly across the ice, cutting frost out of it with my hired blades, looking for patterns, looking for spaces between people that I might fit through. I skated a lot in Russia, on some cheap hockey skates I bought for about seventy-five pence in a state shop called Olimp. And after using them the first time, I did o-limp a lot. They were not great skates. Still, we would glide around Patriarch's Ponds at night, looking for Lara and giant cats and the ghost of Mikhail Bulgakov, and trot home happily in the midnight snow.

Oh Loraz! Where have you been all these years? What are you doing for the rest of my life? We could have been so happy together. In another world, there we are, just you and me, both of us utterly untroubled by the human predicament, me keeping you in full-time employment, and you protecting me from myself. You must have known I'd be good for you when I dreamed my dreamy way through my teens, always off on some great adventure of the imagination, reading books and cycling alone through Thomas Hardy country, where nothing ever happens. I will miss you already, like I miss everything I've lost in this unimportant life: my childhood, Glendene, my packs of friends, my Russia. Loraz, I could sing you love songs, from Nick Drake and Lou Reed. But of course nothing lasts for ever. Everything must pass. We are creatures of habit and our habits do not serve us well, particularly those that afford us pleasure. Nabokov once said that in order to enjoy life we should not enjoy it too much. But then he also wrote 'Lolita, light of my life, fire of my loins', so I suppose we shouldn't trust absolutely everything he wrote.

I am on quite a heavy dose – one milligram three times a day, which is considerable given that Lorazepam is apparently far stronger than Valium. It is clear that, even though Dr Wilkins thought it was a good idea, not everyone did. Every time I mention Lorazepam to Dr Burnie, she winces as though I have told her that her cat has been run over. GPs have got into trouble for prescribing Lorazepam. They dished it out like confetti in the late nineties and a lot of people ended up addicted.

Dr Wilkins suggests tapering gently so as to avoid a bumpy landing. But of course I know better. I'm having my best week for six months, so I just dump the old girl in a matter of days and never look back. I whittle half a milligram off each day, so that by the middle of the week I'm making do with three half-pills and by Saturday I get up and look at the pale blue box with contempt. Sharon is cross with me, thinks I'm reverting to my competitive nature, trying to win a 'who-can-come-off-Lorazepam-the-quickest' contest. Maybe I am. All I know is that thinking about my dependency on Loraz is becoming a problem in itself.

The effect is quite weird. I'm constantly feeling for the anxiety, the vibrating hands, the stomach growl which have been absent for weeks. But they aren't there. There is still a leaden fatigue that makes me fall down into sofas and armchairs with an audible 'ouff'. There are outrageous muscle tremors – an eyelid, my right tricep – and shaking hands, which I try to conceal. I yawn all the time. It's one of the few pleasures I get: I yawn in public places and see who yawns back. There is the tinnitus again, louder in my right ear than my left. Sometimes the timbre of the atmosphere just seems to change suddenly, like they're conducting a secret experiment with the air or something, and there is that high-pitched ring coming in through one ear and out of the other. I wonder what it is. And my headache is back, rattling around my right eye. But for now the anxiety, the insomnia and the dark moods that they generate – all are quiet. A brand new February, my forty-first, is just around the corner. A month ago I was taking five pills to get through the day. Now I am back down to just two antidepressants, one in the morning, one at night. Instead of chemicals I feel something else pipe through my system, something I haven't felt for years. Optimism.

11

Books

I can read again. I can't tell you how relieved I am. Well, perhaps I can. Let me try: *I am so relieved because I can read again.* Not just pulses of the internet blinking in and out of my life. Not just emails. Not just putting one eye in front of the other and marching through simple news stories. I can actually take in information, retain it, hold it in my memory, recall it where necessary. I can follow plot and argument and character. I have a degree in reading books and making sense of them. At last I can do it again. Yesterday I went to see Dr Wilkins. I sat in the waiting room, romping through Robert Harris's *Imperium*. Good old Wilko notices things like that. 'You're reading a book,' he says. 'That tells me all I need to know. You weren't reading a book when you first walked in here.'

It's more than just a distraction, a pleasant half-hour in an easy chair. It's more than just the chance to be that guy on the Tube, nose in a decent tome. Books have lots to say about breakdown, depression and recovery. Is it just me, or is everything I am reading packed full of people with mental illness? Perhaps I'm just noticing them more, the way you notice a new word that suddenly seems to be everywhere once you have properly understood it for the first time. Perhaps I am unconsciously seeking them out; people with mental illness just love to spend time learning more about their condition. As Sylvia Plath's heroine Esther Greenwood notes in *The Bell Jar*: 'The only reason I remembered this play was because it had a mad person in it, and everything I had ever read about mad people stuck in my mind, while everything else flew out.'

It is not just a case of me seeking out stories about madness. Mad protagonists are seeking me out too. I get back to Stieg Larsson, and there is Lisbeth Salander, clearly suffering from some kind of post-traumatic stress disorder and a little bit OCD too. In *On Green Dolphin Street* Charlie van der Linden is clearly so exceptionally depressed I wonder that it takes him until page three hundred and plenty to actually have a breakdown. There is Hanna from *The Reader* and Hans van den Broek in *Netherland* and Hector in *The Slap* and Ma in *Room* and Eva Khatchadourian from *We Need to Talk About Kevin* – all clearly suffering from depression. I pick up a wonderful book by Sarah Waters, called *Affinity*, a compelling yarn that centres on a nineteenth-century character bearing most of my symptoms. Poor love. In those days they gave you laudanum and generally forgot about you. I'm struck by how little has changed.

German authors are good at depression. I read many German books at university and, looking back, pretty much all of them had a protagonist who was broken down, dispirited or otherwise depressed. The song 'Is That All There Is?' is based on 'Disillusionment', a short story by Thomas Mann that centres on a character who 'went out into that supposedly so wonderful life, craving just one, one single experience which should correspond to my great expectations. God help me, I have never had it.' Yes, the Teutonic greats do existential midlife despair like no others: characters like Hans Schnier, Tonio Kröger, Gustav von Aschenbach, Gregor Samsa, Woyzeck, right back to Werther and Faust, all of them tell us a little something about what it is to be an outsider, lost and alienated and unable to see the point in a godless world. Faust is the granddaddy of them all, the ur-depressive, hitting midlife with nothing to show for it, prepared to deal with the devil in order to acquire some experience that might make life *memorable*. No one talks about existential despair any more these days. But it's everywhere I look: in the people who want to be famous, in the famous people who want to be more famous, in the people who want bigger houses, better houses, smarter cars, high-achieving kids. It's there in the people getting older who wonder if that's all there is; in younger people who wonder if they're ever going to amount to anything. Is that all there is? we ask ourselves. Because if it is, we might as well break out the bloody booze.

That was certainly Boris Yeltsin's approach. I re-read his

Midnight Diaries and am convinced that he had some kind of depressive breakdown during his first term in office, which I followed in fascination from the offices of the *Moscow Times* and latterly for the AFP news agency. I wouldn't hold it against Yeltsin. Governing Russia in the nineties would be enough to break most men.

I dip into Alan Bennett's *Untold Stories* and am horrified at the suffering of his mother. (Bennett is brilliant at describing mental anguish: 'Over a matter of weeks she had lost all her fun and vitality, turning fretful and apprehensive and inaccessible to reason or reassurance.') I read Marcus Trescothick's *Coming Back to Me* and find startling similarities between his condition and my own: 'I was jittery, unsettled, shaky and very dull company ... and later spent a third successive restless night worrying, tossing and turning ... This was the night the sleeping pills finally stopped working. It began with me literally pacing up and down the room. I couldn't stop. I couldn't sit down and I couldn't relax ... I started sweating heavily. I started shaking. I felt myself losing control. I was petrified.' I make Victoria Coren's delightful book about poker last as long as possible. Then, bang, within a couple of hundred pages she too is on antidepressants. Yes, books are a great help: they make you realise you are not alone.

I spend a few agreeable weeks in the company of the American post-war novels that also centre on existential depression. There is Holden Caulfield, at war with the vapidity of his own youth; there is April Wheeler, bereft at the emptiness of the American dream; there is Neddy Merrill, suffering a breakdown in the space of an afternoon in which he tries to swim home through the cruelty of suburban Westchester county; there is Esther Greenwood, stuck in the suffocating miasma of the bell jar because of her inability to conceive of her place in a male-dominated world. Her experiences as a young, naive magazine intern in New York stun her into submission: there is no way her dreams can be fulfilled here. She is expected to serve men. No other aspiration will do. It's enough to tip her over the edge.

Sometimes the overlap between what's on the page and what's happening to me is uncanny. Waters gives me a heroine who, like me, is sleeping badly and spending many hours looking out of her window. Plath describes perfectly the feeling of not being able to read: 'Words, dimly familiar, but twisted all awry, like faces in a funhouse mirror, fled past, leaving no impression on the glassy surface of my brain.' In *In Cold Blood*, Truman Capote describes the mental anguish of Mrs Clutter, who suffers 'seizures of grief that sent her wandering from room to room in a hand-wringing daze'. He also renders the undulations of depression: 'She knew "good days" and occasionally they accumulated into weeks, months.' But the illness never truly lets go. At her worst, she tells a confidante: 'I'm missing out on everything. The best years, the children – everything. A little while, and even Kenyon will be a grown-up – a man. And how will he remember me? As a kind of ghost.' I've had the same thoughts about my own little family. How will they remember their father? Am I to miss out on the rest of my life?

But the one that really stops me in my tracks is Boris

Akunin's *Pelagia and the Red Rooster*. There on page 171 is the following passage:

> He had changed, the public prosecutor's wife complained. Something seemed to have got into her Motya – he had become irritable, he hardly ate a thing and he ground his teeth in his sleep . . .
>
> 'When my Antosha reached forty he went a bit odd as well,' said Ludmilla Platonovna, returning to the subject of husbands . . . 'But after a year he settled down and moved on to the next stage in his life.'

I wonder. Will I get to settle down and move on once I'm forty-one? I know the author a little so I ask him about this strangely apposite passage. 'I had seen this happen to older friends and acquaintances who suddenly started doing absurd things: ruining perfect marriages, downshifting, changing sexual orientation, committing suicide,' Akunin said. 'As for my own experience: at forty I started writing a thick volume on the history of writers' suicide; at forty-one I returned to childhood by becoming an author of adventure novels; at forty-four I quit my job and have never worked since. I feel much younger, stronger and healthier now than when I was forty.'

So that's what this is all about. Midlife crisis. Typical. Most guys would get to ride a Harley and a twenty-three-year-old gym instructor from Basingstoke. I get to sit on the floor and do breathing exercises.

I wonder how far back you have to go to find the earliest

mention of a midlife crisis or an existential depression. I don't know *Hamlet* well, but know enough to understand that he went through it too. 'I have of late – but wherefore I know not – lost all my mirth, forgone all custom of exercise; and, indeed, it goes so heavily with my disposition that this goodly frame the earth, seems to me a sterile promontory.' And if you can't imagine what a sterile promontory looks like, believe me it's not a pretty sight.

That was written four hundred years ago. I go back even further, pull down a volume of Dante's *Divine Comedy*. It is on the shelf with Proust and Milton and all those other books I pretend to have read. I really am a dreadful show-off. Anyway, opening *The Portable Dante* at Hell, I am amazed by the opening canto:

> Midway upon the journey of our life
> I found myself within a forest dark,
> For the straightforward pathway had been lost.
> Ah me! how hard a thing it is to say
> What was this forest savage, rough, and stern,
> Which in the very thought renews the fear.
> So bitter is it, death is little more;
> But of the good to treat, which there I found,
> Speak will I of the other things I saw there.
> I cannot well repeat how there I entered,
> So full was I of slumber at the moment
> In which I had abandoned the true way.

So breakdown is Hell; depression is Purgatory; and recovery, well, recovery when it comes will be Paradise.

Perhaps I shouldn't be surprised at all the depression in books. After all, if one in four of us is to suffer mental illness in the course of a lifetime, then I suppose one in four fictional characters will as well. The proportion among authors is probably even higher, if we remember Tonio Kröger's solemn observation that 'healthy people never write, act or compose'.

Depressed parents are harder to find. In *Netherland*, Joseph O'Neill produces as fine a paragraph on the weariness of parenthood that I can find:

> If there was a constant symptom of the disease in our lives at this time it was tiredness. At work we were unflagging; at home the smallest gesture of liveliness was beyond us. Mornings we awoke into a malign weariness that seemed only to have refreshed itself overnight. Evenings after Jake had been put to bed, we quietly ate watercress and translucent noodles that neither of us could find the strength to remove from their cartons; took turns to doze in the bathtub; and failed to stay awake for the duration of a TV show.

Hans van den Broek is not alone in struggling with the demands of parenthood. Eva Khatchadourian hits the nail on the head: before you have children, it is possible to feel special about yourself, your prospects, your promise, your time. After children that sense of specialness evaporates. You are a utility, a cipher, a host, dull, plodding, there merely to serve the interests of others. 'Up until April 11, 1983,' Eva says, 'I had flattered myself that I was an exceptional person. But since Kevin's birth I have come to suppose that we are all profoundly normative.' Not for the first time, it occurs to me that depression and parenthood have much in common: a cataclysmic event, a long slog, and things getting tougher before they get easier. And it doesn't become tolerable until you properly accept and embrace your predicament.

Marcus Trescothick also struggles with the additional demands of family. Suddenly the runs he makes for England are no longer the most important thing in his world. In fact, they may be more important to thousands of people he has never even met than they are to him himself. English cricket may need his dashing strokeplay, his bucket-like hands in the slips, his occasional captaincy even, but not as much as his wife needs him in the house to help with a very young family. Clearly a decent man, he is so conflicted by these competing demands that it literally blows his mind. 'Looking back, I almost cannot believe that I managed to persuade myself that my captain's needs were greater than my wife's, that the England cricket team was more important than my family ... Staying on tour was without doubt completely and utterly the wrong thing to do. I have carried the guilt with me ever since. It almost certainly contributed to the illness that was just around the corner.'

Then there are the books on depression itself. I am drawn to these like a neurotic to a chat room. In the library I would normally drift around fiction, maybe sport and a bit of history. Now I go straight to mental health. I get them out of the library and yomp through them in hours. First up: Sally Brampton's

Shoot the Damn Dog. It's beautifully written, full of wisdom and sound advice about the benefits of yoga, walking, meditation, gardening, kindness to others, gratitude, acupuncture and, most of all, acceptance. 'If there is any lesson I have learned from depression,' Brampton starts her last – and best – chapter, 'it is this. We have to let go – of self-pity, anger and blame. We are what we are. Life is what it is. It will be what it is, however we are, and the best way to deal with it is gently. It took me a long time to learn that.'

The book is terrifying for a depression victim in the early stages of recovery. Brampton spends years battling the thing, tries to commit suicide twice and in the end I'm relieved that she actually makes it to the end of the book. Reading it makes me agitated. Do I have years of agony ahead of me too? Gwyneth Lewis's *Sunbathing in the Rain* is an easier proposition. Lewis looks on depression as an ally not an enemy, not a black dog or a shadow boxer. She says it is trying to teach you a lesson: that something in your life is very wrong and needs to be excised for you to get on and live a happy life. Its purpose, she writes, 'is to teach you how to avoid becoming depressed again. In that sense, depression is a very kind disorder, and will return only if you refuse to learn the lessons it has to teach you.'

In this way it is a friend. It forces you to remove everything in your life and then gradually reinsert things one by one until you find the thing that sets you back. That is the toxin that must be removed. I'm not sure I've found what my toxin is yet.

What do these tortured souls do to get better? I am combing their words and deeds for hints, clues, advice. I need to get better too. I've been in this thing for more than six months now; some things appear to be on the mend; the unholy trinity of insomnia, rumination and bleak moods are subsiding, but in their place I face frustration, boredom, impatience and loneliness. It seems there will be several layers to getting better. Being able to get out of the house, concentrate, read and do gentle chores again is all well and good, but what about work, a social life, some meaningful contribution to the world? Essentially, I'm still washed up here, trying to get well. Unless and until I indicate otherwise, I am always just here, washed up and trying to get well.

What to do? Esther Greenwood is enrolled as a volunteer at her local hospital, little good though it does her. In *Affinity*, Margaret Prior is signed up for visits at the forbidding Millbank gaol. Prisoner Selina Dawes immediately sees through the ruse: 'You have come to Millbank to look on women more wretched than yourself in the hope that it will make you well again.'

I'm not sure that jail-visiting or voluntary hospital work is possible, or even advisable, at this stage. But I have something far more immediate that I can do to help myself, to help Sharon, to give a little back, to make the world a slightly better place. I can start parenting again.

I am wearing pink beads and sitting on a small chair in the shape of a cat, reading a bedtime story to my daughter. She is rather too lively for my liking and I yawn. I have yawned an awful lot through my illness. I don't know why. But I seem to yawn most when I read bedtime stories. Sometimes it's just because reading out loud gets you like that. Mostly it's because I'm still exhausted. Not for the first time I wonder if we haven't got this ritual the wrong way around: she should be putting me to bed.

'Take those beads off, Daddy,' she scolds, 'you look like a girl.'

'You put them on me!' I protest.

'I didn't,' she lies.

I don't have time for this. I start reading a book about a pig who becomes a spaceman. I skip a word or two, but she's too sharp for me.

'Blast off into *outer* space,' she says.

'That's what I said.'

'No you didn't.'

'Yes I did.'

'No you didn't. You said blast off into space, and it should be blast off into outer space.'

'OK, blast into outer space.'

'Blast *off*—'

'Look, I'm not going to argue with you about this.'

'Yes you are.'

'No I'm not.'

By this time I could have finished the book and been halfway through *My Friend Walter* with the boys.

'Look, can we just get on and finish the book.'

'We can't finish it.'

'Why?'

'Because you haven't read every word.'

'Hmm?'

'If you don't read every word, you haven't finished the book.'
I suppose she is right. I read every word.

Sometimes, when I'm in a better mood, when there's light still in the sky and someone has said something kind to me recently, when there's a game of football to be played or friends to be met, or just a simple evening with Sharon at home, then I'm on better form with the bedtime reading, I promise I am. Then I might slip in extra words, silly words like 'bottom' or 'eels' and get them to guess what I've inserted. Sometimes this descends into hilarity all round, and we all laugh deeply and look at each other's laughing faces as if we want to be reminded of what a face looks like when it laughs, in case we don't see it again for a while. Those are the happy times.

The year warms up. 2010. It has a nice even ring to it. It's still cold and dark, but time is on our side now. The evenings are getting longer and, yes, you can notice it even in January if you pay enough attention. By the end of the month it will be light at five, and that makes a lot of difference if you have small children, or even if you don't.

If the onset of depression is a shiver, a shudder, a snap, a crack, then the beginning of recovery feels like that moment when you just know high pressure is building and there'll be fine weather for a few days. Something ridges across the mind, as if a batch of serotonin that got held up in traffic finally arrived to spring the jaded nightshift.

It's happened to me twice so far. The first time was at Hallowe'en, when technically I'd only been in the pits for a few weeks. We were lying on the sofa in the playroom and a delicious autumnal sun, fat and soft as butter, was lapping at the corners of the room where old nails and pen tops lurk, and I felt something imperceptible shift, like a switch changing the polarity so that everything started to circulate in the right direction again. There was a gathering at one of the neighbours' houses, all the kids together with their face paint and sorcery. The steady burble of conversation, the quizzical animation of faces across a room, the lozenges of light in the upstairs windows, the gunmetal sky twilit and constant; for a brief moment there was a feeling that things were not quite so bad.

The second time was a couple of weeks ago. I was walking to the pool to meet the family for a swim. It's a deeply unprepossessing place full of snot and other people's children. We quite like it. There's a big shallow area where Janey can bimble around, talking to fairies and pretending that she can swim, and a deeper bit for the boys to swim and jostle and wrestle and fart and shriek. Every so often, depending on the whim of a spotty teen on minimum wage, they switch on the waves and we all gasp and roar and let ourselves get biffed around until water goes up our noses and in our ears. And I'm lying there in the artificial air, with Janey pottering and darkness falling outside, and the ridge pulls its way across my mind and suddenly I'm just a little stronger, just a little steadier, and I'm right here, right now, in this moment, and it's good. And that's all I need. Tonight I will sleep. Tomorrow I will do stuff. And later on, much later on, I will get back to being me again.

*

Books and children are not the only things I can do again. I am on a bike, freewheeling around Richmond Park, taking on stokers and spokesmen, tailgating motorheads and feeling the fresh thrill of a headwind and a steep descent and a heart that has bounced into action like a puppy. I only do one lap – seven miles – and that leaves me gasping on the grass by the gate in contented exhaustion. The next day I feel a lightness of mind that I haven't felt for a long time. I'm persuaded once again that exercise is part of the solution.

I am watching television again: not too much, for it can still overload me. But that's good. It means we can savour *The Wire* and *Mad Men* over a period of months rather than bingeing. I'm enjoying food again, eating lots more than I ever did. I can approach a hearty meal with a certain appetite, a pleasure that I haven't felt for years.

I still have too much time on my hands, so I meet up with other depressed dads I have come to know. Depressed people love meeting their peers. They can compare symptoms and take heart from the fact that they are not alone. The fact that there is someone else out there going through something similar transforms the depressive's understanding of his relationship to his illness. He is no longer left to the lonely thought that this is some freak turn of nature. Instead, the illness can only be understood as a human condition.

Bill is local, and about a year further down the track than me. Although, as we always say, everyone's thing is different. Our wives have been consoling each other for months. Now he is coming up the hill for a cup of tea. We sit in the garden in the first warm sunshine of the year and compare notes. He went down about eighteen months ago, just sat in a chair for a month, off work for three months, went back, fell down again, and is now getting back to it again.

I ask him what caused his thing. 'It's difficult to pinpoint one single thing,' he says. 'It was a combination of factors that came together at a stressful point and I couldn't cope. Looking back, I think I might have been depressed before, just milder and able to cope. At the point it kicked in (from June 2008) I was in a demanding job I had grown tired of.'

Like me, Bill began to lose sleep. Like me, he began to feel overwhelmed by his work and began to secretly dread the big pieces of work that previously he had relished. He tried sleeping pills, but they only made things worse.

'There was this feeling that my life had spun out of control and there wasn't anything I could do about it. I sat on the sofa for hours, staring into space, trying to reverse the clock in my head, trying to go back and make things better.

'I call depression "the invisible curse". No one can see it. It's not like having a broken leg or a bandaged head. It doesn't feel like a real illness. You feel like a fraud taking time off work. It feels slight and pathetic when you explain the symptoms to non-sufferers.'

Bill and I agree that talking to each other helps. So does confidence that you will recover. 'Believe that you will recover and you will,' he tells me later, when we are both a lot better. 'Stick with your medication. But also try to help yourself. Don't be too hard on yourself. Take things one step at a time. Break up tasks into small, manageable chunks. Try to do at least one enjoyable thing a day, however small. Go swimming. Walk to the shops. Remind yourself of all the things you enjoy. Live in the present not the past, be aware of smells, sights, sounds, taste and touch.' I am struck by how very eloquent this illness can make people.

Nigel's story is quite different, much more tightly entwined with the changes that fatherhood brings. Nigel is a classic case of a dad depressed. It surprises me when he 'comes out'. We've had a fairly jokey thing for a while, giving good banter. I inwardly smile when I see Nigel at a local gathering. He will not let the conversation languish. He will enliven the proceedings with talk of scoring the morning school run out of ten (Thursday was minus two) or getting thrown off the River Thames for unauthorised kayaking.

This feels like the first serious conversation we've had. Nigel says that when they had their first child he felt unappreciated, unloved even, and resented it. 'It was a combination of my own need for fairly explicit demonstrations of affection and appreciation with the fact that my wife was struggling to stay upbeat with the emotional and physical trauma of the arrival of our first child. Broadly, I interpreted anything other than laughter and delight as dissatisfaction with me, so if you add the sheer effort of combining jobs and kids you end up with a slow and unrecognised descent into gloom. All when everything's meant to be great.'

Nigel says there was a clash between how he wanted to be – light-hearted, fun and relaxed – and what he became – dark, grumpy, inflexible, anxious. 'I found myself thinking a lot that this wasn't what I had in mind for myself, that I didn't even very much like myself in my home circumstances.' A marital crisis ensued and they were both prescribed antidepressants. 'Antidepressants helped. My GP very quickly picked up that my light-hearted explanation was a feeble gloss from a struggling bloke.' Nigel says he felt very alone at the time, unable to find peers to confide in: 'I got the impression that the darker side of parenthood wasn't a welcome topic among my dad peer group – it was easy to end up sounding like a downer, and a bit disloyal.'

I commiserate and tell him it all sounds very familiar to me. In fact, Nigel's revelation is making me wonder if my own descent into depression started around the time I first became a parent. 'Early parenthood sucks,' Nigel says. 'There's nothing to be said for lack of sleep, the fact that you simply cannot adequately cover the needs of work, partner, kids and self, the fact that both partners cannot help but feel they're getting the worst of it.' His words remind me of the grumpy old cliché I had become before I fell ill. A bedraggled dad, grumbling about everything, with cheap hair and pink, disastrous eyes, scudding around looking for half-empty glasses to knock over. A night out, once something to anticipate with glee, was now a brave grimace, an effort to get ready at the worst time of day (between five and seven in the evening, when small children disintegrate), a chore to listen to people talking about tedious things (their children, mostly) in an uninteresting venue somewhere.

I'd come to hate birthdays and Christmas. I hated the pointless gimcrack stuff people bought for me and for each other. I seemed to have become someone who got penknives and torches as birthday gifts, even though I've never whittled anything in my life, and am quite happy in the dark. As for Christmas, I dreaded the presents that everyone would get that seemed to serve little purpose other than to sustain another brief wave of false jollity and keep the economy lurching forwards. Christmas was just one long road trip to show off the children, who were invariably sick or hysterical or both. Summer holidays were no longer holidays but just the same old grind at a different, slightly less convenient venue. Weekend gatherings revolved around the kids, and once they were in bed everyone was too knackered to enjoy themselves. Everything was a sigh or a grunt. Even when Sharon bought me a piano for my birthday one year, my first reaction was to think, 'Oh God, who's put that thing there? That's another thing I'll have to deal with.'

The wider world offered few crumbs. Democracy was a vapid, venal waste of time; elections predictable and immaterial. Football was a beautiful game ruined by rich men and vulgarians; pop music was emptier than ever, ransacked by ignorant chancers and their idiotic TV talent contests, so reduced that an entire vocabulary of chords was in danger of becoming extinct. Cars were ruining cities; supermarkets were ruining high streets. Al-Qaeda had ruined faith, celebrities were ruining culture, food giants were ruining food and the cult of beauty and appearance was poisoning values. Television was derelict, cinema was impossible with small kids in tow, alcohol was too cheap. The honours system rewarded sycophants and tyrants. I swore at motorists and radio phone-in participants. But more than that: there was nothing to *be* any more, other than a dad: a short, dull palindrome, uninteresting whichever way you look at it. I measured life not in what I had, which was considerable, but in what was lost. Saturday nights out, spontaneity, me-time, mates. Everything became goal-oriented and functional: the car, the kitchen, the weekly shop, even sex. I'd become someone who, five years earlier, I would have openly mocked.

Three forty-something guys, three very different things. But what we all have in common: we have gone through a metamorphosis, a reinvention of who we are. And in order to do it we had to endure a painful disintegration of who we were. Caterpillars becoming butterflies.

There are more and more things I can do. There is my Sharon, still toiling away with the kids like Ilya Repin's *Troika*, still loving me however unlovable I have become. I start to love her back. We curl up in the warm, quiet embrace of our winter weekends, play board games, cook for the children, move bedrooms around just for a change. We are sleeping in the same bed again. That's another small step back towards restoration. She takes half-term off to redecorate a room, we go out for walks and reassurance. I buy her flowers, she cooks for me on our anniversary. I even take charge of minor situations; I forbid her from driving the kids off to her parents for the weekend after she's had a particularly onerous week. Instead, I go out with them for the afternoon – the first time I've done a 'me and three' thing for months.

There is my garden, where I dig and sow and water and shuffle about pleasantly. I have never been into gardening and I get the impression that my bedraggled plants don't like me very much. I learned little from my mum and her green fingers. She would take great pride in serving meals that were almost totally from the garden. My sisters and I just thought it was wrong.

'Why don't you just buy it in the shops?'

'It's different, things taste better.'

'Still tastes like potatoes and tomatoes to me.'

Now I'm starting to get it.

Our garden is tiny, but I decide surreptitiously to annex a side passageway that runs up alongside the house. It is muddy and marginal and full of brambles and fox poo. I dig it over, compost all the weeds, make some manure tea from all the horse dung out on the street, plant some seed potatoes which burst forth within days. It's like my own little allotment. I sift out compost with an old sieve and take a strange, primitive delight in the alchemy of it all. My daughter helps by fishing out worms and snails with her chubby little fingers, storing them in a small cup.

'Why hasn't it got a eye [sic]?' she asks, holding up a snail.

'Snails don't have eyes,' I reply.

'Why?'

'They have antennae instead, which help them see.'

'Why?'

'It's just the way they are made.'

'Who made them?'

'Er, God?'

'Why?' And so it goes on until she accidentally drops it on the floor with a sickening crack. 'Uh oh.'

I decide it's time for the lemon tree to graduate to the great outdoors. It's a big moment for us both. Technically, I know it'll be OK. It's a tree. Trees are for outdoors. But I keep an eye on it all the same, make sure there are no frosts about to unfurl down from the north. It needs to stay in shade for a couple of weeks because the brightness might induce a shock. But once it's up there on the top level of the garden in the mild spring sunshine, it thanks me with a spectacularly joyful outbreak of blossom, some vigorous new growth and several new fruit. All the older lemons are still green, which seems odd. But apparently you can use them. The fruit is ready. The glossy yellow finish is just for show.

And there, lost for so long that I forgot where I put it, is music. I am downloading Florence and the Machine and Nick Drake and an outrageous Herbie Hancock tune called 'People Music', which probably sums up everything I love in music: startling, jazzy but accessible too and with a groove that just makes me move around the kitchen like it's 1975. Music is reaching me again. There's a nice little Jamie Cullum ditty that I work out on the piano and belt out when no one is around: 'I'm all over it now, I can't say how glad I am about that.' It's premature of course, but it feels good. In a quiet, unguarded moment I noodle my way through the song, the song I dare not even mention, its minor sixths and sevenths, trying to master the left-hand rhythms. And I whisper, to no one in particular, 'Is that all there is?'

It isn't. The hardest thing about recovery is that it is not linear. In the beginning there are no good days. Then, just occasionally, one or two. Then whole weeks when you feel almost normal. But interspersed are great pulses of the illness when you're as bad as ever and still sitting on floors or beds staring at the same old walls, thinking yourself into a corner from which it's impossible to think yourself out. This is more bewildering than the early weeks and months. The swings are so wild that on a good day you don't just feel good, you feel enormous, vaster than the sky, capable of everything and anything, hungry for foods and books and new friendships and good times and action. You overdo it. And so a bad spell sets in. When it does, it feels ten times worse by comparison. This jagged curve of a recovery is so baffling that psychiatrists say it is actually more common for depressed people to kill themselves during this phase than during the depths of the illness itself. Often the ups and downs chase each other through a single day. You can wake up feeling strong, checking yourself and finding blank spaces where the symptoms used to be, and you start thinking phew, today could be a good day. Today might not be all about depression. Then you can be hanging out the washing, or dressing a small child and it suddenly barges in, an *accès de faiblesse,* an unexpected front, some weakness in the legs perhaps or a sudden rumble of anxiety and an obnoxious plunge that ruins the entire morning. What the sufferer needs at times like these is something hard and fast, something incontrovertible that will convince his slippery mind that progress has been made, that it's not going to go on for ever, that he is getting better.

It was time to study the chart.

12

The chart

This is the century of data. Everything can be digitised, reduced to a long string of 1s and 0s, quantified, mapped, reduced, charted. And every chart, every dataset tells a story. Sometimes I find it mesmerising, fascinating, brilliant. Maybe this way we will eventually come to understand everything about everything. Every pattern, every story, every intrigue will be searchable, zippable and unzippable; people who know how to search, compress, unzip, extract, interrogate and extrapolate will be storytellers of the future. But at other times it's frightening. Where do they put all this data? And if it continues to increase at an increasingly increasing rate, how much data will there be by 2020? Presumably this sentence will live on digitally somewhere, but where? And for whom?

When humanity has run its course and a superspecies of the future is sifting through the billions of exabytes of data that we leave behind, they might find a small Excel spreadsheet created by a data nerd that tells a story of its own. It was my GP, Dr Burnie, who suggested more as an afterthought one day that it might be a good idea to score myself daily, to try to mark objectively how well I felt. Then, during a bad patch, when you've lost your foothold and the avalanche is coming, there will be firm tufts of data to cling to. I took it seriously.

I scored myself out of 100 on general overall feeling, four times a day: first thing, morning, afternoon and evening. There were some fairly useful demarcations. Anything below 50 meant I was struggling. Below 40 meant the anxiety was growling and I'd be sleeping poorly. Sub 30 scores were indicative of universal bleakness of mood. And any single figure scores meant I was probably a danger to myself. These were mercifully few. On the bright side, a 60 probably meant I was OK, but probably still ruminative and/or sleeping poorly. 70+ indicated a broader serenity and a dab of colour. Above 80 meant I was feeling good, hearty, vigorous. And 100s meant there was a total absence of all symptoms.

I tried to be objective, but it would be perverse to argue that a 70 today would be the same feeling as it was in October 2009. Then, a 70 was bliss, a marvellous pulse of relief. Nowadays I'm pissed off if I get a 70. It means something isn't quite right.

It didn't stop there. I devised moving averages that would tell me how well the past week, fortnight and month had been. I

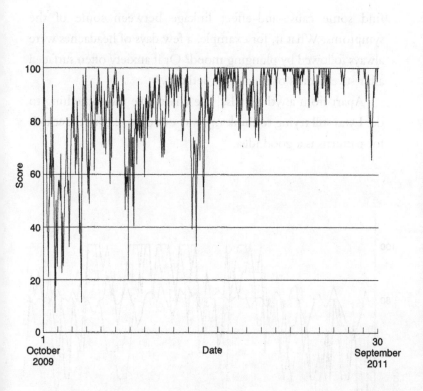

The chart

broke it down still further, scored my eight main symptoms out of 100 once a day, and used the composite to help guide the daily scores. And then, in a simple spreadsheet, I set up graphs to compare and contrast some of these scores.

It was a search for patterns, a quest for some kind of correlation, say between overexertion and insomnia, or between lethargy and mood. I was looking to make sense of it all, trying to work the growing database into narratives. Maybe I might find some cause-and-effect linkage between some of the symptoms. What if, for example, a few days of headaches were always followed by plunging mood? Or if anxiety often surfaced after several days of tinnitus or lethargy?

Apart from anything else, the chart gave me something to do. I was still trying to think my way out of it all. But the search for patterns is a good idea.

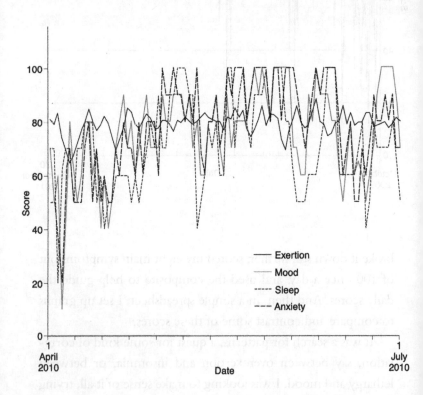

And patterns there were. A dip would often be signposted by mild headaches, early waking or a general lassitude. Then the sleep score would crash, closely followed by anxiety, rumination and mood. Mood scores would recover first, then the anxiety and rumination would fade. Sleep would always be the last thing to restore itself. I became watchful for the tell-tale signs. In the broader flow of things, a natural cycle of peaks and troughs emerged. I calculated the time span between the tops and bottoms of the curve and found that peaks and troughs occurred roughly every two weeks. That meant that, broadly, there was a good week followed by a bad week. Interspersed were occasional episodes, downphases of two or three weeks in which the going got tough. The gap between these lengthened. Average scores lilted upwards. There was a trend, and though it was spiky and slippery there was just about enough there to hold on to. Now, when the waters rise and it starts to get choppy, there is something of an anchor. It doesn't always grip, but it does start to undermine the relentless propaganda of the raging mind. 'I'll never get better,' Marko moans. 'Yes you will,' Roxy replies, 'because on 19 November things were equally bleak, but by 22 November you were steady again.'

Of course, I should have known there would be apps and internet sites that would do all this for me. Moodtracker lets you plot mood (high and low) against sleep and medication changes, all in lovely colourful pink and purple bar charts that seem designed to uplift. There are addictive chat rooms in which people discuss how awful they feel and give each other advice like 'Diet plays an important role', and 'Keep taking the medicine!'

I am often struck by the conclusions that people jump to on these forums. They say things like 'I took sleeping pills for one night, but gave up because they messed with my mood.' But how do they know the sleeping pills affected mood, when there are so many other variables in play? The biggest debates revolve around antidepressants, simply because they are so damned unpredictable. One chat-roomer says he's going to dump them after three days because they don't work. Another implores him to continue because they take time and work eventually. I come to the conclusion that both could be wrong. Without a very large set of data, it's pretty difficult to say anything hard and fast about this illness. During my early weeks on antidepressants I remember envying people who had been on them for months rather than weeks. The general consensus was that there was little uplift in the initial phases – indeed, some people report feeling a lot worse (though of course that may be just the depression flapping its wings a little harder). But many people reported that after eight, ten, twelve weeks they felt more like themselves again. My chart appears to indicate the same thing. Some sceptics make the point that if antidepressants are such a panacea, why don't they work instantly? I believe an answer may lie in the fact that it takes time for them to build up in the bloodstream. The one I take, Citalopram, has a half-life of three days. That means that in three days' time there will be half of it left in your bloodstream. Plus of course around two-thirds of the one you took two days ago and around four-fifths of the one you took yesterday. And so the drug starts to build. I calculated that for someone taking 40mg a day, this will mean that they will peak at just under 200mg in the bloodstream at any time. But, crucially, they won't hit that peak until about three weeks in. This is why, when you come off these drugs, you are advised to taper very slowly.

Data isn't always the answer. It isn't always faithful. Some things are still analogue. And you can read too much into charts. They can be subjective, skewed or wicked, tell you stories that are not helpful. You could be sitting pensively looking at weeks and weeks of top-notch scores, and tell yourself, 'Right, better brace myself for a relapse.' That can become a self-fulfilling prophecy.

Sacha Khan wasn't convinced. He saw the chart as judge-mental, even unkind at times. I would print it off and dutifully show him how the last week had been. He would frown at my low scores and ask if that wasn't adding insult to injury. Wasn't I in danger of compounding the thing by drawing graphs that reminded me of how poorly I was? When things were going well, I couldn't see his point. When they collapsed again, I could.

But I never gave up totally on the chart. It's still going strong.

I have always been something of a chartist, a data geek. It goes back to those long hours staring in fascination at my dad's digital clock. After a while I got bored of that. It was all too predictable. You knew what numbers were going to come up. I wanted something a little more random.

I found it buried in the graveyard of the BBC's summer

programming schedule. Quite by accident, in fact. In those days, television pretty much shut down after the lunchtime blast of *Mr Benn* or *Fingerbobs*. But I must have had nothing to do, because I left it on and then there was some groovy calypso music and then a close-up of a board of glossy, curvy white numbers on a black background. These numbers would flop over every now and then, and sometimes revert back to 0, at which point they would begin another slow crawl up the scale. I had no idea what it was all about, but it seemed to be related to the antics of some men in white clothing. After a while I worked out that one set of numbers on the right appeared to belong to a tall young man with a halo of golden curls. The numbers on the left related to another man, stouter, with a droopy moustache. Each time they ran the board moved in a complex ballet of numbers. Of course I knew about cricket. My dad was a fan, and both my grandfathers were pretty good, apparently. But I never really got it until that afternoon with the numbers clicking over on a scoreboard. From that day until this I've been hooked. Not just by the numbers, but by the rolling narrative of the five-day game that weaves in and out of my summers like a soap opera or a news story. I know when depression has got me again: I have to turn off *Test Match Special*.

Originally, it was all about the data. When I played I would maintain a notebook of scores, averages and charts. They tell their own story. In the early years, 20 was a mammoth individual score and some sides would be all out for 13. Wickets were so easy to get that bowlers would come off with figures like 7 for 4, the equivalent of scoring ten goals in a football match. I coloured my bar graphs, and luxuriated in the fact that my batting average was higher than my bowling average (the hallmark of a good all-rounder) even though both were under 10. By the mid-eighties we were getting bigger and stronger, and usually someone got a 50 in every match. But I had never scored one until one afternoon in Winchester, when it was so hot that no one really cared. The glass was half empty: England had been hammered by the West Indies again. I was struck then – and now – by the strange, self-defeating habit of supporting a team, investing more of my own personal pride in a bunch of men I had never met than I did in my own performance. In 1986 I couldn't hit the ball at all for the first half of the summer; then one day, when the sun came out, it just clicked and I couldn't stop scoring. The next summer I was hitting the ball so well that I needed to change the scale on the Y-axis. But bowling was getting harder. I bowled to several players who went on to enjoy careers as professionals. Once the ball fizzed straight back past my ear and hit the sightscreen without bouncing. I began to realise that cricket would only ever be a hobby for me.

There were other charts too. My dad would bring home a weekly record-sales stats sheet from EMI. I would catalogue them all in a red foolscap book, and work out from sales data where a single might place in the following week's Top 20. I was fascinated by outliers like 'Karma Chameleon' and 'Blue Monday'. And I was infuriated when great records sold modestly and modest records sold greatly. Come year-end, I would be able to calculate pretty accurately which singles were the heaviest sellers of the year, and pass the information around like the valuable currency it was.

Drawing up lists was a particular obsession at school. I still have a small vocabulary book adapted into a book of charts. After about three pages of *la fenêtre*: window, *la porte*: door, *la bicyclette*: bicycle it morphs into Top 20 Albums of All Time, Top 10 Friends, Top 10 Bands I Liked Before They Were Famous, Top 10 TV Programmes (1984), Top 10 Girls I Fancy Who Don't Fancy Me. Later, with a nod to a gathering sense of academic maturity, there were Top 10 Dictators and Top 5 Universities, though the latter on a university application form managed to offend at least three august institutions by not putting them first.

There is another graph I am inevitably drawn to. It charts the rhythm of life, the stupendously regular motions of the heavens. It is a curve that not only describes time, light and season, but appears to move in sympathy with the pattern of light and shade on the earth. It is a wave that has repeated itself since the beginning of time, an infinitely congruent shape that goes on and on for ever. It is the curve of sunrise and sunset.

At the back of my mind lurks an unpleasant thought: that this illness is not some cataclysm of the present, but a visceral rejection of the cadences of the year. I began to falter during that period after the summer solstice when we first perceive that there will not be light evenings for ever. There's always a week in July when some great pessimist says, 'Ooh, isn't it feeling autumnal all of a sudden.' The sunset curve was starting to fall sharply, and so was I. My descent closely mirrored the falling daylight hours, which tumble really quite dramatically from mid-August through to the end of October. The truly dreadful spell culminated at the winter solstice; it wasn't until the vernal equinox that I began to feel more human again. So what if . . . I've read a lot about seasonal affective disorder. No one really thinks that's what it is. But if it is . . . I have to do this

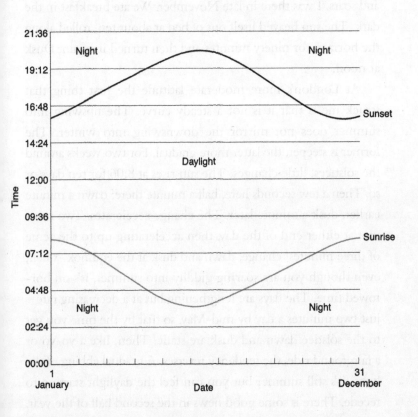

every winter. That thought alone is enough to start the anxiety churning again. I dismiss it out of hand. And then start plotting.

You come across some interesting, even dramatic, things when you look at sunrise and sunset times, provided you don't live on the equator, of course. I once went to the Russian Arctic, where the annual interchange of light and darkness is enough to drive you mad. The light–dark curve really swoops and soars. I was there in late November. We ate breakfast in the dark. The sun heaved itself out of bed at about ten, rolled along the horizon for ninety minutes and then turned in again. Dusk at noon.

At London's more moderate latitude the first thing that struck me is that it is not a steady curve. The upswing into summer does not mirror the downswing into winter. The former is steeper, the latter more gradual. For two weeks around the solstices, little changes. The sun rises at 8:06 for ten days or so. Then a few seconds here, half a minute there; dawn a minute earlier, dusk a minute later. The change accelerates. Two minutes at either end of the day, then accelerating up to the acme of three minutes' change, dawn and dusk at the equinox. Then, even though you are soaring giddily into summer, it's on borrowed time. The days are lengthening but at a decreasing rate – just two minutes a day by mid-May, so that by the time you get to the solstice dawn and dusk are static. Then, like a yo-yo or a fairground ride, the tendency reverses. A gradual ebbing of the light. It's still summer but you can feel the daylight starting to recede. There is some good news in the second half of the year.

Just as the vernal equinox marks the point at which daylight stops increasing at a growing rate, so the autumnal equinox stops the acceleration of the night. It slows down all the way to December. After Christmas, you can congratulate yourself: it's getting lighter again. By Epiphany the darkest month of the winter is already behind you.

I've asked experts in seasonal affective disorder whether it is worse at some latitudes than at others. The science is odd. In America, there is much more SAD in a state like Maine than in Florida. But in Europe the pattern is far more mixed. Finns do not suffer as they should for a people marooned above the sixtieth parallel. Perhaps it's all that vodka. I've been to Helsinki twice. In July it did not get dark. In December, it barely got light. I still haven't decided which is the more disturbing.

I think if I'd done my chart for the past ten years it would have stuck close to the sunrise–sunset curve. Maybe even preempting it a little. I grind through winter, heaving great sighs at the long hours that must be spent indoors doing Noddy jigsaw puzzles and singing 'Wind the Bobbin Up'. I get excitable in March, earlier even, at the rebirth of the year, the promise of summer. Blossom. As a child I would barely notice it. Now I marvel at it like it's something from another planet. Sometimes spring is even a little too much, all that restive energy and so little focus for it all. Inexplicably there is a lull in mid-spring. I've had some bad Aprils in my time. Yes, it's light at eight in the evening. But it can be a forlorn light, when it is cool and wet. May to July is the glorious season, but by late June there is definitely a sense of change in the air. It's a time of year that always coincided with change: end of term, year groups breaking up amid lifelong promises; holidays, drift and disintegration. August is just awful. It seems to mark an end to everything good about the year. October has been kind to me; it gives me a birthday and usually plenty of bonus sunshine to wash over it. There is a sense that all is not lost. But then: November. What a month. Sickness. Skies so low you can touch them – if you can see through the gloaming and mizzle and general low pressure that sloshes over everything like dishwater. No wonder we have Bonfire Night. People were probably trying to set fire to themselves.

I speak to Dr John Sharp, a Harvard psychiatrist and an expert in the 'emotional calendar', about the effect of the year's seasonal cycle on the psyche. His theory is that the patterns of the calendar influence our emotional state in three major ways. The first he calls the 'physical realm' – the play of light, temperature and humidity. The uplifting effect of light on the retina. Excessive heat and humidity make us lethargic. So far, so good.

The second is 'seasonal expectation'. This is the notion that Christmas is fun, that the new football season is exciting, that the *rentrée* of autumn has a whiff of freshness about it, and that 23 November is almost always a dull, dismal, dark day on which it would be great to be a hedgehog.

The third he terms 'event anniversary' and, surprisingly,

says this is the most powerful factor of all. There is something hardwired in us that reacts, consciously and subconsciously, when the year loops around and approaches a time on which something significant happened to us. It can even be triggered by something as ephemeral as the angle of light through the trees, or the kind of food we eat at that time of year.

'It's a survival mechanism,' Dr Sharp says of this subtle animal instinct for the natural cadences of our year. 'Our brains are wired to categorise and cross-reference all the sensory aspects of the seasons. It helps us to know what is likely to be a problem.'

We don't have to be victims of our emotional calendars. Simple tricks like light boxes can help us deal with the physical changes of the season. Event anniversary can be overridden if we take action to demonstrate to ourselves that certain times of year don't have to be dominated by the events of the past. Dr Sharp cites the example of an acquaintance whose mother died at Christmas. The festive season became an annual chore for her – until her fiancé proposed. 'We're rebranding Christmas,' he told her.

'In psychiatry we are starting to take a look at preventive medicine,' Dr Sharp continues. 'Once upon a time, doctors treated problems after they came up. Then we got preventive medicine which has really come in over the past fifty years. But in psychiatry it's only very recently that we have started to do prevention.' For me, he suggests it might be a good idea to do something positive, something assertive when my first anniversary pulls into view later this year.

I think I need to do more than that. I need to decouple, detach my sense of well-being from the inevitable passage of the seasons. I can't change them. I have been too sensitive to daylight and nightfall, summer and winter for too long. So convinced that winter will be dismal, that it invariably is; heaping so much expectation that the heady days of summer will be magical that they can't fail to disappoint.

A day is a day. Forget university research that tells us every year how awful 24 January is. You can have a good 24 January and a rotten birthday. A disappointing summer and a riotous autumn. You might die on Christmas day.

By the spring of 2010 the chart had settled down. Averages were inching above 70. The graph had stopped behaving like a lie-detector at a poker tournament. I jiggled idly with some cells and tried to predict the future. I created a fat 'trend line' that predicted that it would all be over by June. There were still occasional blips that belied the upward trend. I ignored them.

We went away for a weekend for the first time, to see the outlaws. I love going to stay with the outlaws. We sit around a lot and make jokes about the people on TV. We go to garden centres and buy doughnuts for twenty-nine pence. The kids all sleep in the same room. Someone is always making the next cup of tea. The graph gave a little sneeze but settled back into the groove, happy to generate as many 80s and 90s as I needed.

We thought nothing of it. I was becoming impatient for the next thing, the next level on the recovery circle.

'I want to go back to work,' I told Wilko. He agreed. 'You can only get so well sitting around at home,' he said. 'The last little bit of recovery normally comes when you get back into the routine of normal working life.'

13

Relapse

I don't quite know how I've got here.

I am standing in front of the mirror, rested, shaven, show-
ered and scrubbed, in shirt and boxers, trying to fit into last
year's work wardrobe. It's a struggle. My thighs meet in the
middle now. They never used to. In the last six months my
physique has skipped on a couple of decades. After forty years
of eating, finally I can no longer see my ribcage. I'm more than
thirteen stone, compared to just under ten when I last shuffled
out of the office. I will need new clothes.

I will need new clothes because I am going back to work.
It feels like the first day at a new job. I am nervous, ready too
early, dialling up and down the radio, listening to news just in

case I hear something oblique, something that captures my imagination. That's where ideas come from. In the past six months you could count the number of ideas I have had on the finger of one finger. It's like using old muscles again. They feel limber, ready for action. I am buoyant with the kids. They seem surprised. 'Where are *you* going,' asks Edward, as if he's the father and I'm the child. 'Work. Daddy's going back to work.' A pause. 'What is your work?'

I can barely remember. Work seems remote, distant, like a country I once visited in the eighties or a dead person whose face I can no longer remember. I spend a few punishing moments rehearsing some of the negative thoughts that still linger: they won't have missed me, there won't be a seat – or a role – for me, things will have moved on, I'll be superfluous, out of touch with both the news agenda and the fast-moving technology that seems to revolutionise our business every three months or so. I'll be out of the loop. Editors don't just need to be in the loop, they need to be the loop. It's what they are: loopy news-traffic controllers. It takes months to build a relationship of trust with the writers and correspondents who funnel their work through you. I will have to start from scratch.

Then there are the positives:

- I slept well. Normally, before a big day like this, I would have one of those nights when you wake repeatedly through the small hours having dreamed that you have already done the thing that you are apprehensive about. Not this time.

- I feel good. Not just surviving or so-so but formidable and light. I jig around, shadow boxing at Sharon as she dresses. 'Get off,' she says. 'I think I preferred you ill.' See – we can joke about it now. I must be getting better. There are few symptoms left. A bit of nervous excitement, perhaps, but no swooning or panic or anxiety or melancholy or tinnitus or digestive problems or headaches or lethargy.

- I am proud of myself. For long months I never thought I'd make it, and yet here I am. I am recovering the life I loved and lost.

I've been warned to expect a bumpy ride. A colleague who has suffered something similar tells me of numerous false starts in trying to get back to work. Several people have asked me if I'm going for it a little too soon. Six months is nothing for an illness that counts in lifetimes. I take the first train that has seats to spare and sidle down to the Tube at Vauxhall. Did you know that Tsar Nicholas II was so impressed with Vauxhall station that he made the Russian word for station '*vokzal*'? I'm not really sure what he saw in the place. It must have looked a lot grander in the 1890s. I pop up in the tangled knot of concrete and clapboard corridors that is King's Cross. I have read the paper. Gordon Brown is accused of being a bully. Floods devastate Madeira. Oh, and the Pope thinks airport body scanners are a violation. I walk very fast down York Way, crossing as usual by The Fellow, only it's not as usual at all.

Now I am approaching the wavy glass frontage of King's Place. It's a journey I have made hundreds of times, but today it feels a little surreal. In one sense it's like I've never been away, but there is a quickening in my throat and a slight ringing in my ears. Can I do this? People I know have seen me; how many times will I have to briefly and inadequately sum up the past six months when people ask after me? 'Pretty tough/rough, hopefully over the worst/not quite out of the woods yet/just part-time for now/good to be back/don't quite know how I pulled through.' I've imagined this moment – entering the building, approaching the news desk – so many times; how I'd speak to so-and-so if I met them on the escalator; how I'd react if someone else had my desk; a feeling of fear mixed with triumph. There were so many times when I never thought I'd get this far.

People are kind. Someone fetches coffee. Someone else ushers me back to my seat, the desk at which I lost it six months earlier. I spend a gentle hour maundering through news wires and websites. I wander into our open morning conference to hear what's on the collective mind of the *Guardian* staff at the start of another week. Thereafter there are huddles and stories and news lists and checkpoints and conferences. The show goes on. But in another sense, everything is different. I can't undo the last six months. I'm always going to be wary about doing this. I tread very carefully.

I'm going to be leaving at lunchtime for the next few weeks. That's OK. In the afternoons I can concentrate on having a very quiet time. But after day one I have difficulty sleeping again. I can't lie on my left side because my heart is trying to get out of my chest, protesting about the exertions of the day. The ringing in my right ear is quite spectacular. I decamp to the pull-out bed in the spare room. The next day I am dull. I am only going in to the office on alternate days, so I scowl about at home, digging mud and pruning vengefully.

My second day in the office is hard. I can't concentrate and have nothing to say when we discuss the news agenda and big exclusives we could get. I think of all the mental illness that is going unreported. When we write about a bomb attack in Kabul, or the blockade of Gaza; when we write about soldiers waging war or dictators locking up their enemies; when we cover natural disasters and relate the epic scale on which nature sometimes operates: in all these situations there is not the time or space to broach the enormous knock-on effect on mental health. A million Americans tried to commit suicide last year. A million. These are the stories I want to read. Sadly, there doesn't seem to be broad enough appeal to sell them to a wider audience. Unless a story has an obvious dynamic and nice tumescent hook – recession causes increase in depression, or antidepressant prescriptions rise tenfold in a decade, for example – it will struggle to appeal to safe, conservative editors. But what of the hundreds of thousands who kill themselves every year? Or the statistic that says that suicide is the most common cause of death in British men under thirty-five? I know what I want to do, what I need to do. I need to write about this. I need to write about this thing, write something that would have helped me, something that would have made me realise that suicide is never an option, it is just the momentary expression of despair that soon passes. And when it does pass, man, you'll want to be alive to experience how wonderful it is to get a second chance, a reprieve from a death sentence, your life in your hands once again.

My sleep is still fitful. I keep waking up with a heart-stopping jolt. I go back to sleeping in the spare room. A better night ensues. By the end of my first week I'm congratulating myself. I write a note to myself in my diary:

A big pat on the back. So many times when I thought I'd never be able to get near the building, let alone sit down, think cogently and contribute. I need to stabilise at this level then take it further. Here's my post Xmas recovery schedule:

Sleep without Zopiclone: end Dec
Get off Lorazepam: mid Jan
Rid of most desperate symptoms: mid Jan
Start back at work: March
Comfortably handle half days: mid March?
Comfortably handle full days: mid April?
Come off Mirtazapine: May
Crack sleep totally: June
Come off Citalopram: March 2011?

Before I've finished writing it, I know the list is problematic. Depression is not that linear. Just look at the chart. It will not like being frogmarched through a strict timetable like this. It will protest. It may revolt.

The *Guardian* is full of fine people but like any newsroom it's a tough place to do your convalescing. Everyone is sharp, fast and zippy; conversations last nine seconds; a good idea now is forgotten in ten minutes; people are not always clear about what they want, often because they don't really know what they want; the pinball news desk is full of battered ball bearings; I idly wonder why I fell down the hole marked '0' and no one else did. I think some of my colleagues have had the same thought.

This is not specific to the *Guardian*, but to news organisations. News is an impatient master. A newsroom knows only two states: crisis mode and before-the-next-crisis mode. Neither is easy. In crisis mode, everyone is always-on, too few people stretched across too much territory, an electric charge in the air that we're somehow missing something, not being quite clever enough, don't have quite enough people in Jakarta or Devizes or both. Every crisis has its news arc, though, and will sooner or later taper off into resolution, hiatus or indifference. Then before-the-next-crisis mode kicks in. In some ways this is even harder. There is no sense of what or where the story is. Reporters must dig harder to find something good. Editors must grope ever more frantically down the back of the internet to try to find something worth building up. Theoretically this should be the period for people to recharge, take a break, leave the office at five, have a good scratch, soft pedal a bit, decompress. That would be a good way of avoiding staffers having, say, nervous breakdowns. But no one does. No one coasts; it's a tough business, a tough market.

The internet has made it harder. Twenty years ago, when I started out, there was less information to make sense of. The world was finite. It was just about possible for a single human brain to get around all the international news stories that were potentially publishable on any given day. Your competitors' stories were things to read tomorrow; occasionally you'd kick yourself for missing something; more often than not you'd manufacture some contempt at the paucity of their offering. And move on. Getting a proper story was also more straightforward. It was laborious, because you couldn't just cut and paste someone else's quotes from a website, but it was easier to produce something fresh precisely because no one had read it six times on the internet already. Most of the piece would be constructed around conversations you had actually had with real people. And they felt more alive because of it.

Internet-era deadlines have become absurd, a diabolical invention designed to drive purveyors of news mad. It was far easier to pull together a grand synthesis of a snapshot in time – an evening deadline for a daily paper – than to constantly revise, rewrite and respond to the Twitter-era stream of disembodied words that gush forth from the digital machine. Perhaps I've just done my time. Perhaps twenty-somethings see things very differently. They're very young, aren't they, twenty-somethings?

Anyway, it took precisely five weeks for me to fall over again. I hadn't even got up to working full days. I was full of the excitement of news again. Iraq elections too close to call! North

Koreans sink South Korean boat! Lindsay Lohan back in rehab! All that news and only one pair of eyes. I went home at the end of the week with that familiar feeling of knowing something about everything but nothing about anything.

That night there is a random programme about the origins of synthpop buried on BBC2 or BBC4, one of those programmes that make you think you must be one of only about eight people in the country watching it. Everyone else missed a treat: giddy footage of Bowie and Japan and Kraftwerk and Sparks that is simply irresistible. I go to bed with my head fuller than ever.

I awake with a jolt. It is quite a start – like a heart-attack victim getting defibrillated. 23:30. The solo from 'Do the Strand' is on endless repeat in my head. I can't shake it out. I go upstairs, flail around. Sleep fitfully. The next night is worse. I lie, fidgeting, turning and turning in the widening gyre; staring into the darkness. It is tremendously hard not to think, 'Oh no! It's happening all over again. I'll never be properly better. It's just going to keep coming back at me again and again.' Every time I ask 'Is that all there is?' back comes the answer: 'NO!'

It's Easter that is ruined this time. We go to Glendene. There is an Easter-egg hunt for the kids, and a roast, and lots of alleluias at church. But I am going down, sinking fast and can barely endure people speaking to me. I cry so hard at my mum that one of my eyelids turns inside out. I do manage a walk in the woods after lunch, when I tell her I just want a normal life. Why can't I have a normal life? I have booked for Sharon and me to go and stay with Debug in Hong Kong in June. Trying to make something of her fortieth birthday. Now those tickets will be wasted. I will be washed up at home, sitting, staring. A summer, a whole glorious summer will be lost and I will have to grind out another winter and . . .

I am back on Zopiclone; I even dabble with Loraz for a day or two, but she is pissed off with me for not taking her seriously and so doesn't help. There is the wretched bureaucracy of relapse: I must tell my colleagues that I need more time. I must tell the human resources team because my sick pay is running out. I must tell my medical support, go back to costly meetings with Dr Wilkins and Sacha Khan. I am back off work and almost as washed up as I was last time around. The chart makes no sense. It was up there for weeks and weeks, flatlining in the 90s like a temperature chart of Algeria in August. Now it's just a mess. It looks like it was drawn by a child in the back seat of a car.

'Leave the chart alone for a few days,' Sharon says.

'But I can't, it's . . . '

'It's not working. It's just numbers.'

'It's helped before.'

'But it's not helping now.'

We are in the car on the way back home. A glorious April evening unfurls through the Hampshire countryside. Fat sheep amble about with no agenda. Trees burst with newly invented colours. Hollows drip with mist and new life. Sharon is doing ninety. I briefly think of opening my door and diving out. Would it do the trick? It's the last time I will think of suicide as a way out of this.

*

Recovery is hard. Yes, the pits is the worst place to be, because it's bewildering and frightening and above all else you feel wretched. But at least in the pits you know what you have to do. Just sit and be. There is nothing more for you to think about than just getting through the next five minutes. And the next. And the next. But in mid-stage recovery there are harder decisions. Power back up to full-time work or meander a while longer? Use sleeping pills for three days or seven days? Come off them sooner or later? Exercise harder or coast for a while? Book stuff, plan stuff, make arrangements or tread water? Then a bad day hits, out of the blue. And because you haven't had one for a while, it hurts like an infidelity. You wonder, 'Am I ever going to get better? Will I always be damaged?' You look around the office, at all the healthy, vigorous souls going purposefully about their business and you think, 'I want other people to get this. Just so they understand. So that more people understand why I am so frail and half-hearted and not half the man I used to be. I want other people to get this, so that I'm not the only one, so that others know what it is like driving with the handbrake on.' But then I think again, about how hideous it has been and how far I have come, and I look at my colleagues, with their plans and lives and careers and little intrigues, and I can't wish this thing on any of them.

What is this relapse? Is it a new iteration or just an aftershock? Did I actually get properly better there for a while and now it's the sequel? Or is it still the first thing and this is just an afterthought. For weeks things are bad again. It's the most gorgeous April I can remember, but it makes not one iota of difference. I am rickety and thin, sleepless and joyless and baffled at how I could have felt so well in March.

I sit on the floor and meditate. Actually I don't. I think. I think about the pyramid of recovery. On the ground floor, you are just holding out for some respite, a bit of joined-up sleep, an end to the anxiety pangs and the endless, ludicrous chatter of rumination. You tell yourself, 'If I recover, I promise I will not want so much, need so much, do so much, aspire to so much. It will be enough for me just to be myself again, without all the horror. Just me, a person, bimbling around, marvelling at flowers and skies and the changing of the seasons and the power of the sea.' But when you get to the first floor, when you are well enough to marvel at all that stuff, of course you don't. It becomes mundane. It's human nature to want more. Now you are settled of sleep, and the anxiety has gone and so has the rumination and you start to stretch yourself a little – a return to work, some vigorous exercise, a book; and slowly but surely that level becomes humdrum as well. You don't want to just turn up at work, shamble around and then go home; you want to do satisfying things, something to make the day feel like it's been worthwhile. So you do some harder days and it feels OK. You tell yourself: 'I'll be someone who comes in, works hard and then looks after himself in the downtime, to prevent relapse.' But after a while even that becomes dull. You eye up level three. People are socialising up there, taking weekends in Casablanca or Vilnius; playing in a Smiths tribute band or helping refugees. OK, you say, that's the next thing for me. A life is short, and you're dead a long time. I want more. I want travel and excitement and drinks and events and, and, and . . . And before too long you're back in the same old groove, on level six or seven, enjoying life a little too much, making all the same old mistakes. And you look down at level one and it seems a long way and you ask yourself, a croak of contempt in your voice, how you could ever have thought you could be satisfied just ambling around quietly down there. Until you fall, spectacularly and suddenly, into the pits. And boy does that hurt. It's such a long, long way down. And when you've come to your senses and grimly taken in your surroundings, you look deep into the mirror again and make another deal with yourself. Please oh please get me back to level one again. I'll settle there, this time, I promise.

There could be any number of reasons why I relapse. 'It does happen,' says Dr Wilkins, though his intonation and stress on the word 'does' suggest to me that it doesn't happen too often, that I am still something of an outlier. Perhaps we all are. It could be that it was too much work too soon. It could be that I simply went straight back to how things were and failed to change my behaviour enough to give myself a chance. I noticed how quickly I reneged on my promises: to meditate daily, to leave work at work, to walk before I could run. It could be that I hadn't actually figured out what made me ill in the first place. Wilko suggests lithium, which I thought you used to power mobile phones.

'Am I bipolar?' I blurt out.

'Well,' Dr Wilkins replies, 'you certainly don't present as

such. But lithium might help even out some of your mood swings.' I don't like it. I am not someone who has mood swings. That is not who I want to be. Roxy and Marko and mro were such even-tempered souls. I don't want any more pills. I'm at the point where I don't really believe in the medication any more.

Seeing Wilko used to make things better. This appointment has made things worse. I'm more uncertain than ever. Try as I might, I cannot rid myself of the insidious narrative: this is who I am now. I will never be free of my thing. It's always going to be out there, waiting to strike again.

I'd called Sacha Khan two weeks earlier to say thanks for everything and I hope I never see you again. Now I called him back. Sacha, I said, I think we still have some work to do.

The April relapse is not my last. Actually I don't know which was my last relapse. It might not have happened yet. Maybe it's just around the corner, next week, next month. With depression you never really know. This one lasts about six weeks. On a warm spring Saturday I have a sudden epiphany, like pulling the slate clean on an Etch A Sketch. By early May I try again. My sleep is still wayward and I tremble like an old man at times. But slowly the horror starts to dissipate. I have three good months. I build back up to full days in the office and actually start contributing. It's a good time, a World Cup summer. The lemon tree puts on a spurt, grows another six inches, bobs around in the breeze like it's good to be alive. It's a hot summer, fine for tomatoes and green beans. I'm playing football again with the Wimbledon gang, and rehearsing with my little trio. Yes, I'm doing too much, but it's exciting to be feeling so damn well again. We go to Hong Kong, which is a little scary. But it's a wonderful time with our oldest friends; we swim in the South China Sea and catch buses and taxis in the rain, play whist and sing karaoke. I puncture the hilarity of an evening by singing 'You Make Me Feel Brand New' to Sharon, which makes us cry. 'You silly, silly man,' Sharon says, but in a loving way. We fly home.

Things again come to a head towards the end of the summer, as my first anniversary pulls into view. I am on a carousel in Nîmes, bobbing up and down on a plastic horse, when I realise I may have done something stupid. My brother-in-law is standing below, grinning wickedly and holding up a copy of the *Daily Mail*, which has paid to reprint an article I have written for the *Guardian* about depression. As we merrily circle in three-four time in the shadow of the Roman amphitheatre, I catch snatches of the headline. It took three revolutions before I understand it in its entirety: 'How trying to be the perfect dad left me a shattered, helpless wreck'.

'Don't let the kids see,' I mouth at him. But it isn't the kids I am worried about.

I wrote the piece for the same reason I am writing this book. To reach people: to give them hope, to provide the story that I wanted to read when I was in the pits. But the sudden burst of interest it has generated is overwhelming. My phone is bleeping all the time: texts galore, and not just my dad with the updates from Trent Bridge. There are several requests for media appearances, follow-up pieces, Facebook overtures, and long handwritten paeans from fellow sufferers whose plight makes me wonder if I haven't actually been rather lucky. Some I find genuinely touching, others make me smile. All of them make me think, which is probably the worst course of action for someone in mid-recovery.

Experts weigh in. Depression authority Dorothy Rowe blogs about me. She writes of me: 'He did not learn everything that depression could teach him . . . Mark has not learned how to avoid becoming depressed again. Life is never without adversities. The chances are that he will become depressed again until . . . he learns the lesson that his depression can teach him.'

She wasn't wrong. Within three days of returning to work I relapsed again. That ominous quickening in the throat, a ringing in the ears, horizontals and verticals all askew, an alarming semi-detachment from everything around me, words on a screen that I just couldn't take in. That cold flush, as if you have someone else's blood in your veins. I went home for three weeks. This time the relapse comes with a new line in negative thinking. One relapse can look like a random event. Two starts to look like a pattern. I look at the chart. October, November, December, March–April, August. A pattern. Extrapolate it and you can see that I will be suffering again early in the new year. I'll take that. Grind out the relapses and enjoy the times in between, which should get longer and longer.

'He did not learn everything that depression could teach him.' Well, I tried. I tried to learn as much as I could. But it's hard, you know. Hard to know what you need to learn and what is a red herring. Hard to know what bits of me I must reform and what bits I am allowed to keep. Because, to be honest, I pretty much like the whole lot. There's none of it I really want to change. OK, I have a bent nose and dodgy knees and I'd quite like a deeper voice, so I'd change those if I could. But my character suits me just fine. I'm not someone who's always wishing they were someone else, something else. I'm pretty much fine just as I am. So just tell me the bits that I have to change and I'll change them, but let me keep the rest. Let me keep the sense of fun and the ability to love and the enjoyment of company and the thrill of anticipation. Let me keep the eye for the ball and the ear for a tune. Let me keep the family man and the diligent pro. Let me keep all that and I'll gladly tweak some of the other stuff. The over-eagerness to please; the reluctance to confront; the grumpy old man cliché; the superiority. I'll work at all that if you'll just let me be me.

What else do I need to learn, Dorothy? I haven't exactly been complacent. Now I wasn't just depressed; I was cross.

14

The onion

What caused my thing? Everyone has a different theory. Maybe you do by now.

My parents and the outlaws agree: it was my work. The evidence? Simple. My breakdown followed a period of prolonged workplace stress. And each time I venture back, I relapse. My mum has gentle words of comfort. 'There are lots of other things you can do,' she tries. 'You can even stack shelves at Sainsbury's if you need to, just while you are sorting yourself out.' My eldest sister, Julianne, wonders if it might be linked to all the terrible things I have covered as a reporter over the years. I don't like to tell her that I've never actually seen anyone so much as sprain an ankle; the most terrifying thing I ever witnessed was a Bank of England inflation report, and that was only terrifying because I had no idea what anyone was talking about. Sharon doesn't know what is to blame, but knows what she doesn't want it to be: her business. She started it six months before I became ill. We both know it has stretched an already overstretched family. My sister Carolyn thinks it is broader than that. She has three children too. I think she has always admired my parenting, but wonders if all the demands on me have taken their toll. 'You're like a swan. Calm on the surface but paddling like mad underneath.' Friends say I have been a little too serious for a little too long. Too much Mark, not enough Roxy.

As for me, I think all of the above are true. And more. But just as important as what is why. Why am I what I am? What made me the kind of person who worked too hard and half killed himself with domestic drudgery in his spare time? When did everything become such a route-march, and not just when but why? Would things really have fallen apart if I'd just accepted that washing wouldn't get done or that we'd eat a few more takeaways? Why would I always stay late at the office and bend over backwards to make things work and people happy? Why did it always have to be the best? Why do I need to work for a big name like the *Guardian*? Why do I try so hard at my passions, instead of just sitting back and enjoying them? Why do I like winning games? Why can't I read crappy novels or watch whodunnits on the telly?

Why do I do what I do?

Chasing my tail like this isn't good. I feel I need to identify what I was doing wrong, cut it out and then heal over. But such self-examination is like peeling an onion. You don't know where to stop. You don't know where the mucky bit is. If you're not careful you might end up discarding a lot of good, healthy material.

It seems like everything is up for grabs. Maybe it's my personality – perhaps I need to be meaner, or care less. Maybe it's family life – perhaps I'm just not cut out for it. Maybe it's something deeper, darker. Maybe it's really all up for grabs and I have to rebuild me from the ground upwards, at the age of forty.

Sacha Khan stops me before I am surrounded by shredded onion peel. All of us, he says, develop character traits early in life. Sometimes, these can be 'maladaptive' if we are exposed to extremes in our upbringing. The obvious example is of neglected or rejected children, who may find it harder to make lasting attachments as adults. Or the child who gets too much of a good thing may not know how to assert him/herself in adulthood. But there are many more subtle habits that develop. They will be hard to cut out: they have formed early, like the roots of a tree. But it's worth a try.

It's called schema therapy, a programme developed by the American cognitive behaviourist Jeffrey Young. Schema therapy involves examining and trying to straighten out the early tics that may be harmful to us as adults. Think of schemas as clusters of preconceived ideas, prejudices and reflexes that form the core of our behavioural instincts. They are grouped into five broad areas that reflect areas of our upbringing (and I paraphrase): rejection; overprotection; overindulgence; other-directedness (i.e. guided by others' standards, not one's own); and inhibition.

From this soup of abstract nouns a basic idea emerges: if exposed to the wrong kind of nurture in our early years, we develop odd reflexes and coping mechanisms. These are very resistant to change, and don't really respond to logic.

It's quite easy for me to identify my schemas. They are mostly clustered under the group 'other-directedness'. It's a wishy-washy heading, but the subhead is quite brutal: 'An excessive focus on the desires, feelings, and responses of others, at the expense of one's own needs – in order to gain love and approval, maintain one's sense of connection, or avoid retaliation.' Under this heading we get 'recognition-seeking' 'subjugation' and 'self-sacrifice'. I am basically an assiduous but obsequious little toad: I do everything I can to ingratiate myself with other people, whatever the cost to my own self-expression.

I also loosely subscribe to a couple of other schemas under different headings: one called 'unrelenting standards', which is best summed up as an emphasis on 'shoulds' and 'oughts'; and another called simply 'pessimism', a preoccupation with loss, disappointment, might-have-beens and things that could go wrong.

From this it is possible to identify the coping strategies that we resort to in order to mitigate the schema. For me it's often about overcompensating: trying too hard to overachieve, please people, gain recognition.

More perplexing is why I am this way. I had a blessed upbringing, enough attention but not too much, plenty of love, fun and wide open spaces. I am baffled as to why I became someone needful of recognition, praise and status. In a family of four children you quickly learned the opposite: that most of the time, it wasn't your turn for the attention.

Sacha Khan gets me to become heedful of these instincts, to override them, poke my tongue at from time to time and then notice that the world does not fall apart if you behave differently. He cites as an extreme example an obsessive-compulsive patient who could not bear anything to be out of place in her house. He politely asked her to leave a book jutting out of the bookcase overnight. She found it maddening to do so the first time, slightly easier thereafter and, with time and experience, her brain came to realise that bad things would not happen if the books were misaligned on the shelf.

For me, it's different. I need to learn that you can say no to people and they'll still be your friend, your colleague, your wife. That sometimes things don't have to be perfect: good enough is often good enough. That you shouldn't always worry what other people think, particularly as, more often than not, it's not what they actually think that is bothering you, but what you think they might be thinking.

I find a good example from work. Before I became ill, I would often be concerned that I was rather peripheral to the main action of the day. Quite often, when a major story broke, senior editors would take over and I would be assigned all the tiresome leftovers, the bits of world news no one would be reading the next day. Actually, it's still a fun job, still a great intellectual puzzle to work out what is interesting, what fits together well, what will provide the perfect mix of information and entertainment and stick it in a newspaper. But I felt like an understudy, a footballer who can't get a game for the first team. I would get carried away with my thoughts: I'm just an extra here, my expertise and ability is not being fully used, I must have pissed someone off to get sidelined like this. If there are to be staff cuts in our department I will be the first to go because I'm just the desk junior who sweeps up world briefs about dead actors and overweight kangaroos. In reality, I have been told many times what people think of me. In reality, it was just a sensible division of labour. But in my head it was all very different. Now I am to stop this train of thought. Examine it for what it is. Recognise that it's just the way things are; there is no sinister hidden meaning. I don't have to try twice as hard to ingratiate myself in order to avoid being sidelined because I haven't even been sidelined. Instead, now I am to pause and think how far I have come; how lucky I am to have made it back to this; how a few hours of drudgery here or there are so much easier to endure than the thing I have just overcome.

One exercise that I find hard to do is to deliberately make a total arse of myself in public. Sacha suggests getting down to do some press-ups in the GP surgery's waiting room. Or walking into a hardware store and asking for a Cornetto. The idea is that you bring shame on yourself, but it doesn't actually cause you any harm or material discomfort. You realise that it's not so important to feel superior all the time. Within hours it's all forgotten. Unless, of course, you have to go back half an hour later to buy two dozen screws and a spirit level.

*

It was my middle child who invented the concept. Edward has an older brother and thus doesn't win much. It doesn't really bother him – he is pretty even-tempered like that – but occasionally he wants to engage with us without the fear of defeat. So he would say to us, 'This is not a winning game.' James and I would look slightly disappointed, but we'd see his point. Unloading the dishwasher does not have to be a competitive undertaking.

The boys and I are always inventing games. Our latest effort is called TriFoot – it's football for when you only have three players and you can't make fair teams. So you make three goals instead, on a kind of triangular pitch, and each player has a designated goal in which they must score. Anyway, it's quite fun until the first player scores. If it's me, James will sulk. If it's James, Edward will sulk. And if it's Edward ... well, it's never Edward, because he is normally skipping around looking for villains in the undergrowth. And so the game breaks down. Another of our games we call Daddy Can You Find Me? It's a bit of a misnomer because they are doing the finding and I am setting them things to find. It's good for a dismal stopover at motorway services, or a thankless walk to school. Only you have to orchestrate it so that one boy finds the first one and the other the second, and so on. If one of them opens up a two-point lead the other sabotages the game, arguing over a technicality or refusing to play any longer. It's the same with the Whistling Game (I whistle tunes from TV shows, they guess the show) or Guess Who In Your Head, Cheese in the Sky, Wink Murder with Questions or Hide and Seek on Paper, or any of the myriad games I have dreamed up on slack winter afternoons when the telly quota has been exhausted. Someone is going to win. Someone else is going to cry.

Why is winning important? I'm not sure. It must go back to primitive survival instincts. The feeling of superiority that victory brought must have engendered a great sense of security in early humans. A triumph for the tribe meant strength, impregnability, auspicious prospects. Somehow over the generations the feeling has persisted even though the meaning of victory has been transformed beyond all recognition. Now we feel that same glow in victories that mean little or nothing to our broad state of well-being. What does it matter if someone else is slightly better than us at hitting a small white ball a long distance towards a hole in the ground? Who cares if the adjacent table scores better on the 'British Novelty Records of the Fifties' round at the pub quiz? We even feel the glow when we are not directly involved in the competition at hand. It never ceases to amaze me how strongly I can feel about the exploits on a distant sports field of eleven men I have never met, and probably wouldn't like if I did.

I have always had a competitive streak. If anything, it has become wider as I have got older. As a child, I wasn't too bothered about losing team sports, but when it came to test scores it was different. There was a keen sense of loss whenever I was outdone by rivals. On the other hand I adored the attention – from teachers, parents and peers – that came with good marks. The bar has been set pretty high ever since. Funnily enough, for someone who likes to prevail I haven't actually won very much.

A couple of cricket tournaments. Junior Diving 1978 at my school (I remember little of this, just falling off a diving board upside down and coming up to scores of 9s and 10s). A recitation prize for reading 'The Lobster Quadrille'. Apart from the odd game of football, and an office World Cup sweepstake, I really haven't won much at all.

Sacha's prescription is both odd and wise. He suggests I take up things that I am not very good at. I find the idea strangely compelling. Most of us, I am willing to bet, generally amuse ourselves with things that we do quite well. It takes a certain sort of masochist to persist with something for which they have little ability. I quickly abandoned the things I was not much good at: rugby, the clarinet, acting, photography, drawing, running, church, shopping, philandering. Not worth wasting time on. Now I can see that sometimes a thing is worth doing just for the sake of doing it, not for the outcome or the result. There is no pressure.

I need to incorporate something that isn't to be taken too seriously, something light and frivolous that doesn't involve effort or intensity, something that doesn't *amount* to anything. So Sharon and I pick up dancing lessons again. We are hilarious, stepping all over each other on a Monday night. In particular, it is the samba that makes us laugh. When I am learning the Botafogo Sharon says I look like a man with a wooden leg. When we jive it is my skipping motion, like a horse trying on a new pair of shoes, that tickles her. Most dances are hard to do without a little bit of camp. She is never too far away from ribbing me. It is all very light-hearted. And yet still . . . there is

271

a sense in which we don't just want to turn up and dance. We want to improve. We don't want to be laughing stocks. We are not prepared to stick at level one, with boring, predictable movements. We want more. Reverse turns and whisks and a bit of drama to the tango, which I love. After a few months we are dancing a reasonable waltz and cha-cha-cha – and the feeling is so good we want to get better and better. I am worried that dancing is becoming a winning game.

I go back to the garden. The lemon tree is awesome, king of all it surveys. But the potatoes were not a great success. Most of them were smaller than garden peas. I feel disappointment. In the new spirit of non-competitive behaviour, I cradle the disappointment, see that it is really rather meaningless and move on. Next year, I say, next year there will be bigger potatoes. You see – it's difficult not to want to feel some kind of progress in the things that we do.

Other things I take up: chess. And I don't mind losing, honest I don't. Which is just as well as I do it a lot. The computer makes few mistakes. I use the Apple-Z key a lot, to undo my hazardous gambits. Occasionally I drag the setting option down to 1 or 2 so that I can get a rare victory, but normally I lose. It doesn't hurt. From chess it's but a short step to poker. A few hands with mates or an online game. I am neither terribly good nor terribly bad. I do not lose money, but when I lose a game, there is a feeling of such anger, disappointment and despair that I actually think there is some value in persisting. Each time I lose I must sit in that soup of wretchedness and examine it curiously, and come to understand that it's really not the end of the world. A few months ago, for me, it very nearly was. This is just a random moment, success and failure are slippery notions. It's best to frame the things we do in other terms.

And then there is this. This book. When I started writing it, it was for you, my poor fellow sufferer at the start of your thing, bewildered by your rumination, infatuated with your horror, tearing at your hair and staring in the mirror and asking your eyes terrible questions in the night. But now, as I get closer to the end, I realise it's all a ruse, a pretext. Actually, I've been doing it for me. It's another winning game, another thing I can use to prove myself. But prove myself to whom, and why? Where does it come from, this terrifying Napoleonic urge to prove myself? Can't I just be me?

The opposite of competition? Compassion. I haven't really grasped this yet. Sacha helps. We do a little exercise during a session when I am really quite poorly again. He tells me to shut my eyes and try to think of a time when I helped someone else.

... I am on a train in northern Russia, playing magnetic chess against Sharon. We are in a group, six or eight of us who have been to Moscow for the weekend. We have made friends with Russian passengers. Some are watching our game, advising me not to be so stupid with my pawns. Others are chatting with Jo and Neil behind us. One generous soul gives Jo a present, a scarf, I think, or maybe a bracelet. Just like that. Won't take no for an answer. It's very much in keeping with the era: making friends, hands across the water. But what to give back?

We have nothing. Just the clothes we're standing up in. And my chess game. I fold it up. Hand it over. Everyone feels good . . .

. . . We are walking to school when there is a dreadful sound behind us, a squeal of rubber, a crunch of solid on solid. We turn around and there is someone we know sprawled on the asphalt. Her bike is crumpled on the ground like a dragonfly and there is a kiddie trailer behind that's a mess too. She is in shock. The child is all right. 'I didn't take it wide enough,' she says. 'The trailer. It must have hit the car.' We are late for school but that's all right. Her bike won't wheel, so I carry it home for her. 'Thank you,' she says . . .

. . . I am giving blood in a church. How virtuous is that? The waiting time is nice and short, and they've got chocolate biscuits. I fill the bag very quickly. I have brilliant veins, like brake cables on a bike. The nurse is chatty and I talk back. Once I wrote a short story about how a nurse forgot to attend to a man giving blood and all his blood ran out until he was the colour of cement. It makes me slightly uneasy now. 'Well done,' she says. 'You're good.' I am good. That is what this afternoon is about. I am giving blood and someone else will get to use it – marvellous blood this, O negative, a full pint the colour of wine, the consistency of treacle, with a chemical composition that is mostly red blood cells and plasma, but a few hormones and vitamins and amino acids and carbohydrates as well. Oh and probably some antidepressant residue in there as well, I suspect. It will go from here to a blood bank and then be used to make someone else's life a little better. Don't worry, I can make it up again in a few hours. I feel great. Every one's a winner. I am making a difference.

I think of the piece I wrote, the responses I got, the overwhelming messages from people saying how relieved they felt to read about someone else with their condition. I tell Sacha about all these people, people I have deliberately or unwittingly helped. There was Caroline. She wrote to me saying, 'I wanted to write to you personally to say how much I have valued reading your articles about depression recently and your experiences.' Caroline says that, like me, she has been scouring the internet for anything that will tell her more about her own condition. She says it has been like living 'in some kind of fog and surreal world', and that my piece was 'a valuable source of comfort and support'. I'm lucky to have had the platform to be able to reach people like Caroline.

Then there was Catherine, who had suffered several bouts of mild depression in her twenties before she was upended by postnatal depression. She started: 'I felt *exactly* like you described – longing to be someone else, to be lost in a book, to not even want to be on the planet and to think that everyone else would be better off without me.' Catherine says it took her sixteen months before she could really see improvements in how she was feeling. She was sweet enough to conclude, 'If your article makes just one person feel like they are not alone, or gives them ideas for what can help, then you have done a hugely important job. Depression happens to anyone and you have shown that regardless of a high-powered job or a very happy family it can still strike.'

We focus on them, Caroline and Catherine and the many others out there. We feel their respite, their relief at my unwitting intervention in their lives. A wave of something washes through me, flushing out the lump of anxiety sitting deep in my abdomen.

I am back in the office. My colleagues are doing well. The foreign team are excelling. I am nowhere on the roll of honour, but it doesn't matter. I look at my colleagues and try to luxuriate in their triumphs and advances. They are like me. They don't want to be sidelined or stuck doing world briefs. They are intelligent, capable, good folk. From now on I will savour their moments, rejoice at their little triumphs and support and encourage them.

Sacha makes me write a list. Top 10 Worst Things That Ever Happened to Me. It's all a bit parochial, I'm afraid. This thing is definitely number one. A couple of domestic disasters are high up there: we seem to have had a lot of water hazards in our homes over the years, including one that flooded our flat so badly we had to move out for nine months. There were a couple of affairs of the heart that went wrong. And the big watershed moments of growing up: a new school, Switzerland, the first day at university. At number ten I put fatherhood. But it's in the Top 10 Best Things That Ever Happened to Me too.

Sacha gives me another exercise. I get lots of homework now. I've been writing positive data logs and thought–emotion–behaviour reports for weeks. Now I must compose a speech.

Not any speech, but the address I would want a good friend to give on my eightieth birthday.

What do I want him to say? How would you want your speech to sound? What is a life for? What do we want our few short years here to be all about?

I must confess I find it tricky. The speech I would want to hear will vary from year to year, even from day to day. Thirty years ago I would have hoped my life would have been all about playing for England at football, cricket or whatever. Ten years ago I might have wanted a friend to eulogise about my work, not that there's been an awful lot to eulogise about: the places I've written about, the scrapes and escapades I got into. But that's all quite prosaic stuff; it doesn't amount to a whole lot and I'm really not sure that I've made a difference. A life has to be about more than that, doesn't it? Now I have children. They must feature. So do I want my friend to rhapsodise about what a great dad I've been? Have I been a great dad? What is a great dad? A guy who grinds out sixty hours a week to pay for opportunity for his kids, like my father did, or a guy who sacrifices his own career, preferment, enjoyment and leisure so that he can give his children more of himself? I'm torn. I think I want my friend to say that I blazed a trail, showed dads that there is a middle way, a guy who can be a good pro and a good parent.

The trouble with all these approaches is that they centre on things I have already done. In a way, the crux of this exercise is to get you to focus not on your achievements, but the things you still want to do. The thing you want your entire life to be about, not just the story so far. I think awhile on this and come up blank. What is a twenty-first-century life for? Is it to praise the Lord or magnify humanity? To be kind to others or kind to yourself? To do one thing exceptionally, or many things adequately? To blaze a trail, or put out fires? To do good things, or just not to do anybody very much harm. To shine or to endure? I'm not sure what there is left for me to achieve. If, two decades ago, you'd offered me three children, a wife and a house and a good job on Britain's best newspaper by the time I was middle-aged, I'd have jumped at it. I have the job I want and the family I want. I got it all by the time I was thirty-five. Can there really be nothing left for me? Have I truly done all I set out to do? Is that all there is?

15

A new normal

I am mentally ill.

It doesn't mean I will stab you or stalk you or demand a low-calorie recipe for cheesecake when I am sitting next to you on the Tube. It doesn't mean I will dribble or smell or abduct your infants or infect your pets. It doesn't mean I want to rule the world or take risks with your money or corner you at a party and talk about depression.

I am mentally ill. I broke a bit of my brain, like you might break your collarbone. It took a lot of healing. It will always be vulnerable. It could recur. I don't think it's a condition that should invite prejudice. People with lung cancer and heart disease are not ostracised or humiliated or debarred from jobs or opportunities, even though in some cases their lifestyle will certainly have contributed to their affliction. Mental illness is rarely about lifestyle or choices we make or weakness of character. It just happens to certain people, lots of people, for lots of different reasons. It is painful enough; it seems grossly unfair to double the punishment with discrimination. But that's what we do. Because we don't understand it. Because mental illness changes what someone is, who they are. Their countenance is unsteady, something insidious flickers behind their eyes; they always had it coming; this always affects people like them. They have turned into someone we are not sure we can trust: unreliable, unpredictable, hysterical, bothersome. If we employ them they might go off sick for a year. If we make friends with them, they might begin stalking us. Mental illness is best avoided. No wonder most of us keep our thing to ourselves.

'The vast majority of people with mental health problems anticipate getting negative responses from others and this stops them telling other people,' says Sue Baker, director of the Time to Change programme that was set up to change negative attitudes towards mental illness. Baker says nine out of ten people with mental illness say they have experienced stigma and discrimination. She says she even had second thoughts about coming out about her own mental health history when she applied for her job in mental health.

'Yet, paradoxically, "coming out" can be the best thing for someone with a mental illness. It can have a powerful influence,' says Baker. 'If you don't disclose, then people who might help you aren't going to be able to.'

In many senses I was so very lucky. My thing chose its moment very carefully, seemed to wait until my family was fairly settled before it crept in through the back gate and made itself comfortable. As luck would have it, I could afford to be ill in 2009. At any other time it could have been very different. We were done with tiny babies, the children were just about in school and Sharon had taken the plunge with her business. A year earlier and she might not have. Three or four years earlier and we wouldn't have had Janey, our delightful little girl. Pre-2001 and I might not have had kids at all. Pre-2003 and the *Guardian* wouldn't have taken me on, and I wouldn't have wanted to work there. It is almost as if my organism waited for everything to be settled and then said, 'Right, now's as good a time as any for a quick nervous breakdown and spell of depression.'

The chart has made sense. There were moments when it looked misshapen, like a broken accordion abandoned in a mineshaft, utterly without pattern. But now I can see it was exactly how I thought it would be. A ripple, just like any other of nature's ripples. The pattern of aftershocks following an earthquake. The movement of a rope flicked by a ranch hand. The displacement of water when a stone drops into a pond. The initial waves are choppy, but the further away from the event you get, the smoother the curve, until eventually all is still again.

Sharon buys me a memory bracelet. At least that is what I call it. I never wore jewellery. I do now. It is black for the clouds, and silver for the linings. I will wear it for ever.

*

Sharon and I go for a walk. We have bumped into a rare day on which neither of us has anything particular to do. The kids are at school. I am working part-time. Sharon has holiday to take. We put on our walking boots and toddle off into the morning.

We trace the footsteps I have taken on countless occasions: down the hill, into Richmond Park through Kingston Gate, past the playground that we call the 'wee-slide' park, through the penumbra created by ancient oaks, and up the hill, puffing a little near the summit. Then on towards the Ladderstile Gate, overtaken by joggers and dog walkers, cyclists humming by on their busy route from A to A. Then we turn left and head across the open heathland where families picnic in summer. We don't say much. We've done a lot of talking, but for the first time in our lives I don't think we can really know what the other one has been going through. It has been impossible for her – just as it is impossible for anyone – to know what the dark virus of depression really feels like, however much it is etched on my face. It is similar for me: I have no idea what it is like to be married to someone with depression. I suspect that if there's one thing tougher than getting through clinical depression, it's nursing someone through it. Sharon is the kind of nurse you'd want: loyal, dedicated and a delicate mix of sympathetic and resolute.

And so we make time for a proper conversation about it all. I start by asking her what she did to keep herself sane and together throughout the worst months.

SRO: There are obvious things. Make sure you look after yourself. Everyone said that to me and I didn't understand what they meant.

MRO: What did you do to look after yourself?

SRO: It's all about survival. Survival looks different for different people. In the early days, for me it was my parents. They were a lifeline. Talking to them so that I felt there was someone at the end of the phone. And a slight amount of not acknowledging the enormity of it. If you acknowledge the enormity of it then you too could fall over. I kept on going to work and doing what I had to do for the kids. I talked to friends, and with some I found it easier than with others. If I'd tried to hide it from work or family and friends I would have crumpled.

MRO: How easy do you find it to understand my predicament?

SRO: I could see that you weren't making it up and that it was serious.

MRO: Were you tempted to say 'Pull yourself together, man'?

SRO: No. On a couple of occasions I thought a good couple of nights and you'll be over it. If he could just have a couple of nights of rest. I thought it would be a quick fix. And I wanted to say in a couple of weeks you'll be better. Then it became clear that it wouldn't be a couple of weeks or a couple of months.

MRO: How did that feel?

SRO: That was the scariest time. I remember on the night of your fortieth birthday it being very scary when you had the breakdown in the hotel in London and you having a massive panic attack. That was the first time I took it seriously. You don't. You go on and expect the other one to go on. This is our dream evening, in a hotel and pootling off to the theatre and a dinner, something we both love doing. You couldn't do it.

MRO: At that point did you look forward and wonder what was going to happen?

SRO: No. Because at that point I didn't know how serious it was. Over the course of the weekend it became clear that it wasn't just a one-off, that you were struggling more seriously. But the scariest time for me was around Christmas when you weren't really any better and you'd had two or three months of drugs and there didn't seem to be any improvement. And you would go to bed and I would think, 'Fuck! What is going to happen to us?'

MRO: There must be a coping mechanism?

SRO: I kept life as normal as I possibly could. I did take charge, from us having been an equal partnership. When we realised what the illness was I then thought I have to make different home arrangements, employing the nanny for extra hours and taking on a housekeeper to alleviate additional stress.

MRO: But at the same time not knowing if we could afford any of this stuff?

SRO: Yes. But I had to go to work. And that meant getting

shopping delivered and getting someone else to do things around the house. Because you couldn't.

MRO: How do you nurture someone who is mentally ill? How do you nurse them back to health?

SRO: Treat them normally. You accept that they are physically ill, and in the same way that if someone has broken their leg you wouldn't expect them to climb a flight of stairs. You would work around it. That does mean being less selfish and creating space for that person to get better.

MRO: What happens when they ask you for reassurance or tell you for the thousandth time that they can't get out of this?

SRO: We had the same conversation a hundred million times. I tried every tactic. I tried being sympathetic and understanding and going on that journey with you. Sometimes I shouted at you. Sometimes I burst into tears and said I don't want to talk about this any more. I think you have to be yourself.

MRO: It must be strange when they are no longer the person that you have known.

SRO: They still are. They are just very poorly. It's the same as them lying in a hospital bed very ill; they wouldn't be quite themselves.

MRO: Does someone like that become hard to love?

SRO: Different people have different responses. You were never nasty to me or the children. Friends that I have talked to who have suffered the same thing told stories where they were really horrible to their spouses and kids. If you had been, I don't know how I would have reacted. You just withdrew, you didn't give love, you didn't give me any affection and nor the kids.

MRO: Which must have been hard.

SRO: It's all hard, though. It's difficult to put your finger on what is the hardest thing. Having to live and cope with someone that's mentally ill is the hard thing. I found your sleeplessness was the most difficult thing to deal with. I needed to sleep and was acutely conscious of whether you were sleeping or not. Some nights it was like having a newborn baby: you were asleep and I didn't want to come and check in case I woke you up. For five months we didn't sleep in the same bed. I did find that hard. I wondered will we ever be able to sleep in the same bed again.

MRO: Were you thinking this is going to pass, or this is how it's going to be from now on?

SRO: To start with I was constantly focused on when you were going to get better. But then last Easter, when you had another major relapse, I realised it's not about when, it's about how you get better. I stopped thinking, 'Is he back to normal?' I thought instead, 'Is he OK?'

Talking to friends in the same situation helped. Jane for example. It almost felt like they were a year ahead of us. On the one hand you want to know how bad it can be, but you also want know someone else has got it hard and it's not only you.

MRO: Why does that help you, to know that someone else is suffering?

SRO: Because it's the loneliest thing I've ever done. However much you have supportive parents and friends, you had to focus on you getting better and I had to focus on everything else. I couldn't have rational conversations with you about things. We always talked, and that was good, but we were talking about things that you wanted to talk about. For the first time in our relationship I would check myself before I said things to you.

MRO: What sort of things?

SRO: Things like, 'On Saturday, we could do . . . ' I stopped saying anything about let's do this or that because part of it was about the overload. So I stopped planning stuff, stopped sharing it with you. Of course I was never going to say, 'What if you never get better?' but of course I thought it. It's gone now, I don't check myself now. But I did for a good six or eight months.

MRO: Can you learn from this experience?

SRO: Of course you can. It depends on who you are. I never thought that I would be very good as a carer because I'm not the most sympathetic of people, but I have learned that you can get through a hell of a lot. I have learned to be kind to myself. That is an important message. The person that's ill gets better, but the carer has to get better too because it's very stressful. At times around the Christmas period I felt I was going to explode: every time there was a little relapse I felt like a jug of water and every time it happened a bit more of my reserves of water ebbed away. The carer has to refill the tank. I only did that when I when to see Brenda [a counsellor]. It wasn't until six or seven months and then I went and, God, did I need it. Your friends can be sympathetic but sometimes they are too close, too connected, and sometimes you don't want to tell them about everything your spouse has said because you don't want to rupture their relationship. It helps to know there is a safe pair of hands.

I'm really glad that you are better. That we have found a way to live with it. Even this last weekend, when you didn't sleep very well at Glendene, I felt a bit on edge. I used to have this terrible sinking, lurching feeling at night when you were pacing around.

MRO: Do you try to protect the kids?

SRO: No, and I don't think we did. The one thing we did really well was tell everybody. So many people said you're being so brave for telling us. But I don't think there's any other way to deal with it. The kids needed to know. I think you have to protect them from the rawness of it. There was one time when we didn't and you were in floods of tears by the front door and that's stuck in Janey's memory. But if you don't tell them they'll think it's their fault, because kids are egotistical. And we told the school as well. I don't think you wanted to.

MRO: It felt a bit random.

SRO: But it's not at all. They are at school five days out of seven in a week. And if it was going to come out then we needed to have all the bases covered and the teachers needed to know. I wonder if you felt I'd told too many people. You'd say, 'Oh, you haven't told so-and-so, have you?'

MRO: Well there's disclosure and there's full disclosure. You want to be a bit in control of where the information's going. The terminology is so crap, you talk to people about depression and they just don't get it.

SRO: Some people are helpful, but others are always like, 'Oh, how are you?' You want to be treated normally, and if you aren't you'll start avoiding people.

MRO: The thing that annoys me is when people ask if I'm on medication. Well yes I am, but that doesn't tell you very much.

SRO: People use that as a barometer to understand how ill you are, because if you're on medication it must be serious.

MRO: Although some GPs will put someone who is a little bit sad on antidepressants.

SRO: Sure. But people still check with me: 'Is Mark still on medication?' My response is yes, and if he's on it for the rest of his life, that's fine. It's irrelevant.

MRO: And yet it's not really indicative of how things are. But that's because people don't really know about the illness and what it entails.

SRO: It's really hard when your husband tells you he doesn't think he can go on. The first time, I was horrified. It is a cry for help that shouldn't be ignored. The third time I remember getting really cross with you and saying, 'Don't you dare. You'll destroy our kids' lives if you do.' That's how I felt. If you're serious, you're going to screw up a lot of lives.

MRO: I think that goes through the minds of a lot of people who have severe depression. They may have children and can see how an act like that could ripple down through the generations. But at the end of the day, sometimes the illness can be too strong.

SRO: I can appreciate that. I didn't ever think it was too strong for you. I could see it was horrendous. I wouldn't wish it on anyone. But I know you are a strong man. I had no doubt you could cope because you're incredibly strong. And I know that is part of why you got ill. I always had faith in you to find a way. Because I couldn't help you get better.

MRO: But you did.

SRO: I could only help you by doing all the things I did. You were the only person who could get better.

MRO: You do yourself a disservice. My heart goes out to singletons, people without parents, people who don't have close friends or partners. I worry about people like that who fall ill. I wonder what to say to them to help them pull through. Because for me, one of the strongest things pulling me through was you and the kids. I had a conversation with Bill, who told me that if it wasn't for his wife and kids he wonders whether he would have just given up. He's spot on. A lot of us would feel the same way.

SRO: Maybe it is the people who are alone who are the ones who kill themselves.

MRO: It's that daily contact. Sometimes it is quite hard to be with other people. One of my triggers was when we were in bed reading and you would reach out for your bookmark and I would think shit, she's going to go turn her light off. It's time for me to face the night hours on my own. The rhythm of someone else's daily life can be a double-edged sword. On the one hand they are keeping you in some kind of routine, getting up in the morning and going to bed at night; on the other, they remind you of what it is to be normal and human, and how far you are from that.

SRO: I did get cross with you on a few occasions, when I got to understand the rhythm of the illness and I could tell when you were going to have a dip. There were a couple of times when you pushed too hard, worked too hard, and then you would relapse and I could see it coming.

MRO: That was more recently, though?

SRO: Yes, once you were mending and coming out of it. I felt really cross with you: you don't have the right to put yourself through this again. You would always try to come off the drugs more quickly that you should. It was almost like a competition.

MRO: The five or six months in the pits were without doubt the most shocking time. But the steps towards recovery are, if anything, more treacherous. Because it's all trial and error. I am trying to get back to normal and slipping up again and again. And you keep getting cross with me for doing what we both want me to be doing.

SRO: It is difficult. I had taken control of everything. We didn't do anything big. I was in charge. So I felt you didn't have a right to make those decisions. But of course you did. I remember when I first when to see my counsellor, she said, 'You've been gripping the steering wheel like this and you've been hunched over, and I am going to try and help you let go gently and you'll see that the car isn't going to crash.'

Your mum was brilliant. Her alongside me was the constant voice of support there. My parents found it hard. They were extremely worried about me, and about you. And would come at the drop of a hat. But they were asking what is happening. How are we going to cope? Whenever you had a relapse I would be on the phone to my mum and that's a terrible situation for her to be in, with her daughter sobbing down the phone at her. I remember saying to her one time, 'I don't think I can cope.' And she said, 'Well you will. You just will.' And you do.

MRO: People cope with all kinds of extraordinary things.

It's almost like it has to be a period of months, because coping isn't something you do in a day. It's a life-changing process and you go through it over a long period, then you come out the other side with a few more wrinkles and grey hairs, and another experience tucked under your belt.

SRO: Work was absolutely crucial for me. There were times when I thought I'd got it wrong. We'd just set up the company a few months earlier. And I wondered, 'Have I got my priorities wrong here? I've got three kids and a poorly husband.' I asked Mum and she said no, you've got to keep going.

MRO: My dad said the same thing. Talking to him at one of the blackest moments. He said I don't care what you think, Sharon has to keep working, it's the central pillar of family life and if she gives it up you'll all be inwardly focused.

SRO: At the time it was a funny feeling. It was the best thing to get on the train in the morning and know that I didn't have to see you. Because it was really hard. Really hard to be around you.

MRO: I would call you up—

SRO: Yes, you never call me, you never use the phone unless you really have to, and I could tell from the way you said hello whether it was a good or bad day. But generally if you called me it was bad. You'd say, 'I don't know what to do, I don't know how to get through the next hour.' But there weren't many days when I felt I couldn't leave you. We got your dad up a few times for lunch. And Sparky and Tim would call up and ask if I wanted them to go over. They really cared and were a real help.

But I wouldn't wish it on anyone. It's a horrible, horrible thing.

MRO: You wouldn't want to do it again. But if it happened again would it be different?

SRO: The nature of the illness is that it would be different. I would take heart from the fact that it would never feel as bleak for me as it did the first time. I guess it could be worse. You might never recover from it. But I think we've incorporated it into our lives now. So that we won't let it happen again.

There's a Chet Baker song I used to whistle during better times. 'Everything Happens to Me'. It's a wistful shrug of a song. You can take it both ways. Bad stuff happens and good stuff happens. Who knows which is which?

I am walking up the hill towards home, a golden September sun pouring down like part of a glorious experiment to find the perfect temperature for life on earth. And suddenly I bump into an old friend who has recently retired. We speak of gardening and grandchildren, work and leisure. Then I say I haven't been well.

'I know,' he says. He tells me how he had something similar in the mid-eighties when he was doing night shifts, haring up and down the M3 in the early hours, making do with four or five hours' sleep. 'Thatcher was doing it, so I thought if she can, why can't I?' How it all unravelled and he had to build up from ground zero.

'The most important thing is acceptance,' he says.

His words stay with me for a long time. The most important thing is acceptance. It's that I am me and you are you and we're both all right really. We do what we can to the best of our ability, but the rest, well, we just have to accept that things are the way they are and no amount of agonising or striving or wishing or thinking or trying will change the things that are beyond our control. In fact, a lot of the energy and agony we expend on such things will just make things worse.

The often-cited example is that of the slave Epictetus, who was shackled in chains by his master but made no effort to break free. He knew it would only hurt him all the more if he chafed and rubbed his skin against the metal fastener. If you're bound in chains, don't make things worse by breaking your leg to try to get free. Accept it. If it's pouring with rain and you're huddled in a shelter, don't agonise about how bad it is that you're going to get wet, or how good it might have been if the sun had been shining. Get wet and see how it really makes you feel. That's the ultimate truth about this illness, a paradox I have only just come to understand: it's only when you truly accept that you'll never be properly well again that you start to recover; as soon as you tell yourself it's all over, you relapse.

A friend died a few weeks ago. He'd been ill for a while, but that's no consolation. He was forty-four, with two children at that brilliant age when everything is opening up for them, for the family.

His wife tells me, soon after he died, that Kevin never said, 'Why me?' of his hideous illness. He would always say instead, 'Why not me?' That's a crisp example of why the world is poorer without him. The human tendency is to blame, to find fault, to bewail circumstances beyond our control. In actual fact, what Kevin articulated was a polar opposite of this: we shouldn't moan about how unfortunate we are; we should celebrate how well we are. We should marvel constantly, each day, each moment, at the bizarre and precarious nature of our existence; at the improbable geometry of the earth's place in the solar system; at the delicate zoological balance that allows seven billion of us to survive each day; at the serendipity that has allowed all those reading this book to be born in this time and not a thousand or even a hundred years ago; at the continuing run of good luck that spares most of us from deadly illness or murderous villainy or the vicissitudes of nature. Our lives are a miracle. Our continuing happiness is not a given, but a stroke of outrageous fortune. We should ask, 'Why me?' not when we suffer some wretched setback but every day we wake up and the world is still there and our lives stretch ahead of us, marvellously improbable.

A dip.

They will come, Marko, remember that. A day or two where you are flat and can't get into the book you are reading. Tiredness. A bit of leggy lethargy, some indigestion, a lot of farting. Yawning. Headscrew. A sudden disinterest in things. Then a first night of wakefulness. Erratic concentration; that mild panic in the upper chest that feels like blue cobalt in your collarbone. The stomach buzz. Thinking … It's a dip. They will come. They will stay. And they will pass. Everything does.

James is ten. Fancy that. I have a ten-year-old son. I shall write a poem to commemorate the moment.

> Ten long years of parenting
> Has sometimes been a scary ting
> And even a despairing thing
> When fully analysed
>
> It started in a maternity ward
> The little chap we both adored
> We didn't know that our reward
> Would be so well disguised
>
> Peekaboo we played and played
> While babies dozed and toddlers brayed
> And soon we'd lost a whole decade
> Completely atomised
>
> Bugs and fevers all contagious
> Temper tantrums quite outrageous
> None of them are yet teenagers
> Only little guys

And yet it hasn't been so bad
To be a most bedraggled dad
I can teach them the capital of Chad
And plenty more besides

In fact it has been beautiful
To parent kids so dutiful
Particularly when you're all in school
Or watching something really cool
That has been televised

The lemon tree died. It had been unhappy for months. It had to come in for the winter, of course, and seemed generally perky about things until late in the year, when the darkness started to tell. I tried potting up, feeding it and generally fussing over it, but that just seemed to make it worse. I moved it: into the sun, out of the sun, into a warmer part of the house, but it was no use. The fruit was green and hard. Leaves began to fall, a few at first then a lot all at once. Eventually there were only about nine left. An inauspicious scale began to climb the branches, turning green into light brown. Perhaps it was depressed. If this was a novel we could get all naturalistic about it, linking the blossoming tree to my own decline and my revival to the death of the plant. But it isn't, so let's not do that. Instead there was me and there was a tree. One of us died. I'm glad the tree got it.

I, on the other hand, have wintered well. It was nothing to do with light and clocks and the curves described by ancient celestial bodies. It was just my thing, that's all. My thing. It came, it stayed a while, a long while, a dark and difficult interlude. And over the past nine months it seems to have acquiesced. My symptoms fell quieter and quieter, taking it in turns to fade out. Finally they fell silent, unable to muster anything. The chart flatlined at 100. As I knew it would eventually. There are still occasional blips and slips. But it was either going to converge on 100 or 0. If I add a trend line now it becomes apparent what's been going on. I tried to recover too soon. The upsetting months in the middle of last year were all about me trying to do too much too quickly. I thought I was up at 80s and 90s when I wasn't quite. No wonder I relapsed. Depression doesn't like being shown the door before it's good and ready to leave. Recovery is another of those diabolical passive verbs. You don't recover from depression: recovery comes to find you. When it's good and ready.

I am noticing things – beauty, seasons, people. I buy birthday presents on time. I eat apples with a certain wonder. I don't rush. I'm never the first or last at parties. I drink, but carefully: too much alcohol will keep me awake. I read, write songs, plant seeds. I have rediscovered my genuine interest in other people, the thing that made me want to be a journalist. I find ways to be useful at work, though I have to play well within myself. It's been the most exciting season of news I can ever remember. I've been lucky enough to get back to it again.

I've been writing too, as you can see. Not really as a means to an end, but just as a way to relate to the world. If you're reading this, however, which I can only assume you are, it means I have also got this book published, which is another silver lining to the cloud. In fact there doesn't seem to be a cloud at all now. It's all one big shiny halo of gold.

These are the best years of parenting too: three little ones no longer toddlers, not yet teenagers. I tell them things – about dictators and diamonds and jazz and tax, about accents and myths and Moscow and the seventies – and they soak it up like little sponges. I tell them about breakdown, depression and recovery and they nod solemnly. I relate to them the convulsions of the Arab world and they re-enact the ousting of Mubarak ('No, I'm the police, you're the people!'). We play the Whistling Game at bathtime, and laugh as Edward does something with a flannel that makes it look like he is waterboarding himself. We play TriFoot in the park until we're exhausted and we lie happily in the grass staring up at the sky, asking each other where it stops, what goes beyond the edge. We play capitals and 'What-country-is-next-to-what-country' and 'Play Your Cards Right!' We pick up rubbish on the way back from school. We listen to Edward relate an entire episode of *SpongeBob*, complete with accents. We laugh when Janey points to the driver's pedals in the car and says, 'Do you need three legs to drive it?' We make up lateral-thinking riddles for each other to solve. (I am pleased with this one: 'A man is working his last day in a library. He is not retiring or moving to another job, but he is not unhappy about being let go. Why?' It takes my boys twenty minutes to get to the answer. Tweet me on @markriceoxley69 for more clues).

We have sprawling, random, surreal conversation.

'Dad, how long would it take to go around the world?'

'Depends how you go.'

'By plane?'

'Ooh, twenty-four hours.'

'By car?'

'Well, a month, maybe two.'

'By foot.'

'Oh gosh, I don't know, two years?'

'What about by fence?'

'By fence?'

'By hat?'

'Now you're just being silly.'

'What about by grasshopper?'

I show them some of the joys of being alive: a fine view, a sublime chord change, a burning fire, blackberries. I show them these things and while they inspect, I observe them. When they smile or make big eyes at something amazing, or relax their features in a sudden moment of understanding that I have helped bring about, I feel happier than any man ever has, and I know that everything has been worthwhile.

Is that all there is? I ask, of myself, of the illness, of the world. And I know the answer.

It isn't.

It never is.

But it no longer matters.

To buy any of our books and to find out
more about Abacus and Little, Brown, our authors
and titles, as well as events and book clubs,
visit our website

www.littlebrown.co.uk

and follow us on Twitter

@AbacusBooks
@LittleBrownUK

To order any Abacus titles p & p free in the UK,
please contact our mail order supplier on:

+ 44 (0)1832 737525

Customers not based in the UK should contact
the same number for appropriate postage
and packing costs.